Service Before Self

A Journey of Conviction, Courage and Commitment

Vinod Prakash

As narrated to Ramesh N. Rao
Edited by Andrea Wolfe

Library of Congress Control Number:		2020905062
ISBN:	Hardcover	978-1-7960-9439-8
	Softcover	978-1-7960-9438-1
	eBook	978-1-7960-9515-9

Printed in the United States of America

Rev. date: 08/21/2023

To order additional copies of this book, contact:
Xlibris
1-888-795-4274
www.Xlibris.com
Orders@Xlibris.com
803106

Dedicated to my family in India
For instilling empathy, endurance and ethical values,
And to my family in USA
For wholeheartedly supporting my aspirations

Vinod at his 75th birthday party in August 2008.

CONTENTS

Foreword xiii

Tribute xvii

Preface xix

Author's Note and Acknowledgments xxi

Chapter 1: Early Life (1933-1947) 1

1.1: Birth of the Youngest Child into a Tumultuous World 1
1.2: At Home and Around the Neighborhood 3
1.3: My Siblings and Me: Putting Education First 8
1.4: Working in the Family Business 15
1.5: Family Values and Political Activism 17

Chapter 2: Coming of Age (1947-1960) 22

2.1: Tragic Reverberation of India's Partition 22
2.2: Risking the Future by Standing Up for My Values 25
2.3: Making Optimal Use of Limited Educational
      Opportunities 27
2.4: Chasing My Career Far Away in Calcutta 29
2.5: Working for the Planning Commission 32
2.6: Opting for Studies in USA 34
2.7: Marriage and *Bon Voyage* 37

Chapter 3: Early Married Life and Studying Abroad (1960-1967) 42

3.1: Life in Boston 42
3.2: The Birth of Our First Child 46
3.3: Return to India 48
3.4: Renewed Service to the Government of India 50
3.5: Life in Delhi 52

3.6: Prioritizing the Best Medical Care for Our Son 53
3.7: The Short Tragic Life of Our Daughter Leena 54
3.8: Coping with Family Challenges.................................56

Chapter 4: Settling in the U.S. and Working at the World Bank
      (1967-1988) 59

4.1: Return to MIT...59
4.2: Work and Family Life in Rhode Island 60
4.3: Joining the World Bank...64
4.4: The World Bank – Some Recollections............................66
4.5: Traveling for Work and Home Leave 69
4.6: Indian / U.S. Citizenship 76
4.7: Hospitality to Friends and Relatives 77
4.8: Connecting to Indian Culture 78
4.9: Travels to Cultural and Historical Sites in India..............80
4.10: State of Emergency in India...87
4.11: Support for IRF and Reconnection to RSS....................88
4.12: Impact of the Raid on the Golden Temple
      at Amritsar 90
4.13: India's Worst Industrial Disaster – Bhopal 92
4.14: Embracing *Vanaprastha* 92
4.15: Closing of IRF and Founding of IDRF 94

Chapter 5: Serving India: Nurturing IDRF (1988-2019) 96

5.1: An Inspiration for Giving Back 96
5.2: Overview of IDRF's Contributions 98
5.3: Disaster Relief and Rehabilitation 99
5.4: Development and Economic Self-Reliance 104
5.5: Formative Years 106
5.6: Challenges in Managing Volunteer Network 108
5.7: Streamlining Operations 110
5.8: Smear Campaign...111
5.9: Enticing Donation Received...114
5.10: Standing up for the IDRF Charter 115

5.11: Adherence to Compliance Impels Filing a Court Case ...116
5.12: Sarla's Ardent Support 119
5.13: Choosing Whom to Help...121
5.14: Overhauling Governance and Management................124
5.15: Modernization of IDRF 126
5.16: IDRF's Recognitions and Awards 126

Chapter 6: Family Life 130

6.1: Joy of Living in a New Home *(Grihasth Jeevan)*............130
6.2: Sanjay's Medical Complications, Education and Career...131
6.3: Gautam's Early Life, Education and Career 135
6.4: Sanjay's Wedding...138
6.5: Gautam's Wedding 141
6.6: Unique Tradition for Wedding Gifts............................143
6.7: Joyful Life as Grandparents 145
6.8: Engaging with a Vibrant Network of Friends 150

Chapter 7: World Gone Dark: The Harsh Hand of Fate
            (2010-Present)...155

7.1: Cataract Surgeries..155
7.2: Corneal Transplant: Ophthalmologists' Blunders..........156
7.3: Medical Catastrophe 157
7.4: Treatment at Johns Hopkins Hospital.........................158
7.5: Retina Surgery Reveals the Inconceivable Truth............160
7.6: Confronting a New Reality: Blindness.........................161
7.7: Combating Social Isolation 164
7.8: Split Thoughts on the Legal Battle 166
7.9: Medical Malpractice System is a Mockery! 168
7.10: Discovering Avenues of Learning and Sustenance.......170
7.11: Unavoidable Accident 174
7.12: Impact on Relationship with Grandchildren.............174
7.13: Silent Cry and Tenacity...177

Chapter 8: Reflections on My Life 182

8.1: Looking Back 182
8.2: Reflections on Career 183
8.3: Inheritance of Ethical Values 185
8.4: Reflections as an Indian American 186
8.5: Reflections on Sarla's Role 186
8.6: Values Inherited by Children and Grandchildren 188
8.7: Reflections on IDRF 188
8.8: Reflections on Europe's Role in India's History 190
8.9: Reflections on Self-Identity 192
8.10: Reflections on Contemporary American Politics 193
8.11: Reflections on Contemporary Indian Politics 194
8.12: Reflections on India's Economy and Development 197
8.13: Reflections on the Pandemic 198
8.14: Reflections on Total Visual Impairment 199

Chapter 9: Sarla's Reflections 202

9.1: Sarla's Upbringing and Family Tragedies 202
9.2: Marriage and Voyage 206
9.3: Life in Transition: Delhi 209
9.4: Managing Our Child with Disabilities 210
9.5: Settling in the Washington, DC Area 212
9.6: Our World Travels 219
9.7: Enduring the Cruel Realities of Life 221
9.8: Closing Thoughts 222

Afterword: Reflections from a Few Friends 225

Narender and Aruna Jain 225
Carol and Peter Lowe 226
Malini and Hemant Joglekar 227
Jaipal and Sheila Rathi 228
Ashok Bhagat 229
Achala and Anil Singhal 230

Appendices..232

    Appendix 1 – Family Tree..232
    Appendix 2 – Glossary...235
    Appendix 3 – Arya Samaj...237
    Appendix 4 – The Rashtriya Swayamsevak Sangh (RSS).....239
    Appendix 5 – My Research Works 241
    Appendix 6 – My Favorite Books 243
    Appendix 7 – Important Events (1959-2010) 245
    Appendix 8 – IDRF's Grants for Disaster Relief and
        Rehabilitation, 1993-2022...248
    Appendix 9 – IDRF's Finances, 1988-2022.........................250
    Appendix 10 – Awards and Recognition.............................252
    Appendix 11 – Our Daily Prayer 255

FOREWORD

DR. VINOD PRAKASH and his wife Sarla tell a fascinating story of their purposeful journey in life. For Vinod, it begins in 1933 in the city of Meerut in the historic heart of Hindu India. His is a fascinating story that relates life's challenges, with its many triumphs and an equally large number of setbacks, to what is happening in the larger world around him. It is a story that demonstrates, as the title says, a continuous aim to serve. He grows up in a traditional *vaishya* family engaged in business, with a devotion to Hindu ethics and the goal of an independent India. Informed by his nationalist orientation, Vinod came into contact with the Hindu nationalist Rashtriya Swayamsevak Sangh (RSS) in his youth and was inspired by its focus on service in a Hindu cultural context, even going to prison for two months in his youth to protest against a government crackdown on the RSS. He learns early on the value of self-discipline and it was to serve him well as he launched a career that concluded professionally with a position at the World Bank in Washington D.C. Sarla also had professional credentials in mass communications, though she ended up devoting much of her life to caring for the family, initially a son with cerebral palsy and years later Vinod when he lost his sight.

While pursuing a successful career in the USA and providing well for his family, Vinod, in partnership with Sarla, sought to provide services to help the poor and marginalized in their homeland. What stirred them to take a more public role was the 1975-77 State of Emergency declared by Indian Prime Minister Indira Gandhi which resulted in mass arrests of her political opponents and a virtual cessation of democracy. Vinod was one of many overseas Indians outraged by this assault on democracy and he took an active role in the American activities of the Friends of India Society (FISI), set up to help those seeking a restoration of democracy in India and the release of political prisoners. He also played a major role in giving shape to the India

Relief Fund, now the India Development and Relief Fund (IDRF). Its role initially was to provide financial help to the families of those arrested during the Emergency. Under Vinod's guidance, it became increasingly focused on development, especially education and health care for the poor. From its formal inauguration in 1988 to 2019, it had raised 39 million dollars and was tightly managed by Vinod and Sarla to maintain efficiency and a low bureaucratic overhead.

But its very success generated opposition, ranging from the ideological left to opponents within the RSS itself. The leftist critics charged it with fascism (motivated in part because of its friendly ties to the RSS and its commitment to Hindutva, a set of ethical rules grounded in Hindu traditions). Overlooked by its critics is the fact that Muslims and Christians have always been recipients of its philanthropy – and that it has worked to break down barriers created by religion, economic status and culture. Within the RSS and its American offshoot were people suspicious of the IDRF's independence and highly centralized control. The book has a fascinating discussion of the internal infighting by elements within the American affiliate of the RSS (the Hindu Swayamsevak Sangh) and Vinod and Sarla over who would control the organization. Some of the opponents in the RSS seem to have been motivated by a desire to take control of the IDRF because it had a record of fund raising; others were antagonized by the firm centralization of decision-making in the hands of Vinod and Sarla. One consequence of this internal tension is that the IDRF now maintains a certain distance from the RSS. Yet, Dr. and Mrs. Prakash have continued to host visiting RSS leaders and meet with them in India. Despite this challenge to the role of Vinod and Sarla within the IDRF, their commitment remains strong and clearly gives them both a strong sense of purpose.

This book tells the tale of the growing internal tensions within a part of a much expanded and socially diverse RSS – and so a necessary read for those seeking to understand the challenges facing the RSS in contemporary India. One has only to realize the importance of this narrative when considering that the RSS is by far India's largest NGO, and among the 100 plus organizations affiliated to it are India's ruling party and its largest service network. How the IDRF and the RSS work out their relationship will tell you much about the future trends in both.

Dr. Walter K. Andersen, with a doctorate in Political Science from the University of Chicago, retired in 2003 from the US State Department, having served both overseas and at headquarters in Washington. He joined the School of Advanced International Studies of Johns Hopkins University in 2004 and retired as head of its South Asia programs in 2019. His two books on the RSS are considered the most authoritative on the subject.

TRIBUTE

Dear Mom and Dad,

SOME YEARS AGO, I read a phenomenal book called *All the Light We Cannot See*. It is a compelling story about a young blind girl trying to survive during World War II in France. The title's reference to light and vision directly alludes to the girl's blindness but also signifies so much more.

The narrative captures the theme of light found in the darkness of wartime. Specifically, one of the soldiers in a war bunker hears a late-1930s broadcast about the rare scientific phenomenon of the brain's power to create light in darkness. That even in pitch black, the brain can somehow "see" without the use of one's eyes, through the force of memory, willpower and imagination. This concept so captured my imagination that I felt compelled to share this with Gautam. And we were both struck by how much that metaphor – the idea of seeing light in darkness – reminds us of both of you.

We celebrate and honor your power to create light in darkness. It is after all, your namesake, Prakash. And you have both cultivated this ability for many decades. When your family resisted the British occupation of India, you were creating that light. When you started IDRF many decades ago, you understood that a bright spot needed to exist in what was a dark void. And to be sure, that challenge was made even more difficult when Dad lost his eyesight. But the light of your spirit and vision did not waver – you did not stop doing what you had already been doing. And now, you are there to help cultivate that same power to see light in darkness, guiding the way for those like-minded in their commitment to serve.

A few years ago, we took the kids to see the Broadway musical, "Hamilton." It is a phenomenal work on many levels – musical, artistic, historic. An overarching theme in the story is the question of legacy – how much control do we have over the story that is told of our life after we leave this world – as one of the signature songs in the musical goes, "who lives, who dies, who tells our story." We feel blessed to bear witness to your life story, and now to have the gift of your life story in this book. Rahul and Tara already know your story of *seva*, of service and sacrifice, and I trust that understanding will deepen with time. We hope that we can honor you both during your lifetime and the years that follow in a way that does justice to all the light you have brought into this world, and all the light that has yet to shine through the legacy of your life's work and example.

We love you.
Anjali and Gautam (daughter-in-law and son of the author)

Anjali and Gautam in their younger days!

PREFACE

ALL OF US have stories to tell because all of us have led lives of some interest, some challenges, and some triumphs – however big or small. As a boy growing up in a small town in North India, I did not know that eighty years later I would sit down in America and narrate the story of my life to a friend. This book is the result of those conversations, after careful transcription and many edits.

Many believe, falsely, that narratives of only the rich and powerful, or the accomplished and gifted, will resonate with the reader, who will be inspired or awed by those tales. In many ways, my story from the backwaters of colonial India to the capital of the richest country in the world is both an ordinary and an extraordinary tale. My attempt here is not to list my woes or to celebrate my successes but to share with you some of the details of my life so that you can relate to me in some way: as a fellow traveler, as one who aspires to do good in a demanding and sometimes cruel world, and as a citizen of the world that has changed so fast over the past few decades and can leave many behind struggling to make ends meet, or lead some to unimaginable wealth and power.

Being born in India, and nurtured in that old cradle of civilization, I have tried to pay heed to my country's sages and to my community's values; and as a resident of the United States for over fifty years, I have learned to appreciate what our new place of abode and abundance has enabled me to learn and offered me the opportunity to give.

Unlike a typical Indian immigrant, I was impelled to settle in the US as early as the 1960s, not primarily for my professional career, but to take care of my child's health. While all this had gone well, just a decade ago I had a virtual death blow – losing my eyesight completely due to a medical blunder, which led to my confinement to the four walls of my home. This memoir shares the secret of my sustenance, and how I overcame the inevitable state of deep depression by continuing to serve the marginalized in India, Nepal, and Sri Lanka.

I hope you will indulge me and read my story. If, perchance, you find something inspiring, that will justify my conviction that we are all part of one global community.

AUTHOR'S NOTE AND ACKNOWLEDGMENTS

BORN IN A family that could not afford my education at an engineering or medical college, I was expected to extend a helping hand in the family business of selling books and stationery. Upon recognizing my aspiration for a professional career, my family agreed that I could go for my studies to Calcutta (now Kolkata), far away from my hometown of Meerut. The Indian Statistical Institute, Calcutta, turned out to be the launching pad that enabled me to fly to Boston for my PhD at MIT and get settled into life in the United States. I am truly grateful to MIT for offering me a Ford Foundation Fellowship and, in particular, to my thesis advisor, Professor Richard S. Eckaus, who was instrumental in turning me into a proper economist.

Unfortunately, we had to bear some heavy burdens over the years, more than many households. That we prevailed, prospered, and kept our sights clear is a lesson that I hope our children and grandchildren will cherish. By the time my family (specifically, our son Gautam) recognized that we may have an interesting immigrant story to share, the task was no longer ordinary or simple because I had lost my eyesight completely. Hence, Gautam took it as a family project and involved himself in every stage of this memoir.

Fortunately, Prof. Ramesh Rao came to our rescue when he was teaching at Longwood University, in Farmville, VA. He took up the arduous task of commuting three to four hours each way to interview me many times in my home. All the interviews were transcribed in India, enabling him to prepare an initial draft for my biography. His recommendation that Sugam Garg design the cover page turned out to be very valuable. The next task was to find an appropriate editor and my grandniece-in-law, Ruchika Indrayan's guidance was very helpful as was some early editing by Anamika Dugger, the grand-daughter of one of my World Bank colleagues. We were lucky enough to make arrangements with a professional editor, Andrea Wolfe, who suggested a major change:

turning the manuscript from a biography to an autobiography, leading to a more persuasive message.

The draft of the biography as well as the autobiography has been reviewed by various readers – Marvin Haber, Malati Gopal, Renu Rajvanshi Gupta, Geetha Rawat, Shishir Kant, Abhay Indrayan, Vandana Matravadia, and Niti Duggal. I am thankful to each one of them. I am also grateful to Walter Andersen for preparing the Foreword and to Ramgopal Agarwala, and Padma and Narayanan Komerath for sharing their thoughts about the memoir. Throughout this process I was helped by Taylor Augustine, a long-time employee who has become a cherished and much-loved member of our extended family. Last but not the least it was the hard work and commitment of Chaitanya Lamu and her painstaking efforts in coming to our home in her spare time to read and edit along with me, that ensured the book was ready for publication.

This memoir reflects my journey with my life-partner, Sarla Prakash, who has enriched my life in ways that words cannot convey. Her unwavering support, love and encouragement have kept me going, even in my darkest hours. It was her idea to write this memoir and her meticulous record keeping and annual letters provided invaluable factual information throughout the process.

Finally, I take full responsibility for any errors or omissions.

Sarla and Vinod with Ramesh Rao (narrator for this memoir) and his wife Sujaya and son Sudhanva. Ramesh was critical not only in the production of this memoir, but also in being one of the first people to defend IDRF against the leftist attack in 2002 and was the lead author of "IDRF: Let's the Facts Speak", published in 2003.

Vinod with his immediate family — wife Sarla, sons Sanjay and Gautam, daughters-in-law Renu and Anjali, and grandchildren Anisha, Rahul and Tara, December 2018.

Every individual is a center for the manifestation of a certain force. This force has been stored up as the resultant of our previous works, and each one of us is born with this force at our back.
Swami Vivekananda

India was the motherland of our race and Sanskrit the mother of Europe's languages. She was the mother of our philosophy, mother through the Arabs, of much of our mathematics, mother through Buddha, of the ideals embodied in Christianity, mother through the village communities of self-government and democracy. Mother India is in many ways the mother of us all.
Will Durant

CHAPTER 1

Early Life (1933-1947)

1.1: Birth of the Youngest Child into a Tumultuous World

I WAS BORN on March 9, 1933 in Meerut city, Uttar Pradesh (UP), which is about 50 miles northeast of Delhi, en route to the renowned Hindu pilgrimage shrine (*thirth*) of Haridwar and Rishikesh. I was delivered, as babies were in those days, by a midwife at home – deliveries at the local hospital were very rare.[1] The year 1933 was momentous, marked by events that were grand, dangerous, frightening, troubling, and intriguing. It was the year in which the label "Pakistan" was coined by Choudhary Rehmat Ali Khan and accepted by the Muslim League of India. It was the year in which Adolf Hitler was named Chancellor of Germany, and in which President Franklin Roosevelt survived an assassination attempt. 1933 was also the year in which Mohandas Karamchand Gandhi (who had already then become popularly known as Mahatma Gandhi), whose life and philosophy would guide me throughout my life, began his 21-day hunger strike against British oppression. 1933 also saw the births of Amartya Sen (Nobel Laureate 1998 Economics, Bharat Ratna 1999) and Dhirubhai Ambani (Padma Vibhushan 2016, posthumously) who went on to create Reliance Industries, the biggest and wealthiest business-house in India.

I was the ninth and youngest child of Raghuveer Sharan and Saubhagyawati.[2] In addition, two siblings died during infancy before

---

[1]   My birth was later backdated to September 9, 1932, so I could appear for the 10th grade High School Board examination. It became the norm that the 10th grade marks memo issued by the state government was used as a birth certificate.

[2]   See Appendix 1 – Family Tree

1

my birth. My eldest sibling, Yashomati *jiji*, was the only one who was married before my birth. In order of birth, my other siblings were Mahesh *bhaisaheb*, Satya *bhaisaheb*, Santosh *jiji*, Savitri *jiji*, Dharam *bhaisaheb*, Gayatri *jiji*, and Sarla *jiji*.[3] Our family belongs to the *Vaishya Varna* (business community), sub-class (*jati*) of *Rastogis*. According to Hindu mythology, we are descendants of *Harischandra-Vaṃśa*. *Raja Hariśchandra*, popularly celebrated as *Satya Hariśchandra*, is known in India's *purāṇas* as the king who adhered to the truth in face of extreme adversity.[4] My family has always honored this tradition of honesty.

Vinod's mother, Saubhagyawati, in 1962. She died around one year later at age 72 (no picture of Vinod's father is available).

---

[3] See Appendix 2 – Glossary
[4] Encyclopedia of Hinduism, Volume E-H, page 444

1.2: At Home and Around the Neighborhood

In 1926 my mother received a new house as a gift from her parents (my *nana, nani*) and it was near her in-laws (my *dada, dadi*), in flourishing Meerut. I frequently visited my *nana/nani*'s home in Mawana, which was only 15 miles away from my place. Just seven to eight miles from Mawana is the historical town Hastinapur, the capital of the Kuru Kingdom mentioned in the *Mahabharata* epic. Lord Buddha as well as Mahavir Swami (founder of Jainism), it is said, visited Hastinapur, indicating its historical significance on the banks of the river Ganga (Ganges). King Hastin was the fifth successor of Bharat, and India is named after him, identifying with his kingdom.[5] No wonder Meerut is also renowned for initiating the First War of Independence in 1857 (known to Britishers as the "Sepoy Mutiny"). Meerut is renowned for its sporting goods, handloom cotton, textiles, and *rewari*, the deliciously crunchy sweet made of *guḍh* and *thil* (hard brown sugar and sesame).

My parents happily resettled in Meerut, close to our uncles, aunts, and cousins, who lived nearby. Meerut was a typical town for our region, with neighborhoods joined by labyrinths of narrow, unpaved *gallīs* (alleys) in which little children played with sticks and stones, and men strolled leisurely to places of business or pleasure. Most residents of our *mohallā* (neighborhood), *Baniya Paara*, were traders and merchants. I remember long early morning walks with my father to the temple's well, used by locals for bathing with *lotā bālṭī* (tumbler and buckets), and which was surrounded by *neem* trees. People would chew on *neem* twigs on the walk back from the well to clean their teeth and tongues. The *"daathaun"* neem twig is naturally antibacterial and

> **I remember long early morning walks with my father to the temple's well, used by locals for bathing with *lotā bālṭī* (tumbler and buckets), and which was surrounded by *neem* trees. People would chew on *neem* twigs on the walk back from the well to clean their teeth and tongues.**

---

[5]   Encyclopedia of Hinduism, Volume E-H, page 458

eco-friendly, an all-in-one natural toothbrush, toothpaste, and tongue cleaner.

I have a sweet memory of walking down to *Nauchandi mela* (festival) several times during the early spring of every year. It started in the mid-1850s with several entertainment programs and a huge variety of shops dotting the fairgrounds. We used to purchase many non-perishable home commodities. The most exciting event at the *mela* was watching the motorcyclist in the *Well of Death*: a huge wooden well with iron mesh would be assembled for the expert motorcyclist who would go around the well in tune with the music. Even to watch him was most scary, but of course it was also thrilling! The *mela* had shops preparing the two-and-a-half-foot round *sabu paratha,* which was most famous as *peshawari paratha,* and it was a rare treat for people to buy and eat at the *mela*.[6] People used to stand in long lines for their turn to buy that *paratha*.

Our neighborhood had ubiquitous open drains, on one or both sides of the *galli,* which seemed to carry the detritus of humanity, as well as of nature. There was no electricity or running water supply in the neighborhood, but streets had electric lights then. Eighty years later, Meerut's open drains are still there, but countless other changes have taken place: I find that my memories of India don't fade easily. Traveling in my mind to my childhood neighborhood at the age of 85 evokes the same feelings I had as a five-year-old boy.

Our home at #3 Jatan Street, in *Baniya Paara,* had two stories, each with two bedrooms, a living room with a separate entrance, a kitchen, a storage room, and a courtyard open to the elements, with a covered veranda where we could sit and watch the rain pelt down. On rare occasions we saw hail fall along with the rain, and it was fun watching and playing with those collected hailstones as a child. There were two sets of stairs to the second floor, each opening onto a tin-roofed balcony and a bedroom. We slept on portable wooden cots woven with thin strings of jute, which we stacked against a wall during the day.

---

[6]   Extra-large, whole-wheat Indian flat bread stuffed with vegetables including potatoes – typically served as a treat at outdoor fairs during British India. Peshawar, then the capital of northwest frontier province in British India is now in Pakistan. It is over 500 miles away from Meerut.

The mattresses were made of *dari* (cotton) and covered by washable bedsheets. Two sides of our house shared a common wall with the neighboring houses, and so there was little privacy as voices and noise easily passed through the walls. Our kitchen had a huge door made of tin strips and a side door connecting to the bathroom. My mother and sisters cooked on earthen stoves fed by wood supplied by a wood-seller just a minute's walk from home. Later, we used dust that came from the wooden logs while they were sawed for fuel, and eventually, low sulfur bituminous coal, or "coke" as fuel in the coke-burning stoves.

I can still picture our hand-pump, at first outside in the open yard, and later, inside, so that it was easier for the family to draw and store water. At about the same time as the pump was moved inside, our indoor bathroom was built. For the first time, we had privacy, bathing with our *balti, lota* (bucket and tumbler). Very few households had access to running water in those days, and the hand-pump itself was a luxury. I remember the two big *chhatri ka kunwa* (covered wells) in my neighborhood to which neighbors came with their *gharas* (metal or earthen pots) to draw water with a rope and bucket.

Ours was a traditional family, and as was common in that day and age, the men in the family would sit down to eat first, followed by the women. We had neither a table nor chairs; we sat on the floor for our meals which were served in *thālīs* (metal plates). We did have small tables to serve meals and refreshments to guests. My family talked about family, business, and work while we ate.

I loved to watch my mother grind wheat at home using a *chakki* (portable traditional millstone), which she did while sitting on a comfortable stool. In those days, middle class families bought 100 *seers*, equivalent to 95 kilograms (almost one quintal) of wheat (in North India) or rice (in South India) to store in gunny sacks in the house. As the youngest child, I was sometimes sent to the local mill, where a canister full of wheat would be finely ground into *atta* (flour) for making *roti* (flatbread). It was not uncommon to have rats and mice at home, an unavoidable byproduct of storing grain. We used traps to catch them. I vividly remember the dead rats being taken to the fields, far away. I also carried *suji* (semolina), *ghee* (clarified butter), and sugar for baking biscuits to the nearby bakery, where wood and charcoal were used as fuel, and no electricity was needed. My mother made her own soap, with palm oil, for washing our clothes at home. The clothes were dried in the sun on a clothesline stretched across the length of the yard. After they were dried and folded, we placed the clothes under a pillow as an alternative to ironing since we did not have a coal-heated iron press. We also had a *dhobi* (washerman) who used to come home and take our clothes weekly.[7] He used to soak the clothes in hot water mixed with soda ash (sodium carbonate) and boil them on an earthen stove using wood, and later beat them on a stone and dried them on rope strings directly under the sun.

I remember so many sights and sounds of our neighborhood, like the two huge *pani ki tanki* (water-tanks) which were so high up on the hill they were visible from all over the city. These tanks were our main source of municipal water. In between these huge water tanks was the city's main *kothwali* (police-station). From these *pani ki tanki*, the sloped city's roads led in all four directions. A front road, *Subhash Bazaar*, led to my family's bookshop, and a back road led to my neighborhood, accessible through three slanted pathways. On both sides of the back roads were hawkers selling vegetables and fruits. We bought some of our groceries from general (convenience) stores. These were old-time vendors. They used hand-held weighing scales and officially issued weights (or weights made of stone and metal to approximate the official ones), which are still part of life in India. At that time there were no automobiles, motorbikes, or scooters in Meerut. We travelled by horse cart, cycle rickshaw, and bicycle.

At that time there were no automobiles, motorbikes, or scooters in Meerut. We travelled by horse cart, cycle rickshaw, and bicycle.

Even after 80 years, I have vivid memories of things or situations which have either become nonexistent or altogether changed in nature.

---

[7]   The *dhobi* had his own unique pattern of remembering our clothes, as he never mixed or misplaced our clothes with others. He would collect dirty clothes and return the items we had given him the previous week, similar to the way many American families use a dry cleaner today.

For instance, there was no ready-made garment industry, and all our clothes were custom-made by the local tailors. Today, by and large a typical middle-class family heavily relies on ready-made garments, and only poor/rich rely on custom-made tailoring. Similarly, I was always wearing custom-made shoes but today the ready-made shoe industry is flourishing, and customization of shoes may be rare. I still can visualize a hand pump (*Piyau*) that was on the roadside in the neighborhood near our family shop, enabling passersby to quench their thirst by providing safe drinking water to those who walked from distant places. In the same way, there was no hotel industry and visitors use to stay in a community- or temple-sponsored *dharmshalas* (place where travelers used to rest during the nights while they were travelling from far away).

As a boy, I played *gilli-danda* in the street. *Gilli-danda* is a game still common across India, requiring nothing more than two pieces of wood, one about five inches long (the *gilli*) and the other about 12-18 inches long (the *danda*). The small piece, usually placed on the ground, would be hit on one end with the bigger stick, flipping the *gilli* into the air. Then the nimble player would hit the airborne *gilli* with the *danda* forcefully to fling it as far as possible, and one's opponent had to hop on one leg to retrieve it. There was also the team sport of *lagori*, in which a player piled up seven flat pieces of stone, moved back ten paces, and tried to hit the pile of stones and topple it with a ball. One would often see little boys scurrying to put the stones back up in a pile, while the opposing team of boys sought to hit members of the other team with the ball before they finished reassembling the pile and shouted "*lagori!*" These simple, rustic games very much resemble cricket and baseball as played today.

None of my siblings watched movies, nor did anyone play or listen to music at home, since there was no electricity or extra money, and the idea of having a radio was inconceivable.

At home, I played with *kancha* (marbles), in the courtyard, using my thumb and middle finger to aim one marble at another. No one at home played cards or other games. I practiced drawing in school, but I did not have the luxury of pursuing such things at home. Reading novels and storybooks was considered frivolous for all family members. None of my siblings watched movies, nor did anyone play or listen to music at home, since there was no electricity or extra money, and the idea of having a radio was inconceivable. In fact, the first radio at my home was the one I bought with my salary in 1957. I had already taken care of getting our home connected to the electric grid by then.

1.3: My Siblings and Me: Putting Education First

Growing up in a family with modest means, I knew little of special privileges, but I did have the luxury of being the family's adored little boy. The range in ages of my siblings was so wide that four of my nieces and nephews were older than me. My nephew, Suresh, even lived in the same home as I did while he studied for his Bachelor of Commerce degree at Meerut College. Yashomati *jījī* was very fond of me. I traveled the dusty, noisy bus route to her home in Muradabad, seventy miles away from Meerut, quite often. My second oldest sister, Santosh *jiji*, and her husband Chandra Mohan *jijaji* lived only 48 miles away in Hasanpur, and they always enjoyed my visits.

Vinod's siblings. Front row (l-r): Yashomati (eldest sister), Santosh, Savitri, Sarla. Back row: Mahesh (eldest brother), Vinod, Dharam. Missing are Satya Prakash and Gayatri. Picture taken around 1979.

In 1935, my brother Mahesh *bhaisaheb*, a freedom-fighter, married Shakuntala Devi, the daughter of another freedom-fighter, known as '*Mahashay ji*' who lived in Hapur, an hour away from Meerut.[8] He owned a *Khaddar Bhandaar* (Khaadi Emporium) where handspun and woven cotton cloth was sold. Shakuntala *bhabhi* (sister-in-law) had been accustomed to a much higher standard of living than my brother. I was close to Mahesh *bhaisaheb* and *bhabhi*. They knew how much I loved them, and they loved me similarly. Sarla and I have remained in touch with Mahesh *bhaisaheb*'s eight children, now all highly educated, married, and well-settled.

During this time, we socialized with a vast network of relatives, uncles and aunts (addressed as *chacha – chachi, mama – mami, mausa – mausi, phupha – bua*, depending on whether the relation was from my father's or mother's family), many of whom lived in close proximity to us. My *mamajis* (maternal uncles) were *zamindars* (landlords) who lived in Mawana town, 15 miles away. My elder *mamaji*, Paramathma Sharan Dublish, was elected to the ICS (Indian Civil Service, predecessor to the IAS – the Indian Administrative Service) because he had earned a BA degree that was rare in those days, had a good physique, personality, and was from a good family background; however, my *nanaji* (maternal grandfather) was a staunch patriot and did not allow his son to serve the British Government, so he was forced to turn down the position. Both *mamajis* lived next to each other. They had many cows, bullocks, and bullock carts that were well cared for, and kept in a separate adjoining compound. The families relied on milk, yogurt, and *ghee* from the cattle they maintained. I cherished bullock cart rides to their farms and can still remember these childhood visits to my *mamajis*' homes, as well as the *dhotī* (a traditional Indian boy's garment) that my *naniji* gave me which I wore with great pride. Even well-to-do homes in the town had no electricity; they had hand drawn 'pulley fans' (*pankha*) in the living rooms, and used individual hand fans made of *taddy* (palmyra) leaves and others with bamboo twigs that were foldable, and, especially for women, beautifully handcrafted.

As a retired headmaster, my father used to tutor women from elite

---

[8] This is an interesting example of an engagement between freedom fighters' families, despite huge economic differences.

families in their homes. Though he could not himself earn a bachelor's degree he made sure his younger brother, Mahaveer Sharan (my *chachaji*), completed his. My *chachaji* joined the prestigious NAS High School in Meerut as an English teacher and retired as its principal. My sisters Santosh *jiji* and Savitri *jiji* finished high school at Raghunath Girl's School and then married and started their own families. Among my three brothers, only Satya *bhaisaheb* had a master's degree, while Mahesh *bhaisaheb* and Dharam *bhaisaheb* had just a high school education. Satya *bhaisaheb* went all the way to Allahabad to earn his teacher program certification (L.T. or Licenciate in Teaching) and was the first one in the family to travel that far (450 miles). His wife Satyabala *bhabhi*, completed a BA with her husband's encouragement, and later worked as teacher.

Following Satya *bhaisaheb*'s footsteps, my sisters Gayatri *jiji* and Sarla *jiji* also completed their master's degrees as well as L.T. certification. Both worked as lecturers in girls' intermediate colleges and stayed with Satya *bhaisaheb*'s family at Muzaffarnagar, two hours driving distance from Meerut, for some years. Later, Gayatri *jiji* moved to the Municipal Girls' Intermediate (10+2) College quarters. Sarla *jiji* had been afflicted by smallpox as a child and carried its telltale pockmarks. It was not uncommon to see many across India who carried the ravages of this old, deadly disease, as smallpox was not eradicated in India until 1975. Sarla *jiji* never married. In the early 1950s, she resigned from her teaching position at Sanatan Dharma Intermediate College in Muzaffarnagar, to join the *ashram* (hermitage) of Sri Aurobindo at Pondicherry (now Puducherry), South India.[9] As an *ashram* resident, she learned French and Tamil. She renounced all her belongings and possessions to the *ashram*. As an integral part of her spiritual growth blessed by The Mother, she gained expertise in a variety of handicrafts such as hand painting, embroidery, and

> **By educating the women of our family, we set an important example of women's empowerment, which was rare in those days.**

---

[9]   Renowned Hindu philosopher, Dr. S. Radhakrishnan (President of India 1962-67) called Aurobindo "the greatest intellectual of our age." In 1926, with the help of his spiritual collaborator, Mirra Alfassa (referred to as "The Mother"), Aurobindo founded the Sri Aurobindo Ashram, *Encyclopedia of Hinduism*, Vol A-B, page 36.

---

making of *dhoop* (incense) sticks. By educating the women of our family, we set an important example of women's empowerment, which was rare in those days.

My family's strong inclination towards education led to the establishment of the Prakash Educational Store in 1934. The bookstore was the first business enterprise for the family. Of my three brothers, Satya *bhaisaheb* was not interested in business and remained an educator while Mahesh *bhaisaheb* preferred to have his own business (newspaper and insurance agency), so Dharam *bhaisaheb* took charge of the family store and became the breadwinner. We are ever grateful to Dharam *bhaisaheb* for taking care of my parents, along with conducting the marriages of my sisters. He made sure that the other siblings were financially secure and well-settled. Dharam *bhaisaheb*'s youngest son, Arun still runs the business. In view of socioeconomic transformation, it is not surprising that Arun's children have chosen a professional career in information technology. Thereby, the future of my family business may be uncertain.

In 2014 our son Gautam and his wife Anjali, along with their children Rahul and Tara, visited the Prakash Educational Store. The kids were excited to see the shop where I once used to sit!

Prakash Educational Stores – Our grandchildren, Rahul and Tara, visiting the family bookstore which was established in 1934.

They also visited my ancestral home in which I grew up. My family doesn't live there anymore. Dharam *bhaisaheb* and *bhabhi* lived in this home until 1994-95 and then moved in with their son Lalit in Delhi. By then, all my nephews and nieces had already moved to their homes in new housing developments.

Family planning was not widely publicized or practiced in India when I was growing up. With the exception of Sarla *jiji* (since she remained unmarried), my other siblings had forty-one children altogether. That is an average of six children per couple. However, these nephews and nieces all have small families, usually with two children (all these together now have ninety children). This reflects the dramatic success of the family planning movement among educated families in urban India.[10]

When I was old enough, I began attending the *Rastogi Patashala*, the local elementary school, which taught students up to the fourth grade and was located just at the end of *Baniya Paara*. The *Rastogi Patashala* had no playground, being surrounded by houses, but it did have a hand-pump to draw water. There was no electricity, so we had to sweat it out on hot, summer days. There was no paper, so we did not have journals or notebooks, except for special ones to practice handwriting. Instead, we wrote on black slates with chalk, or on wooden planks called *takhti* (small wooden planks painted white on which one wrote with charcoal pieces). At the time (and even largely today), the educational system in India was focused on memorization – just as our ancient scriptures had been handed down through oral tradition and memorized, so too was the approach to primary education. For example, by the 2nd grade, I had memorized the multiplication table up to 40x40!

Elementary schools such as mine were supported by local communities, and the teacher, a Brahmin like most teachers in India,

> **There was no paper, so we did not have journals or notebooks, except for special ones to practice handwriting. Instead, we wrote on black slates with chalk, or on wooden planks called *takhti*.**

---

10   For details, see Appendix 1 – Family Tree

or another school employee would go from door-to-door to collect four *annas* (one quarter of one rupee) to support the school.[11] At the end of each school year, during the full moon in the lunar month of *Asadha* (June–July), we celebrated *Guru Purnima,* a festival celebrating and honoring teachers. Students and their parents would honor teachers with a gift, called *Guru Daksina* (usually one or two rupees), along with a coconut and a mixture of betel leaves and areca nuts. It was not unusual for village schoolteachers to bring gifts, like *ghee* or *ganna* (sugarcane), to the local Inspector of Education as a gesture of goodwill, respect, and of course, appeasement. During Satya *bhaisaheb's* tenure as Sub-Inspector of Education, he insisted that schoolteachers (of his jurisdiction) leave the gifts that they brought him outside the house and only then enter the house, and when they departed, they must take the gifts back with them. The ethical standards were very high in our household. I have vivid memories of my *bhaisaheb* wearing a saddle leather apron to protect his hips while getting trained in horse riding, which was a requirement to be appointed as sub-inspector, because most rural roads were not paved, and inspectors traveled by horseback.

Once I completed 2nd grade, I joined the Deva Nagri School and stayed through high school.[12] Deva Nagri was one of the many government-aided but privately managed schools where the standard of education was superior to what was offered in the government schools, but still could not match the more elite, westernized education offered in the so-called "public schools" (as per the British tradition) run by Christian missionaries. But these missionary schools were far away and expensive. Even Deva Nagri, being privately managed, had some tuition cost which my family could not afford; fortunately, I received a partial tuition waiver because I was a diligent student and my family was well-respected by the community. And the quality of education I

---

[11]   India adopted the metric system in 1958. One *rupee* = 100 *paise* = *16 annas:* four *annas* was rounded up to 25 *paise*

[12]   The principal of the school knew Dharam *bhaisaheb,* because of our educational store. It also happened that the head clerk at the school was Jagdish Sharan *chāchājī* (paternal uncle). He was very helpful to our family.

---

received was certainly better than what was offered for free at the one government high school in Meerut city.

Deva Nagri was a Hindi-medium school where English was taught as a secondary subject. Hindi was spoken in our home, and I have been told I still sometimes speak with my Uttar Pradesh accent. I walked to school, which was about one mile from home, either alone or with some neighborhood children, carrying a sling bag on my shoulder. The Deva Nagri School, unlike the *Rastogi Patashala*, had large playgrounds where we played cricket, football (soccer in the U.S.), and field hockey. The open spaces were also used for physical training classes, now universally known as *Yoga*.[13] I participated in all kinds of children's sports competitions that were common in India at that time – like the potato-in-a-spoon-running contest, sack races, three-legged races, or racing with a blindfold on. I also remember something – it may have been unique to the Deva Nagri School – a separate class hour when we were allowed to garden as part of the classroom curriculum. Each classroom had its own little plot of ground in which the students' planted flowers and vegetables.

In those days, even though it was a co-educational school, most of the students at the Deva Nagri School were boys, as there were two other schools exclusively for girls in Meerut. In all subjects, the teachers emphasized good handwriting: we had to use specially lined notebooks and *takhtīs* for practice. We stayed in the same room for all our classes and in the lower grades, the same teacher taught all subjects. In the upper-level classes, different teachers, with expertise in each subject, would come in to teach us math, science, and so forth. I remember that my cousins and I received special tutoring from my elder *chachaji*, (paternal uncle) Mahaveer Sharan, who was a senior English teacher at Nanak Chand High School.

---

[13] I still can hear the echo of my school bell ringing for the change of every class period and visualize large open drainages just around the two entrances of our school compound. Yet there were no incidents of students falling during my school days.

My fondest memories of my early school years are of mathematics. From as early as age nine or ten-years-old, I loved numbers, and often worked out math problems by writing them out with chalk on the stone floor of our veranda at home during the day, and at nights I used a kerosene lantern to study. There was no dearth of chalk, which I could easily get from the family bookstore. I would soak a rag in water and wipe out the sections of the problems I had mastered on the veranda floor.

I loved numbers, and often worked out math problems by writing them out with chalk on the stone floor of our veranda at home during the day, and at nights I used a kerosene lantern to study.

1.4: Working in the Family Business

While other children and their parents rushed to the local bus stop to pick up the newspaper that reported the results of the 10th and 12th grade board examinations, I simply took it in stride when my *chāchājī* came home and announced, "Look, Vinod has achieved distinction in the exams!" I did not have much time outside of school for sports or spending time with neighborhood children or classmates, as I would often spend a couple of hours at the bookstore helping my father and *bhaisaheb*. As I got older, it was expected that I would assist Dharam *bhaisaheb* in the management of the business.

The shop had no formal book-keeping system; it was mostly a cash-and-carry business, and whenever money was needed for household expenses, it was taken out of the cash register. We kept track of everything, but profits and losses, incomes and expenditures were just in Dharam *bhaisaheb*'s head. Unfortunately, there was not much money to be made from selling books and stationery. The store was renowned for its fixed prices and ethical business practices, and it was the only place in Meerut District where one could get Government of India and UP State Government publications, sold at the government-set prices. On the so-called "supplementary books," including books that compiled old examination papers with answers, there was a little bit more money to be made. No books of fiction were sold in the shop, and so I was not distracted from my studies by the fantasies of novelists. We invested in a German engraving machine that was used to engrave names on fountain pens, which could be given as awards or gifts to young adults, or even as wedding gifts. These fountain pens were mostly used by the elite, or highly educated people, and were imported from Britain and Germany. We would charge eight *annas* (half a *rupee*) for the engraving, which was quite a bit of money in those times. The store was also reputed for supplying required books to school libraries, without indulging in any greedy business practices.

> No books of fiction were sold in the shop, and so I was not distracted from my studies by the fantasies of novelists.

Almost immediately after starting the business, Dharam *bhaisaheb* (along with Satya *bhaisaheb*) began publishing books, which were printed on the local *Nishkaam* Printing Press. Unlike today, printing back then was an arduous, labor-intensive, and noisy task using a composing stick.[14] The manuscripts were prepared by authors, longhand. Drawing upon the family's connections, we invited freedom-fighters, who also happened to be teachers and professors, to write textbooks and school and college guides. As World War II commenced, the publication business ran into serious trouble, because all printing paper was imported. The government-imposed quotas on the distribution of paper, but my brothers refused to pay the bribes necessary for their share of the rations to be approved and released on time. So, while there were customers for the books and there were authors willing to write them, there was little paper for printing the books. I still remember the local paper inspector, who often came to the bookstore to read the daily English newspapers, *Hindustan Times* (English) and *Hindustan Dainik* in Hindi free of charge, would have enabled the business to grow with a bribe of 50 rupees, but we refused to engage in bribery.

---

[14] A composing stick is a tool used to assemble pieces of metal type into words and lines. It is loaded with metal movable leads for printing and typesetting.

I remember we sold *The Indian War of Independence* by Veer Savarkar, which had been denounced and banned by the British. This war for freedom was initiated at Meerut Cantonment in 1857, spread like wildfire throughout North India and was crushed by the British. First published in 1909, the book portrays the British at their cruel and cunning worst, and I remember that this illicit volume was much sought after by the public.

I enjoyed my work at the bookstore, and I believe I was good at it. Since I have a good memory, it was easy for me to learn how the books and stationery were organized throughout the entire store. If a book was not available, it was my job to run to a nearby store or wholesale merchant to pick up whatever was necessary, while the customer sat and chatted with other shoppers or read the newspaper.

1.5: Family Values and Political Activism

Our family maintained an austere and disciplined home. Our means were modest and our values strictly Hindu, patriotic, and nationalistic. The family's sense of discipline and honesty was ingrained in the children. I remember one day at school, Satya *bhaisaheb*'s teacher asked the class if anyone smoked cigarettes. True to his name, Satya (in English, "truth") guiltily raised his hand to admit to this transgression, even though he had only picked up a discarded cigarette from the ground – out of curiosity – and then immediately threw it away. Such was his sense of honesty and integrity – merely touching a cigarette constituted, to him, a moral lapse.

> **Our family maintained an austere and disciplined home. Our means were modest and our values strictly Hindu, patriotic, and nationalistic.**

The family's practice of modest and honest living was influenced by a Hindu reformist movement called the *Arya Samaj* as well as by Gandhiji's movement for independence.[15] *Arya Samaj* was founded in 1875 by Swami Dayananda Saraswati (1824-1883) and was based on the

---

[15]   See Appendix 3.

idea of the infallibility of the *Vedas*. His book, *Satyartha Prakasa* (The Light of Truth), published in 1876, became the guiding philosophy of the *Arya Samaj*. My mother, sisters, and *bhabis* were all ardent followers. As far as our formal religious practices were concerned, we had a *tulsi* (holy basil) plant in the courtyard but there were no idols and pictures of Hindu gods or goddesses in our house. We did celebrate the Hindu festivals of *Holi* (spring festival of colors) and *Raksha-Bandhan* (celebrating bonds of protection between brothers and sisters, including cousins). I have fond memories of our annual visits to my female cousins on the auspicious occasion of *Raksha-Bandhan*. After my cousins tied the *rakhi* (cotton bracelet), I would give them one silver rupee as a gift. Other festivals we celebrated included *Janmashtami* (commemoration of the birth of Lord Krishna), *Vijayadashami* (festival celebrating the triumph of Lord Ram over the demon Ravana), and *Diwali* (festival of lights). During *Janmashtami* I relished my mother's cooking, which included a huge variety of traditional sweets and savories. I have a sweet tooth! As an adolescent, I did not go through the traditional *janeu* (sacred thread) ceremony, and my brothers, who may have gone through that ceremony, ultimately gave up on any of the rituals connected with it because of their active participation in the freedom struggle and their pursuit of the ideal of a casteless society.

This spirit of patriotism deeply affected me. I remember the groups of men who visited our house to discuss events and strategy, all dressed in white *khaddar* (home spun cotton tunic). Our family was so well-respected for its efforts in the freedom struggle, that neither the local homeopathic doctor, Dr. Chaudhari (who would visit our home to attend to anyone sick), nor a very prestigious allopathic doctor, Dr. Bhopal Singh (with his white jacket, coat and arriving in a horse-carriage), would accept any fee or payment for their services.

Even before my birth, Mahesh *bhaisaheb* and Satya *bhaisaheb* had participated in *Satyagraha*[16] during the 1930 Salt March against the British Raj and were carted off to prison. While Mahesh *bhaisaheb*

---

[16]   *Satyagraha* is a Sanskrit word – "*satya*" means truth and "*agraha*" means insistence – and refers to a particular form of passive and nonviolent resistance.

---

stayed at Meerut Jail, Satya *bhaisaheb* was moved to Faizabad Central Jail for 30 months of rigorous imprisonment; he refused to accept a pardon despite pressure from the government to do so. Later, he decided to join the Education Department in his endeavor to serve the nation. We still have the official certificates of imprisonment for each of them.

Lakshman Dutt *mausaji*, my mother's brother-in-law, participated in the 1921 Non-Cooperation Movement. He was a fellow prisoner with Lal Bahadur Shastri, who would later serve as Prime Minister of India from June 1964 to January 1966. During the 1942 Quit-India Movement, several members of my family were imprisoned for participating in public demonstrations, including Mahesh *bhaisaheb*, our mother, Savitri *jiji*, Gayatri *jiji*, Sarla *jiji*, and Satya *bhaisaheb*'s wife, Satyabala *bhabhi*. The women spent several months in jail.[17] Satyabala *bhabhi*'s infant baby, Sharad, was in jail with her until they released her because the baby fell ill. Dharam *bhaisaheb* also

Dharam *bhaisaheb* also participated in the resistance by going "underground" to escape arrest while providing information to party activists.

participated in the resistance by going "underground" to escape arrest while providing information to party activists. We understood that the local Congress Party leaders advised Dharam *bhaisaheb* and a few others to avoid arrest so that they could continue to provide important information to the party and the public. Dharam *bhaisaheb* would secretly write news on stencil paper and make mimeograph copies to be circulated throughout Meerut. I remember going door-to-door

---

[17] Upon India's independence, the new government wanted to make sure that the freedom fighters, who had risked their businesses/professional careers, were provided some means for their livelihood. In this regard, they were given monthly pensions to be paid until the end of their lives. The amount of this restitution was determined by both the length of their imprisonment and the severity of their sentence. For example, some prisoners of the central government were given permits that allowed them to receive an income, such as fares from a government-controlled bus line or sales from a state-regulated business, like the coal used by families for household fuel. My family members who were imprisoned were naturally beneficiaries of this policy.

---

distributing the leaflets/pamphlets and standing on the side of the street to hand them out to passersby.

I was the first in the family to join the Rashtriya Swayamsevak Sangh ("RSS").[18] I attended the *Brahmapuri Shakha* (Branch) of the RSS. The founder, a doctor and patriot, Dr. K.B. Hedgewar (1889-1940), was on a mission to teach young Hindu men to be courageous and self-disciplined and fight for Hindu ideals. Dharam *bhaisaheb* was afraid that participation would distract me from my work at the bookstore, but I was not willing to give up either one, and I found a way to balance my commitments to patriotism and to my family.

In late 1946, while I was at the RSS Training Camp about 20 miles away from Meerut, communal riots broke out in North India, in response to the Muslim call for "Direct Action Day." I vividly remember being taken home from the camp in a truck with armed guards. Our home in *Baniya Paara* was surrounded by Muslim neighborhoods. Our house was so close to the local mosque that we could hear the muezzin's call for *namaz* (Muslim prayer). Some of our neighbors who were out during the riots were unable to make it home before the nightly curfew. Unable to find safety, some of them were badly hurt and others even murdered. I have the distinct recollection that our community had hired two or three watchmen who walked through the streets in the nights tapping their *lathi* (bamboo stick) on the roads and making sounds, assuring safety. Eventually, the politically motivated communal violence, generally initiated by Muslim leaders, led to India's tragic partition on August 15, 1947.

---

[18] *"Rashtriya Swayamsevak Sangh"* is a Hindi phrase which translates to "National Volunteer Organization." My parents and all my siblings believed strongly in the RSS as an organization which was promoting pride in the nation and pride in our Hindu culture. See Appendix 4 for a detailed explanation of the RSS.

The great secret of true success, of true
happiness, is this: the man or woman
who asks for no return, the perfectly
unselfish person, is the successful.
Swami Vivekananda

As the fruit ripens, so does man mature,
after many rains, suns and blows.
Jose de las Luz y Caballero

CHAPTER 2

Coming of Age (1947-1960)

2.1: Tragic Reverberation of India's Partition

THE FAR-REACHING IMPACT of events surrounding partition of undivided British India into post-independence India and Pakistan still haunts me.[19] This partition was responsible for the largest migration in human history of over 15 million Hindus and Muslims. Violent riots started erupting – for example, I vividly remember the Noakhali riots which were a series of semi-organized massacres, rapes, abductions, and forced conversions of Hindus to Islam, and looting and arson of Hindu properties perpetrated by the Muslim community in the districts of Noakhali in the Chittagong Division of Bengal (now in Bangladesh) in October and November 1946.

I was just 14 years old when Lord Cyril John Radcliffe was charged with the task of determining which territories belonged to which nation. Pursuant to the Indian Independence Act of 1947, each of India's 565 Princely States (also called "Native States") were free to choose whether to join one of the newly formed independent countries of India or Pakistan, or to remain outside.[20] Lord Radcliffe's announcement of the borders between India and Pakistan was met with bloody territorial

---

[19] August 16, 1946, the 'Direct Action Day' was announced by the Muslim League Council in Calcutta to show the strength of Muslim feelings towards its demand for an "autonomous and sovereign" Pakistan. The "action" resulted in the worst communal riots that British India had seen.

[20] According to the Independence Act, the formal names of the two countries were Bharat, West Pakistan and East Pakistan. Punjab state on the west and Bengal on the east were divided, thereby east Punjab and west Bengal belong to Bharat. Effective March 26, 1971, East Pakistan became independent and is called Bangladesh.

rioting. The implementation was no less hasty than the process of drawing borders. He submitted his partition map on August 9, 1947, which split India in half. The new boundaries were formally announced on August 14, 1947, the day of Pakistan's independence and the day before India became independent of the United Kingdom. When Independence finally came on August 15, 1947, following a full year of violence, it came as bittersweet relief.[21]

> **When Independence finally came on August 15, 1947, following a full year of violence, it came as bittersweet relief.**

As a young boy belonging to a family of freedom fighters, independent India's first Prime Minister Jawaharlal Nehru's speech on All India Radio echoes in my ears even now. On August 16, 1947, at 5:00 pm, the Indian and Pakistani representatives were given only two hours to study copies of the maps, before the Radcliffe Award (or demarcation line) was published on August 17th. This was terrifying. Our worlds had been turned upside down on either side of the line. I strongly believe that the Indian National Congress Party should have never acceded to the partition of India, an ancient culture and civilization spanning thousands of years across the entire sub-continent of South and South-East Asia. It is a great national tragedy that Mahatma Gandhi, whose Muslim appeasement policy in large measure led to violent bloodshed and partition, is now hailed as the "Father of the Nation." So much of the work and sacrifice of others, who toiled and gave their life to getting India liberated, has been ignored, marginalized, or forgotten. My greatest remorse, which I cannot fully express in words, is about the fact that the world's most ancient urban centers – Harappa and Mohenjo-Daro – of our Indus Valley Civilization (1300 BCE, UNESCO World Heritage site) now belong to neighboring Pakistan. There the word "Hindu" has become anathema, and any connection to the long, living, unbroken tradition of *Sanatan Dharm* is wiped out of their history books and educational curriculum.

---

[21]   I had visited Sarla *jiji* in Pondicherry several times and was impressed by Sri Aurobindo's vision reflecting the unity of India and Pakistan eventually, as per his speech on All India radio August 15, 1947.

I can still picture the meals I brought for the Hindu refugees living in the camps at Meerut. They were forced to migrate from Pakistan-acquired-Punjab and were typically known as Punjabis. These refugees, of whom there were tens of thousands, were generally hard workers and soon landed on their feet. Some started small businesses selling vegetables and fruits or became 'one *anna* partners' (one *rupee* is equal to 16 *anna*, so this meant becoming a 1/16th partner in a business). Gradually, they became two, four and eight *anna* partners in local businesses and many succeeded surprisingly quickly in Meerut's textile or retail bookselling industries. The refugees gradually gained the confidence of the local populace and entered the *sarafa* (jewelry) industry.

Of course, it was natural for the local business community to feel threatened by the business takeovers by Punjabis. Yet socio-economic differences did not create any long-term barriers and eventually there was integration, including intermarriage, as Punjabis became part and parcel of Meerut life. Moreover, our relationship with the local Muslim community remained harmonious. Though we did not socialize with them, they continued to be our barbers, bookbinders, drycleaners, photographers, washer men (*dhobi*), and watch repairers. It seemed to me that Meerut, with its core of freedom-fighters and RSS *Swayamsevaks* (volunteers), was adapting well to the newly-won independence.

The assassination of Mahatma Gandhi, also popularly known *Bapu,* on January 30, 1948 by Nathuram Godse, at Gandhiji's evening prayers at Birla House, Delhi, shattered this brief respite and sent a cold shiver down my spine. Gandhiji's death stunned the nation and the world. The RSS was accused by the Indian government of complicity in the assassination, and on February 4, 1948, the RSS was banned. I suspect Gandhiji's insistence on India's repatriation of 55 crore (550 million) rupees to Pakistan was one policy that led Godse to assassinate the Mahatma. Millions of Hindus and Sikhs had already suffered enormous losses during Partition when they were driven out of Pakistan, and their lands and businesses confiscated and redistributed to Muslims. This might also have fueled Godse's gruesome murder of Gandhiji. The assassination of Mahatma Gandhi remains India's most horrible event since she gained independence.

In hindsight, I am convinced that secularism in India was implemented improperly. *Dharma Nirpeksata* (religious neutrality) was misinterpreted by our lawmakers and, consequently, some governmental policies pushed Hindus into an uncomfortable zone. For instance, the Government of India has taken control of major Hindu temples while allowing mosques and churches to be self-managed. Similarly, divorce cases of Hindus and Christians are addressed in civil courts, but not those of Muslims because they are not subject to the Uniform Civil Code which applies to all other religions in India. For example, Muslims can have multiple wives (permissible under Muslim Personal Law called *Sharia)* while other Indian citizens cannot (and should not, I firmly believe). Another example is that the Muslim *Hajj* (pilgrimage) has been subsidized by the Indian government while no such subsidy is available for other faiths.[22]

2.2: Risking the Future by Standing Up for My Values

On New Year's Day of 1949, Indrabal Gupta, Krishna Gopal Rastogi and I took part in a *Satyagraha* protesting the government's harassment of *swayamsevaks* (RSS volunteers) and the banning of the RSS. We marched to the main police station, where we three *satyagrahis*, all of 16 or 17 years old, presented ourselves for arrest. Our procession was for a mile and people garlanded us and showered flowers on us, hailing our bravery. My fellow RSS volunteers never hated Gandhiji, though they 100% disagreed with some of his policies. In my view, Prime Minister Nehru had a very strong disliking of the RSS because he perceived it as a potential political threat to Congress's supremacy and waited for an opportunity to defang it. I marched to the police

---

[22] India's Supreme Court has wisely instructed the government to take appropriate actions to abolish the *Hajj* subsidy by 2022. The government gradually reduced the subsidy and eventually eliminated it in 2017, instead using it for Muslim girls' education. In 2017 the Supreme Court deemed instant *"Theen Talak"* (Islamic verbal-based divorce) as unconstitutional and in July 2019 the Modi government finally succeeded in nullifying *"Theen Talak."*

---

station without the approval of my family because I believed it to be a true and just cause. I disappeared from home without a word, joined the *satyagraha* and was arrested at age 16, shocking my family and putting my future at risk, as my 12th grade UP Board Examinations were to take place that March.

I marched to the police station without the approval of my family because I believed it to be a true and just cause. I disappeared from home without a word, joined the *satyagraha* and was arrested at age 16, shocking my family and putting my future at risk.

Family members were allowed to visit us in prison once a week, but they were not allowed to bring food. We ate prison food, which was *gudiyani* (cereal) for breakfast and *daal* (lentils) and *roti* (bread) for lunch and dinner, and we slept on the floor. I believe we were considered idealistic youth rather than hard-core political activists, and this is why we were treated decently in prison. I was released from prison in the third week of February 1949, just in time for my exams. Fortune smiled on me that year – examination papers had been leaked and, consequently, the exams were postponed for six weeks. This gave me sufficient time to study. I am humbled to say that I earned distinction (A/A+) in all three subjects: mathematics, physics, and chemistry.

In those days, exam papers were frequently leaked. The government took measures to curb the rampant cheating by replacing the names of students with roll numbers, an attempt to reduce the impulse to cheat by eliminating favoritism in grading (by caste, religion, or nepotism). To curtail prevalent cheating in exams, teachers and invigilators were shuffled among schools. However, cheating remained persistent despite the government's efforts, sometimes with violent consequences: my Satyabala *bhābhī*'s father, Charan Das Mittalji, was murdered in 1942 while serving as headmaster of the government high school in Bijnor. He was murdered by a student in broad daylight for refusing to allow the student to copy during the board exam. This incident left the whole family bewildered. The assassin, who happened to be a Muslim student, was executed after two years by the government through due judicial process during the British Rule.

2.3: Making Optimal Use of Limited Educational Opportunities

I had taken my 10th grade Board Examinations in 1947, the year India won independence. By this time, the Deva Nagri High School had added 11th and 12th grades and had become an Intermediate College. Pleased with my academic record, my family decided that I should attend a full-fledged college in which I could earn both bachelor's and master's degrees. At this point, I still dreamt of becoming an engineer. Students whose families could afford to send them to faraway colleges left Meerut to attend engineering or medical colleges. Due to financial constraints, this was not an option for me as at that time as there were no engineering and medical colleges in the local area, though now Meerut College is a full-fledged university, and the city has many medical and engineering colleges today. Still, I needed to find another way to obtain an education. During those years, my family lived a simple life. We had two square meals a day, but I remember we often had little *ghee*, and few fruits or other extras. Despite our financial constraints, my family was well respected by the community for our active involvement in the freedom struggle due to our principled and disciplined approach to life.

Unlike during my time, it is now easy for the local students to get into their choice of desired educational programs. Seven decades later, Meerut city has become an educational hub; there are many engineering and medical institutions such as, Meerut Institute of Engineering and Technology, Lala Lajpat Rai Memorial Medical College, Netaji Subhash Chandra Bose Subharti Medical College, Chaudhary Charan Singh University (formerly known as Meerut University) and so on.

I chose to study MPC (mathematics, physics, and chemistry) for my B.Sc., a two-year degree program and a logical choice for me since I had focused on science in the 11th and 12th grades. At Meerut College, affiliated with Agra University, I attended classes during the day and then went to the bookshop in the evenings to help my brother, just as I had always done. This schedule, during my B.Sc. final year, caused an unanticipated problem. I had courses scheduled for the first four periods but nothing during periods 5-7. I left campus after fourth period to work at the bookstore, which meant I regularly missed the eighth period. This would ordinarily not have been a problem, as long as I understood the lessons and passed the final exams. But due to a newly promulgated rule that year, students with poor attendance were barred from taking the final examinations – that meant me! This was very embarrassing for me, especially since I was such a diligent student. I did not want my family to be looked down upon by our community because I lost an entire year.

My family was deeply saddened about the outcome of my missing the eighth period, leading to the loss of a whole academic year, but I did not feel deprivation of any love from them. I studied at home the following year, while working at the bookstore, and, in 1952, I was able to pass the B.Sc. exams as a private student. This delay turned out to be a blessing in disguise: I realized that year that I am not suited for business and instead chose to pursue an academic and professional career. However, I did enjoy my time at the shop. I frequently travelled to Delhi by bus to purchase college books and some stationery. In those days there were barely any checkbooks, never mind credit cards. The system was basically a "cash and carry only" system. In some instances, due to our sterling reputation and the goodwill of shopkeepers, I bought supplies on credit. While returning from Delhi, all road transport had to stop for inspection by local Meerut authorities to pay a toll tax *(octroi)* based on the invoices to that municipality, which was common and fair during those days. I used to walk up to the bus station every time I had to go to Delhi and while coming back hired a cycle rickshaw.

I loved math more than any other subject, and so it seemed logical for me to enroll in the two-year M.Sc. program at Meerut College. I remember how our professors would give lectures while we assiduously scribbled notes which we would later memorize for our exams. I have a distinct recollection of how I learned the theory of real variables from Professor Banwari Lal, using a rare book by British mathematician E.W. Hobson (1907). The idea of going to libraries and working on our own was not common at all, and there was no counseling incorporated into the high school or college systems in India either, so

I loved math more than any other subject.

I received little guidance about my studies or career options.[23] In 1954, I passed my M.Sc. exams in the first division, but did not have the privilege of going to Agra for the commencement ceremony, again due to financial constraints. I knew that pure mathematics was unlikely to lead to any career except teaching, but I had higher aspirations than teaching.

2.4: Chasing My Career Far Away in Calcutta

Through a local family friend, I learned about the Indian Statistical Institute (ISI) in Calcutta (now Kolkata). I applied for admission and was called for an interview and eventually selected. The competition was stiff, and students applied from across the country, but only 15 students would be admitted into the program. Until the 1950s, statistics was not a well-known field of study in India, but it suddenly gained importance after independence. ISI is a unique institution devoted to the research, teaching, and application of statistics in the natural and social sciences. Founded by Professor Prasanta Chandra Mahalanobis in Calcutta in December 1931, ISI was the first institute deemed an "Institution of National Importance" by an act of the Indian Parliament in 1959. Professor Mahalanobis was invited by Prime Minister Nehru to be an Adviser to the Planning Commission. He was also the first non-white person to receive the prestigious FRS (Fellow of Royal Society, London) in 1945.

It took 24 hours by train to travel from Meerut to Calcutta. I would be the first in my family to travel so far from home, in 1954. This was a two-year diploma program, and I needed financial support, as the fees were a princely 125 *rupees* a month (for boarding, lodging and tuition). Gayatri *jiji* and Sarla *jiji*, generously stepped in to support my education. The program became a three-year program during my

---

[23] The M.Sc. program at Meerut College was less rigorous and the professors not as highly qualified as I had expected: for example, except for Dr. Banerjee, the head of the Mathematics Department, none of the other professors in the department had a PhD degree.

time at school and every student was given 125 *rupees* as a monthly stipend, no matter the distance from home. I was thrilled to have the opportunity to attend Professor C. R. Rao's classes, then the Director of the Research and Training School, and who was among the first people in the world to earn a master's degree in statistics and remains, to this day, one of the most distinguished statisticians that India has ever produced. [24] It was an honor to be at the school during his tenure.

First year ISI students lived in two separate hostels (dormitories) about three blocks from the main academic campus, at No. 203 Barrackpore Trunk Road. One dorm was for North Indians and the other for South Indians. There were stark differences in food habits between us: we North Indians ate *chapatis* made of wheat, while South Indians ate rice. Our cuisines differ wildly from region to region in India – from our spices and condiments to our choice of breakfast foods (e.g., *dosas*, *idlis*, *uppma* and buttermilk for South Indians; *poori-paratha* and *sabji* for North Indians).

For the most part, the students were open-minded and accepting of cultural and religious differences. However, some Hindu students were unwilling or unable to accept the Muslim students in our community. I remember one infamous incident when a Muslim student, named Pasha, from Hyderabad in South India, sat on the bed while visiting the room of a North Indian student, named Arora. It was rumored that after Pasha left, Arora had all the bedding washed, simply because Pasha was Muslim. Arora's family had lived in what was then Punjab (later a part of Pakistan) and had suffered personal trauma at that sad time during the bloody partition of the country. In the mid-1950s emotions were still raw among some Indians, like Arora, who had suffered directly or even indirectly during Partition. At the beginning of the year following the incident with Pasha and the bedding, our

---

[24]   Unfortunately, the sad demise of Prof. Mahalanobis in 1972 led to a serious decline of standards at ISI due to strong feelings of regionalism. For example, Prof. C.R. Rao was not allowed to administer the institute because he was not Bengali, notwithstanding his global prestige and outstanding credentials – he was a Fellow of the Royal Statistical Society (1965), awarded the Padma Bhushan (1968), and the Padma Vibhushan (2001).

cafeterias and dorms were integrated. The cooks prepared a variety of meals in the same kitchen, perhaps to encourage intermingling between students from different backgrounds.

Our ISI campus was far from the city center: we had to take a crowded bus (well managed by private contractors), and then an old-fashioned trolley to meet our friends for a walk around the lake or to shop at New Market. There were limited options for us to have fun, mainly because of academic pressure and the strict policies at school. For example, the school gave us a one-day leave to attend Prime Minister Nehru's convocation address at Visva Bharati University[25] as we were very excited to see the Prime Minister in person. But a few students stayed too late and missed class the next day. The school docked these students an entire month's stipend!

I remember, as if it was yesterday, waiting for my turn to go on stage to write a calculus symbol on the blackboard for the blindfolded Sorcar to read with the power of his mind. Sorcar correctly guessed the symbol – to great applause.

One of my happiest memories of this period was attending a performance of the world-renowned magician and hypnotist P.C. Sorcar.[26] He was known for being able to mesmerize an entire audience. I remember, as if it was yesterday, waiting for my turn to go on stage to write a calculus symbol on the blackboard for the blindfolded Sorcar to read with the power of his mind. Sorcar correctly guessed the symbol – to great applause.

I was honored that, perhaps due to my high ranking, Professor Mahalanobis took a special interest in me while I was at ISI. During my final year, I began to work with Professor Moni Mukherjee, then an authority on India's National Accounts, who oversaw my research.[27] I

---

[25]   The University was founded by Rabindranath Tagore, the first non-European to win, in 1913, the Nobel Prize in literature.

[26]   Protul Chandra (aka P.C. Sorcar) was a magician who performed internationally and on live television throughout the 1950s and 1960s.

[27]   All graduate students at ISI took the same courses during their first two years, but in the third year we could choose courses in official statistics, economic planning,

was so proud, in 1959, to be among the first few students in the country to earn a Masters in Statistics degree.

By 1959, I had completed several research papers focusing on national income and wealth, as well as economic planning.[28] The British statistician Frank Yates, one of the great statisticians of the 20th century, was a keen conductor of sample surveys. Professor Mahalanobis and Yates, together, helped India become one of the top nations in planning and conducting

> **I was so proud, in 1959, to be among the first few students in the country to earn a Masters in Statistics degree.**

large-scale sample surveys. This success set an important example for our newly independent nation. We needed to grow beyond our colonial dependency and plan for our own growth and development. My focus at ISI was the study and analysis of national income and wealth, and later of economic development planning. Even before my monograph on Gold Stock in India was published, it was used by the Reserve Bank of India. It was such an honor to have my research on the estimation of National Income and on Reproducible Tangible Wealth of India published and relied upon. I have been told that my work was even cited by Professor Simon Kuznets of Harvard University, who won the Nobel Prize in Economics in 1971.

2.5: Working for the Planning Commission

On the advice of Professor Mahalanobis, a special unit of ISI, called the Perspective Planning Division (PPD), was created at Yojana Bhavan (on Parliament Street in New Delhi) in the office of the Planning Commission of India, to be headed by Pitambar Pant. Pantji, like Mahalanobis, was trained as a physicist and brought scientific rigor to planning. Considering my area of specialization and my work on Indian

---

or sample surveys for specialization. The third year enabled us to gain first-hand insight into real-time experience of statistical applications and to earn post-graduate diplomas. My papers were a part of my independent study in the 3rd year.

[28] See Appendix 5 – My Research Works

holdings, Mahalanobis advised me to join the PPD, which I did in 1958. To do so, I moved from Calcutta (now Kolkata) to Delhi. I was happy to be moving closer to my hometown, Meerut.

At the PPD, I focused on industrial development. I was asked to devise an input-output table (inter-industries relations table) for India, and to study the infrastructure and employment potential of small-scale industry. I was pleased that my research was used in the preparation of India's perspective planning.

My work was done at a desk with the use of a Facit mechanical manual calculator and reams upon reams of graph paper. I did not have the benefit of computer technology, but I did have several assistants helping me with the project. Our work became an integral part of India's plan for industrial development. Centralized planning, based on the Soviet model, was a guiding force in the development of a newly independent India. While most countries at that time aligned either with the capitalist democratic West, or the communist Soviet Union, Nehru chose to keep India non-aligned. As part of his program of economic reform, Nehru nationalized private businesses such as the airlines and insurance industries. Tata Airlines, established in 1932, was nationalized and renamed Air India in 1953, and 243 private insurance companies were amalgamated into the Life Insurance Corporation of India in 1956. Though the existing steel industry was left alone, the nation embarked on building new, huge iron and steel industrial plants in the public sector.[29] The Tata Iron and Steel Industries (TISCO) in Jamshedpur, Bihar (now Jharkhand), and the Iron and Steel Industry (IISCO) in Asansol, West Bengal were given permission to remain privately-owned.

Shaped as the country was by its colonial past and inspired by the Soviet Union's rapid economic growth, it seemed logical for Indian leadership to endeavor and to establish an ideal combination of Soviet-inspired centralized planning and Gandhian decentralized production.

---

[29]   The Bhilai and Bokaro steel plants were set up with the help of the Soviets, the Durgapur unit with the help of the British, and the Rourkela unit with German expertise.

This strategy was meant to ensure economic self-reliance for India, but it was only partially successful. Looking back, however, I believe the import substitution strategy (i.e., protecting "infant industries" from predatory outside forces and from the international market), did not fully take into account the consequences of a command-economy. I am convinced that private enterprise should have been encouraged much earlier. The Indian economic system was on the verge of collapse by the late 1980s, after which India finally liberalized its economic policies. At that time, even the British refused to offer credit to India. For instance, in order to obtain a loan in 1991, the Government of India had to secretly airlift 67 tons of gold to be pledged with the Bank of England and the Union Bank of Switzerland.

Furthermore, I would like to share my personal experience on questioning the efficacy of the nationalization of private insurance companies. Upon settling in USA, I started paying the annual premiums for my four separate life insurance policies at the same time in advance by usual mail, using a single check, and a letter mentioning the policy numbers, due dates, and the premium amounts. My checks were cashed, but were put in "Suspense Account" instead of applying the total to my respective policies. Consequently, all my LIC policies were cancelled due to "non-payment of premiums." Thanks to SM Dugar, (a colleague of mine at the Monopolies Inquiry Commission) who arranged our meeting with the Regional Director of LIC. We were warmly welcomed with a nice cup of tea as was the tradition, and I received my money back in due course. However, the government of India realized the limitations of Nationalized Insurance and opened up the market for private sector in the year 2000.

2.6: Opting for Studies in USA

From 1957 to 1960 experts from all over the world were visiting New Delhi to assist India in its quest to develop in a thoughtful manner. This was an exciting time. We were close to the center of power in Delhi, and so my office in the PPD was an active hub. I was in exactly the right place at the right time. I was lucky to have many opportunities to use my hard-earned knowledge, and virtually every foreign expert was impressed by my command over India's statistical data. I was soon nicknamed "the Walking Encyclopedia" for my ability to recall key statistics quickly, without consulting papers or books. I feel elated every time I think about it. I was honored to assist one such expert, Jan Sandee from Holland, who worked for the United Nations Program of Technical Assistance, and who helped India prepare a long-term plan.[30]

I was soon nicknamed "the Walking Encyclopedia" for my ability to recall key statistics quickly, without consulting papers or books.

During this time, I lived in a rented room in *Vinaynagar*, a government employees' residential colony, and commuted to work by bicycle four to five miles each way, six days a week. I usually ate dinner at a *ḍhābā* (roadside restaurant) on the way back. I ate lunch with other fellow workers at temporary food stalls near the office. I worked constantly as work was my only passion. My social life was comprised of occasional meetings with some family friends, and my friendship with one of my associates, a statistician named T.V. Grace, who was a Christian from Kerala. Grace was staying at the YWCA women's hostel very near our office, and sometimes after work, when the weather was good, we would walk down to India Gate where we would sit and talk. It was a platonic relationship that did not go beyond watching the sunset and talking about life, but I saw the potential for a life partner in this good friend and colleague, and so I proposed to her. Grace softly rejected the

I saw the potential for a life partner in this good friend and colleague, and so I proposed to her. Grace softly rejected the proposal, saying she would like to remain just friends as she was considering becoming a nun.

---

[30] Jan Sandee, "A Long-Term Planning Model for India," United Nations, Bureau of Technical Assistance Operations, 1959. I later visited Jan's family in Holland in 1962 with baby Sanjay on our way from Boston back to New Delhi.

---

proposal, saying she would like to remain just friends as she was considering becoming a nun. We remained friends for many years.

Things could not have been going better for me professionally. All visiting experts praised my work; and several even offered me opportunities abroad. For example, Professor Trevor Swan from the Australian National University, considered the greatest economist Australia has produced, offered me a place at his university. I considered this offer and even visited Canberra but, in the end, I declined the offer. Professor W. B. Reddaway, visiting from the University of Cambridge, invited me for a one-year program at Cambridge, but I declined this offer as well. Finally, Professor Don Humphrey of the Fletcher School of Law and Diplomacy at Tufts University, who was stationed in India as a representative of both the Massachusetts Institute of Technology's (MIT) Center for International Studies and the Ford Foundation, offered me a fellowship of $400 per month for a one-year special studies program in economics at MIT. Excited to have the opportunity to study at MIT, given its international reputation as a flagship science and technology university, I accepted. It was enticing for me since I didn't know anyone personally who had gone abroad.

When I shared my intention of accepting MIT's offer with my boss, Pitambar Pant, he laughed at me and ridiculed the idea of studying economics: "Why waste time studying economics which assumes that all other things remain the same?" he asked. I knew better but didn't want to be argumentative. "Mahalanobis and I are not economists, but we are all doing this work in economic planning," Pantji insisted.

I knew that studying economics would help me prepare the development plans I had been charged with creating. Thankfully, others agreed and encouraged me to accept the offer, especially my colleagues, Dr. Amartya Sen and Dr. Jagdish Bhagwati, both of whom I had met at the Planning Commission in New Delhi. Dr. Arun Kumar Gupta from the Ministry of Commerce helped me prepare my resignation letter and my application to MIT. Pant was still unhappy about my decision to go to MIT. When I approached Professor Mahalanobis, he asked: "You are doing all this for India, right?" I explained that studying abroad would better equip me to contribute to India's growth and prosperity. Mahalanobis considered this. "We will give you a one-year leave-of-absence with full pay, but we will *not* accept your resignation. Go study at MIT and come back."

Now Pantji had no choice, so Boston bound I was!

2.7: Marriage and *Bon Voyage*

The offer to attend MIT was especially attractive because I could take my new bride, Sarla, with me to Boston. We had met and married in the typical Indian manner of that time, by arrangement through family contacts. Our families belonged to the same community, and both subscribed to the *Harishchandra Vansh Patrika*, a monthly magazine published in Hindi with a section devoted to matrimonial advertisements. Sarla's family saw the ad my family had placed, and her relatives also happened to know my cousin Indu *jiji*'s husband, Hari Shankarji. Indu *jiji*'s older sister, Ravi *jiji*, was in Lucknow, about 60 miles from Kanpur, where Sarla was studying at the DAV College. Ravi *jiji* was able to meet Sarla in Lucknow. She then reported back to us by letter. As telephone service in those days was very scarce, everything was done by "snail-mail."

In November 1959, I went with Gayatri *jiji* to meet Sarla in Kanpur. Sarla's brother, Satya *bhaiya*, arrived from Bihar Sharif to be her chaperone. I was especially nervous because I knew Sarla was a very smart young woman and that she was used to a standard of living far superior to my own. But this difference between our families was ignored in the matchmaking. I think I was an attractive groom to Sarla's family because of my academic background and professional achievements, and my position at Yojana Bhawan. No one talked about whether we were compatible, nor was there was any attempt to match our horoscopes, as it is traditional in India to this day. However, our families made sure that we didn't belong to same *gotra*.[31] Sarla's eldest brother, Om *bhaiyā*, who was visiting from UK, had met my boss Pant and heard about me. Apparently, and much to my satisfaction, Pant had mentioned my "strong work ethic" and my "impeccable personal conduct," which impressed Sarla's family.

Sarla was born in Bihar Sharif on July 16, 1939 and was the seventh of eight children.[32] She was given the nickname *Chintu*, the Hindi word for 'worry,' because she was born two months prematurely. Her father, Mahesh Lal Arya, was president of *Arya Samaj* in Bihar, and had inherited his family's jewelry business in Bihar Sharif, which was started in 1884 by her great-grandfather, Munnalal, and is still thriving today. Sarla's father was just 49, and her mother just 44, when they died. Sarla and her siblings were sent to *Gurukul* (boarding school) from age nine, which provided them with self-confidence and independence. Sarla studied at the *Kanya Gurukul Mahavidyalaya*, Dehradun, a strict *Arya Samaj* boarding school far from home. She was a bright and hardworking student, and she received several gold medals for her accomplishments in exams. She studied Hindi and Sanskrit for her bachelor's degree, but then chose English-medium education for her master's degree in political science, for which she was studying when we met. I was impressed with her intelligence and realized that she would be a wonderful companion and wife.

We were married on May 16, 1960, in Bihar Sharif, Sarla's hometown. My wedding procession involved a 24-hour train journey one way, besides a 50-mile journey by road. As a result, only nine members from my family attended the wedding.

---

[31] In Hindu society, the term *"gotra"* is commonly considered to be equivalent to *clan*. It broadly refers to people who are descendants in an unbroken male line from a common male ancestor. Marriage within the same *gotra* is prohibited by custom, being regarded as incest. *Source: Wikipedia*

[32] See Chapter 9 for more on Sarla's upbringing.

Vinod on his wedding day, riding a horse in the baraat (wedding procession). Location is outside Vinod's home, with his mother (in sari with glasses) standing behind him.

We were greeted by the bride's family at the Kanpur train junction. My family had made no dowry demands; as freedom fighters embedded with social reformist ideals, my family was dead set against dowry. According to Sarla's Satya *bhaiya*, who managed their family affairs, the wedding budget was eighteen thousand *rupees*.

Vinod and Sarla at the time of their wedding in May 1960.

Three months after our marriage, we left for MIT. The Ford Foundation's Delhi office made travel arrangements for us and even provided some pocket money for our trip. Family members from both sides came to the airport to see us off.

We still smile when we remember how, during our layover in Zurich, we were mistakenly served beer when we asked for water. I was a little familiar with Western ways from my time in Delhi because of my interaction with foreign experts. I had tasted alcohol before, so I sipped the beer, though not without a little discomfort, but poor Sarla threw up the bitter drink after just a sip or two. What foreshadowing of the challenges we would encounter in our new life in the U.S.![33]

---

[33] For important events in our life (1960-2010), see Appendix 7.

You cannot believe in God until you believe in yourself.
Swami Vivekananda

That quiet mutual gaze of a trusting husband and wife is like the first moment of rest or refuge from a great weariness or a great danger.
George Eliot

CHAPTER 3

Early Married Life and Studying Abroad (1960-1967)

3.1: Life in Boston

WE ARRIVED IN Boston ready to tackle the adventure of living abroad. Our first view while landing was something we had never seen before – a huge number of cars and virtually no people! A representative of the International Students Office at MIT met us at the airport and brought us to our new home, a studio apartment at 80 Marlboro Street, across the Charles River from MIT, in Boston. The rent was $80 per month and the apartment was furnished with the basics: we had a bed, a dining table, dishes, cookware, a few chairs, and a refrigerator in the kitchenette.

We were careful to bring our woolen clothing from India as we planned to spend as little as possible and maximize savings for our future because we were bound to return to Delhi. Our savings in the US were naturally going to provide us financial security. As a young Indian couple belonging to the middle class, it was imperative for us to lead a simple lifestyle. For instance, I purchased two 50-cent bags for shopping at the weekend Hay Market (involving considerable walking and metro rides), where the prices for fresh vegetables, fruits, and eggs were about half what the supermarkets charged. There were no Indian restaurants in Boston and few, if any, places to buy the powdered spices necessary for Indian cooking; fortunately, we had come prepared with a small quantity of spices that would fit in our two suitcases.[34]

---

[34] Sometime later, we discovered a specialty store, Kalustyan's Wholesale Spices in

We soon met our official hosts, Professor Norman Padelford, who taught political science, and his wife Helen, who had started the host-family program at MIT for international students. Mrs. Padelford was instrumental in helping us settle down at our new home in Boston, and she and her husband even invited us to join other international students at their home for Thanksgiving and Christmas.

The Padelfords, lifelong friends and mentors, visited Vinod and Sarla at their apartment in Kingston, RI in 1970.

We also became acquainted with a brilliant Indian visiting professor at MIT, Sukhamoy Chakravarty, and his wife, Lolita. As they were the only Indians we initially knew in Boston, they soon became an informal host-family for us as well. Later, Professor Amartya Sen arrived as a visiting professor, as did Arjun Sengupta, as a student in a special program. They became our good friends. Sarla wore *saris* regularly at

downtown Manhattan, which changed our lives for the better. They shipped Indian spices to us in Boston.

this time, which made the Americans we met curious. Oddly, people tended to ask if we were from Pakistan. We knew Pakistan featured as a prominent topic in the American news at the time, but India was discussed often as well, especially in progressive Boston.

We also made friends with an American PhD student at Harvard University, Bill Johnson, who had posted a note on the bulletin board of the International Guest House around Harvard Square in Cambridge seeking a tutor for Hindi. He had won a Ford Foundation fellowship to visit India with his wife Margie, to complete his dissertation on the Indian steel industry. Sarla helped him learn Hindi, through the Berlitz School of Language. Bill became such a good friend that when our son, Sanjay, was born in 1961, it was he who brought Sarla and the baby home from the hospital in his car and helped us get a used crib from the MIT student furniture exchange. While Bill passed away in 2014, we are still friends with his wife Margie.

Boston weather proved to be as cold and snowy as we had expected. I have a vivid memory of my heavy winter coat and snow boots, that I bought for just five dollars through a program at MIT that allowed international students to donate their used clothes, utensils, and other items. To save money, I would trudge by foot through the snow to my classes, armed only with this warm coat and a hat. During the heaviest snowstorms, only a few of the twenty or so students would show up for class – all of them international students. The American students knew that classes were likely to be cancelled, so they would stay safe and warm at home while listening to the weather report on the radio.

> To save money, I would trudge by foot through the snow to my classes, armed only with this warm coat and a hat. During the heaviest snowstorms, only a few of the twenty or so students would show up for class – all of them international students.

I soon became immersed in my schoolwork. I usually took three classes per semester and audited a fourth: auditing a class involves attending the class without sitting for examinations or receiving a grade or course credit. As I had studied math and statistics previously, I had virtually no background in the study of economics as an academic subject, so the classes were difficult. Plus, my command of English was still tenuous, since I had not studied it beyond the tenth grade, but I was used to working hard and knew that I could succeed if I gave my studies my full attention.

I joined MIT for my special studies because I hoped to gain insight into the theoretical bases of economic growth in both developing and developed societies, without the distracting obligations of teaching or working as a research assistant. My fellowship was initially for one year, but my professors understood that my knowledge of economics was not well-developed. By the end of my first year, I realized that I would need further study of economics if I wanted to make a significant contribution towards India's development planning. Extending my stay by one more year would also allow me to complete the qualifying examinations for my PhD degree. My advisor, Dr. Paul Rosenstein-Rodan, frequently visited India as a development expert and was able to convince Professor Mahalanobis to extend my stay. MIT and the Ford Foundation made it possible for me to stay by extending my full fellowship for another year. Dr. Rosenstein-Rodan taught at MIT from 1953 until 1968: he proposed the "Big Push" model, in which he argued for "planned, large-scale investment programs in industrialization in countries with a large surplus workforce in agriculture."[35]

---

[35] He was the department's expert in economic development, along with his colleague Professor Charles Kindleberger, in charge of international trade and finance, Professor Franklin Fisher, in charge of econometrics, Professor Evsey Domar, who took on comparative economic systems, Dean Richard L Bishop, microeconomics, and Robert Solow (Noble Laureate 1987), sources of economic growth. I recall that Professor Paul A. Samuelson (Noble Laureate 1970) would rarely cover the planned material during Macro Economics class because he had so many fascinating anecdotes to share. Moreover, he had to quite often miss classes due to his external commitments. Therefore, he would conduct extra classes during weekends which all students attended.

Sarla and Vinod at an MIT function, circa 1961.

While at MIT, I buried myself in my books, spending hours at the library; I often came home only to eat and sleep. Meanwhile, Sarla worked toward her M.S. in Mass Communication at Boston University. She was an outstanding student and was awarded the 1961-62 Kaltenhorn Foundation Fellowship. We studied most of the time, but we did manage to attend some cultural events at the Kresge Auditorium at MIT. We were even able to see a movie once in a while.

> **While at MIT, I buried myself in my books, spending hours at the library; I often came home only to eat and sleep.**

3.2: The Birth of Our First Child

I remember how excited we were to host our friends Sukhamoy and Lolita Chakravarty, Amartya and Navneeta Sen, along with Ramesh and Shanta Gangoli, at home one evening in late May 1961. Sarla, already an excellent cook, made *aloo paratha*, *sabji* and *daal*, *mooli-paratha* (radish *paratha*) and all the nice side dishes that go with an Indian meal – despite the fact that she was nine months pregnant! After seeing our guests off at around 10:00 pm we went to bed, but Sarla soon went into labor. Our dear friend, Lilian Bono, accompanied us in a taxi to the hospital. The next day, May 31, 1961, we welcomed our first child, Sanjay, into our lives. We took his name from the epic battle in *Mahabharata*, which was fought in Kurukshetra, not too far from city of my birth, Meerut.[36]

Sarla, Vinod and Sanjay, March 24, 1962 in Boston
while Vinod was doing his PhD at MIT.

Sanjay seemed, initially, to be a healthy and normal baby. However, when he started crawling unusually, Sarla noticed a lack of coordination and, later, frequent falls when he started to walk. Sarla was only 22 and a graduate student, along with me, and this was a real harsh blow to us. We could not understand why he was growing well but his motor skills were not improving, and this alarmed Sarla's motherly instincts. Even our family doctor, who had served as both obstetrician and pediatrician, had no idea what was wrong with Sanjay. Later, he referred us to Boston Children's hospital where Sanjay was diagnosed with cerebral palsy.

---

[36] Sanjay is the charioteer and minister of King Dhrtarastra (father of Kauravas) in India's epic poem, the *Mahabharata*. He narrates every move of the war between the Kauravas and their cousins the Pandavas to the king. Sanjay was blessed by Veda Vyasa Mahrishi and had divine vision wherein he could see every incident that occurred in the course of the war in Kurukshetra though he was 110 miles away in Hastinapur (Meerut District). He was like the eyes and ears to the king. He was also the first one to narrate the *Bhagavad Gita* to the king, apart from Lord Krishna himself.

During this time, we were both busy 12 to 14 hours a day with our graduate studies, taking care of Sanjay, and doing household chores. I remember we moved to a bigger apartment, in married graduate student housing at Boston University (at 14 Buswell St), and we spent $10 a week on food and $10 a week on babysitting. We hired our new neighbor, Jean Swinney, to sit for Sanjay. She became a dear friend and even attended Sanjay's wedding, though she and her family had moved to California by then. We remained in touch until her death in 2010.

In more ways than one, 1961 was a difficult year. My father passed away in the latter part of 1961, while I was still at MIT. Because there was no telephone in our Boston apartment or in my home in Meerut, I learned of my father's death by airmail letter several weeks after the fact. We were deeply saddened and felt helpless since we had no access to modern communication such as a telephone. We shared this grief with a couple of our Indian friends.

> I learned of my father's death by airmail letter several weeks after the fact.

3.3: Return to India

Looking back, I see that the challenges we faced during this period could have easily worn us down. But Sarla's energy and faith saw us through these difficult early years in the U.S. It cheered us to think about returning to India after my studies were complete. As a young adult in India, I was a bright star in my profession and was appreciated and respected throughout the field of economic development. Whereas, at MIT, I was a mere graduate student and was almost a novice because I had barely studied any economics before arriving; I had been a science and statistics student till then. Thus, it was a mighty task for me to keep up with other graduate students, but I completed my PhD program well in time.

> Looking back, I see that the challenges we faced during this period could have easily worn us down. But Sarla's energy and faith saw us through these difficult early years in the U.S.

So eager was I to return to India that I packed my bags immediately after passing my PhD qualifying exams and, with infant Sanjay in my arms, I returned to Delhi in September 1962. After much discussion and cajoling, Sarla moved to New York City to complete her master's thesis (on the history of United Nations Radio) for which she was supposed to visit the UN library many times. She was reluctant to be separated from Sanjay and probably more than a bit anxious about living on her own in New York City. Mrs. Weiss was a human rights activist volunteer at the UN, and fortunately saw Sarla's ad on the bulletin board that she was seeking a place to live. Mrs. Weiss contacted Sarla and offered her a place where, in lieu of rent, Sarla would attend to Mrs. Weiss' phone calls for three hours each evening. This arrangement worked perfectly for Sarla. We are forever grateful to the Weiss family who befriended Sarla the moment she arrived in the city. The Weisses hosted her and took great care of her and became wonderful mentors.

While Sarla was in New York and I was in Delhi, Sanjay was taken care of by his *taiji* – wife of Satya *bhaisaheb*, then Inspector of Education in the villages and towns of Bulandshahr district (near Delhi) – as well as by his *dadiji* (my mother), who passed away in 1964. It is painful to think about how, when Sarla returned to India in February 1963, Sanjay did not recognize her for many days. This was heartbreaking to Sarla.

October 12, 1962, Satya Prakash (Vinod's brother) and Satyabala
(Vinod's sister-in-law) with Sanjay who was 1-year old. They took care

of Sanjay for five months while Sarla was finishing her master's thesis in Boston and Vinod was in New Delhi at the Planning Commission.

We had shipped our household goods from Boston to Delhi in preparation for our return to India. We had known this moment was coming and we were well-prepared for it; we knew the customs limits and we had meticulously kept all our invoices and related records. What should have been a straightforward exercise turned into a nightmare which was, unfortunately, typical of India in the 1960s because of the corrosive effect of corruption. I refused to bribe the Customs Inspector, as was expected of me, and so I made more than 35 visits to the Customs House in Delhi to try to reclaim our belongings. The Customs Inspector even had the audacity to invite me to his home (at 28 Malvya Nagar) in South Delhi. But I would not budge. Ever the idealist, I preferred to spend more money in three-wheeler *autorickshaw* (scooter) and taxi fare to-and-from the Customs House than I would have paid in bribes. Eventually, I was forced to pay extra customs duty since I was charged a penalty of Rs.18,000 – a fee for the difference in value between how much I paid for an item in the U.S. and the "list-price" (similar to MSRP in the US) of such items in India. I could not, however, abandon my principles, so I fought the case through appellate jurisdiction in Delhi and won. Still, this was not the end of the ordeal as the money we were owed remained stuck at the Customs House. Ultimately, I had to rely on personal contacts of Sarla's brother Vishu (the renowned Dr. Vishva Prakash Ayra) to have it released without paying a bribe. Even now, sixty years later, I feel India still runs primarily on bribes and personal contacts.

> **I refused to bribe the Customs Inspector, as was expected of me, and so I made more than 35 visits to the Customs House in Delhi to try to reclaim our belongings.**

3.4: Renewed Service to the Government of India

I had kept in touch with Pitambar Pant throughout my time at MIT. Pantji had even visited us at our home during an official visit to the States. Upon my return to Delhi in September 1962, I resumed my work with Pantji, at Yojana Bhawan. Along with my normal assignment concerning India's Preparation Perspective Plan, I was asked by Professor Mahalanobis to work also on the Distribution of Income and Levels of Living Committee, which he chaired. As the second assignment was high-powered and time sensitive, I was not granted leave to go to Bombay (now Mumbai) for customs clearance or to accompany Sarla and Sanjay for medical checkups in other cities.

I felt honored to be deputized as the Joint Director in Economics and Statistics at the Monopolies Enquiry Commission, chaired by one of the Supreme Court Justices, which was a very high position for a 31-year-old. The position at the Commission lasted about 18 months and the work was both interesting and challenging. I especially appreciated the fact that it allowed me to address the genuine fear of monopolistic tendencies in India. My recommendations were incorporated in the Commission's Report. Later, a permanent Monopolies and Restrictive Trade Practices Commission (MRTPC) was established by the Central Government to make sure that Indian entrepreneurship was not constricted by corporate interests. Certain rules and regulations had to be formulated so that there was a legal and regulatory edifice to guide the growth of Indian industry and trade in a fair and competitive environment.

During this period, I also compiled and analyzed the data for my PhD dissertation. I wanted to work on a practical, meaningful topic, so I chose to focus on inventory management, which blended concepts from both macro- and microeconomics. I was particularly interested in finding methods to save economic resources by optimizing the levels of inventories, especially in public-sector enterprises. I developed a questionnaire, which I sent to MIT for feedback. I also received some informal guidance from Amartya Sen (Nobel Laureate 1998, Bharat Ratna 1999) who was aware of my professional expertise and academic aspirations. The questionnaire was then mailed to select industrial business companies so that I could do a meaningful empirical study. However, the response I received was not encouraging, due to bureaucracy as well as the innovative nature of resource optimization, and I could not complete the follow-up interviews I had hoped to rely upon. In view of this challenge, my advisers at MIT suggested I choose a more manageable topic for my thesis, and so I narrowed my focus to the macroeconomic aspects of inventories.

3.5: Life in Delhi

We lived at 25/14 East Patel Nagar, Delhi, and paid a monthly rent of Rs. 230 for four and a half years, until we returned to the U.S. in 1967. We had brought a propane cooking range back with us from Boston, which was much cleaner burning and safer than the more common coal or wood-burning stoves that were then available in India.[37] We had a refrigerator, modern cookware, dinnerware, and utensils, and other unusual items that prompted the neighborhood children to call Sarla an "American auntie." Despite our relative affluence, we did not have a telephone: getting telephone service was virtually impossible for anyone not involved in senior levels of government service. In fact, before leaving for the U.S. in 1960, I paid a Rs. 1,000 deposit to be on the phone line Priority List, and later learned that there was still a ten-year wait. When we needed a telephone, we relied on our next-door neighbors, Mr. and Mrs. R.L. Gandhi, who were warm, kind, and cordial. Mr. Gandhi was an income tax officer and so he had an official telephone at home.[38] We hosted many family members during this period, as we were the only ones from either side of the family located in Delhi.

The years we spent in Delhi were a tumultuous period in Indian politics. First, there was the Indo-Chinese War, from October 20 – November 21, 1962, followed by Prime Minister Jawaharlal Nehru's death on May 27, 1964, which bewildered and saddened the whole nation.[39] From April to September of the following year, India and

---

[37] Our Delhi home was unique in my social circle because of our kitchen and American products. Decades later, environmental consciousness has increased so much that the Indian government is encouraging the masses to use liquefied petroleum gas (LPG).

[38] We are still in regular touch with their daughters Anita and Alka, who currently live in California.

[39] Emotionally millions of Indians worried about the nation's future without Nehru because *Bharat* (India) and Nehru were considered virtually synonymous.

Pakistan were involved in the Indo-Pakistan War of 1965 (also known as the Second Kashmir War). I remember the air-raid sirens and nighttime blackouts in Delhi. The new Prime Minister, Lal Bahadur Shastri, emerged as a national hero during the war. In January 1966, he traveled to

I remember the air-raid sirens and nighttime blackouts in Delhi.

Tashkent in the Soviet Union (now Uzbekistan) to sign the Tashkent Agreement, a peace treaty between India and Pakistan. He died there of a reported heart attack, though many still believe there was a conspiracy involved in his death.

Prime Minister Nehru's daughter, Indira Gandhi, was appointed as the next Prime Minister by the old guard, the senior-most political leaders of the Congress Party, after Shastri's death.[40] This prompted a split in the Congress Party, with the socialists led by Indira Gandhi and the conservatives by Morarji Desai. My own political support leaned towards the Bharatiya Jan Sangh (BJS) founded by Shyma Prasad Mukherjee in October 1951, whose ideology was similar to that of the RSS (the BJS was against communism, not keen on the close ties with the Soviet Union that Nehru had built, and not inclined towards appeasement on religious grounds).

3.6: Prioritizing the Best Medical Care for Our Son

Sarla had excellent credentials in Mass Communications and yearned to join the Indian Institute of Mass Communication (IIMC). Mass Communications at that time in India was in its infancy. However, the IIMC was a great distance from our home. Sarla made Sanjay's medical care her top priority and gave up her heart's desire and aspiration of working at IIMC for our son's well-being. Staying at home gave Sarla the flexibility to take Sanjay for treatment at various hospitals and clinics around India.

Sanjay needed treatment for right hemiplegic cerebral palsy, a developmental disability. He had to wear a brace on his right leg. He

---

40   Cartoonists had a great time in picturing Mrs. Gandhi standing on the shoulders of the men of the old guard.

also had to be taken to the orthopedist regularly so that his leg could be stretched, and the doctor could record the changes in his growth. At one point, Sanjay's doctors recommended he be taken to the renowned Christian Medical College in Vellore, Tamil Nadu. I was not given leave from my office due to my work on the high-profile study led by Professor Mahalanobis. Sarla and toddler Sanjay visited the doctors all by themselves. Sarla faced this ordeal on her own. We were frequently advised by the medical community that Sanjay had no future to lead an independent life and may be left at an orphanage. These heart-breaking words reinforced our commitment to see that he led a normal life.

> **We were frequently advised by the medical community that Sanjay had no future to lead an independent life and may be left at an orphanage. These heart-breaking words reinforced our commitment to see that he led a normal life.**

3.7: The Short Tragic Life of Our Daughter Leena

Our second child, daughter Leena, was born on April 28, 1964.[41]

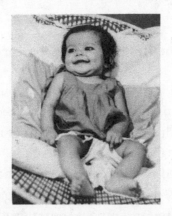

Vinod and Sarla's daughter, Leena (April 28, 1964 –
February 6, 1965), who died of leukemia.

---

[41] My family in Meerut was of very moderate means, whereas Sarla's sister Saras *jiji* was living in a relatively wealth household. So, we decided to have Leena delivered under her care.

Upon her return home with us, we were happy to be able to employ a temporary helper to assist with Leena's care in addition to our established full-time household help. Shortly after her birth, Leena was diagnosed with the dreaded disease leukemia. In the 1960s, the medical treatment of cancer was rudimentary. Leena was treated in Delhi with Dr. Prem Kakkar (Padma Shri, 1987) after a close friend of Sarla's brother, Dharam *bhaiya*, made arrangements at the Irwin Medical Hospital for her treatment. Dr. Kakkar was a professor at the Maulana Azad Medical College, which was attached to that hospital. He was such a good friend to us and so concerned about Leena, that he donated his own blood for transfusion to save little Leena, but she could not survive. She succumbed to the disease on February 6, 1965.

We were distraught. How many challenges should we have to face? Yet we authorized the medical college's hospital to preserve Leena's organs for use in research, which was not a common practice at that time. One of our closest friends, Shravan Kumar, helped organize the Hindu ceremony to send little Leena off by immersing her body in the waters of Yamuna River.

Shravan Kumar and family (including wife Sunita, son Mukul, daughter-in-law Abha, grandchildren Manya and Madhav). He was Vinod's colleague and close friend since 1957 and is like an older brother for Vinod.

While I was driving to the *ghat*, Sarla sat on the pillion seat of our Vespa scooter, with our baby's corpse in her arms. This event remains as clear in our memory as if it happened just yesterday. Even after 50 years, when we happen to recollect Leena's tragic demise, we become emotional and feel tremors passing though.

> **While I was driving to the *ghat*, Sarla sat on the pillion seat of our Vespa scooter, with our baby's corpse in her arms.**

Sarla's eldest sister, Sharda *jiji*, came from Bhagalpur, Bihar to console us and help us in our attempt to find some kind of normalcy following this tragedy. I regret that there was little help from my side of the family, especially since in those days telephones were uncommon, and whatever access there was seemed very limited for my family. We had little to help us through this time except, perhaps, the hope that our pain would lessen over time.

> **We had little to help us through this time except, perhaps, the hope that our pain would lessen over time.**

3.8: Coping with Family Challenges

In 1966, we decided to return to the U.S. for Sanjay's care. Medical care was much more advanced and attitudes toward people with disabilities were much healthier in the U.S. than in India. I wrote to Professor Max Millikan, who had visited us in Delhi, to request that I be allowed to register again at MIT in order to complete my PhD. My request was instantly approved, effective September 1967, and I was given a $275 per month stipend. This was the normal stipend given to graduate students without an outside fellowship.

Amid all this, Sarla became pregnant again. We were eager to fill the void left by Leena's death, but the timing could not have been more tangled and complex. Since we had already lived in the U.S., we knew how hard it would be to have a newborn child in the midst of the challenges of moving and managing Sanjay with a full academic workload. Ultimately, we made the very difficult decision to, quietly and privately, abort the pregnancy. This was possible only because of our friend, a female family doctor named Krishna Rastogi. It was another sad and severe blow. Looking back, I see that we were strengthened by the challenges we faced during our young lives, and, perhaps, we were better equipped to forge ahead in the U.S.

This life is a hard fact; work your way through it boldly, though it may be adamantine; no matter, the soul is stronger.
Swami Vivekananda

This country, with its institutions, belongs to the people who inhabit it. Whenever they shall grow weary of the existing government, they can exercise their constitutional right of amending it, or exercise their revolutionary right to overthrow it.
Abraham Lincoln

CHAPTER 4

Settling in the U.S. and Working at the World Bank (1967-1988)

4.1: Return to MIT

WE RETURNED TO Boston in 1967 via Montreal, Canada. I still recall our first impressions of Canada: we were overwhelmed (and also overjoyed) by the International Expo67, and we immediately noticed and admired the courteousness of Canadians. It was just the two of us, as 6-year old Sanjay had stayed with my sister Sarla *jiji* at Sri Aurobindo Ashram in Pondicherry (now Puducherry).

1967, Sarla and Sanjay (age 6) with Vinod's sister, Sarla, who took care of Sanjay for 15 months while Vinod and Sarla were in Boston as they could not

afford to keep Sanjay with them. Due to right-side hemiplesia (cerebral palsy),
Sanjay is wearing a leg brace and his right arm is shorter than his left arm.

Just like before, MIT's representative received us at the airport and brought us to our new home at 135 Clark Street, Cambridge. It was fully furnished, affordable, and within walking distance to the campus. This reflects the excellence of MIT's International Students Program. I worked full-time at MIT on my dissertation during the academic year 1967-68. My thesis involved empirical work pertaining to the macroeconomic aspects of India's industrial sector. At the MIT computer lab, I used a time-sharing IBM 1401 computer with the programing language Fortran IV to develop and design my program. I had to punch numerous IBM cards having 80 columns and 12 rows (7 $\frac{3}{8}$ by 3 $\frac{1}{4}$ inches exactly). It was only through these punch cards that I could feed computer input data designed by me. Prior to initiating the statistical analysis, I had to make sure that there were no errors in the program and data input. This process involved printing on reams of paper. Looking back, the computing process was extremely tedious, but there was no other option in those days for empirical research. As my dissertation took shape, I accepted a position as assistant professor at the University of Rhode Island (URI), mainly due to its proximity to MIT where I could meet my professors and complete my dissertation. This move would also enable us to resume Sanjay's treatment at Boston Children's Hospital, once he returned from India.

4.2: Work and Family Life in Rhode Island

Just before moving to Rhode Island, we bought a new 1968 Chrysler Valiant (turquoise color) with manual transmission (automatic was far more expensive) for $2,300. Owning a car represented an achievement of a distant dream for me. Our friend Sharad Rastogi drove us to Kingston in the new car, since neither of us was confident to drive on highways. Good old days those were, when

Owning a car represented an achievement of a distant dream for me.

we made just one direct trip from Boston to Kingston with all our belongings in this car. During our first year in Kingston, we lived at the University Garden Apartments. I recall that there were no other Indians in the economics department, but there were a few in other departments at the university, including Professor G. R. Verma in the Department of Mathematics. Professor Verma and his wife lived on the floor above us when we moved into the faculty apartments after the first year.

Seven-year-old Sanjay arrived from India in late August 1968, just in time for the beginning of the academic year. My sister Sarla *jiji* flew with Sanjay to Delhi from Madras (now Chennai), and that was her first time flying! From there Sanjay was accompanied on the flight to New York City by Mrs. Asha, wife of Professor Prem Aggarwal at the University of Pittsburg, a close family friend. Sarla and I drove to JFK airport to pick up Sanjay and that was my first long drive on the interstate. I was completely unaware of other states' traffic rules. For example, in Connecticut, the left-most lane was for passing only and not for normal driving. As a result, while driving back through Connecticut from the airport at around midnight, we were pulled over by a police officer because I was driving in the passing lane. We did not make it home that night until 4 a.m. We were shaken by the experience, but relieved to have been let off with just a warning. Once settled, Sanjay started second grade at the local elementary school. He had picked up French at Pondicherry (now Puducherry) but had almost no exposure to English.

I stayed at URI for three years teaching economics courses, including a basic course for freshmen and sophomores on macroeconomic and microeconomic theories, and an advanced course for seniors and graduate students on economic development. I designed the latter course with the help of colleagues from two other departments. It was built upon the work of the Swedish economist Gunnar Myrdal,[42] (Nobel Laureate 1974, Economics), one of the experts who had worked as an advisor to the Government of India.[43]

---

[42] *Asian Drama: An Inquiry into the Poverty of Nations* was published in 1968.
[43] See Appendix 6 – My Favorite Books

It is an American tradition in higher education that students write evaluations of their professors at the end of each semester. I received some complaints that students had difficulty following my lectures because of my heavy accent. The Chair of the Department of Economics, Professor Richard Sabatino, was kind enough to simply acknowledge the students' concerns and encouraged me to adopt a more American-sounding accent. He remained a close family friend of ours until his death some years ago. Life in Rhode Island was pleasant and comfortable overall. Though I was the only non-American faculty member, we were treated so warmly by other faculty members that we felt like it was our second home.

Vinod's colleagues and their spouses from the Economics Department at University of Rhode Island. Photo taken in 1985 when we visited Kingston, RI to meet with our old friends. From L to R: Vinod, Jean Rayack, Rick Sabatino, Bertha Sherman, Elton Rayack, Ruth Heller, Sarla, Ben Sherman, Bill Heller, Sanjay, Gautam.

I even recall my exact salary – it was $11,000 per year. I earned some extra income teaching summer courses. There was not much to do in the small university town of Kingston except to entertain friends and spend time with family. Life there was certainly less chaotic than in Boston. Sarla enjoyed hosting Indian graduate students from the

Departments of Engineering, Pharmacology, and Mathematics. One of them, Alakananda Paul, was the first woman to earn a PhD in engineering from URI. We continue to be close family friends.

Our second son, Gautam, was born in a Warwick, RI hospital 20 miles away from our home on May 13, 1969.[44] Mrs. Verma, wife of our mathematics professor friend, was so affectionate to our family that she offered to take care of baby Gautam and insisted that Sarla do something and make use of her education since she had an advanced master's degree. We remain very close family friends with both the Vermas. I enjoyed my three years at URI and consider that period as the second-best phase of my life, after the early days in New Delhi. Sarla and I led a more enjoyable and balanced life, and we are still in touch with many of the friends made in Rhode Island at that time.

> **I enjoyed my three years at URI and consider that period as the second-best phase of my life, after the early days in New Delhi.**

The Prakash family in 1971 in Kingston, Rhode Island.
Sanjay is 10 and Gautam is 2½ years old.

---

[44] Lord Gautama Buddha, born as *Siddhartha Gautama*, is the founder of Buddhism. After he came across the four heart-rending scenes of agony, misery, disease and death, he gave up his princely life and set off to find a solution for these troubles. He got enlightenment *"Sambodhi"* in 'Bodh Gaya' under a Banyan tree in Bihar, near to where Sarla was raised. He shared the path of supreme knowledge to his disciples.

4.3: Joining the World Bank

The International Bank for Reconstruction and Development (IBRD) is an international financial institution conceived in 1944 at the Bretton Woods Conference in New Hampshire for the purpose of aiding reconstruction of those countries affected by World War II and, more generally, to assist in the development of what were then called Third-World (developing) countries. The IBRD is the first of five member institutions that comprise the World Bank Group and is headquartered at 1818 H Street NW, Washington, DC. The Bank maintained its focus on reducing poverty in the developing world by providing loans for building schools and hospitals, improving literacy, and reforming agriculture and infrastructure. Despite the common goals shared by delegates, the power differential between those from developing and developed countries remained intact.

In the spring of 1971, during my third year at URI, Professor Hollis Chenery (Harvard University), was working as Vice President for Developmental Policy at the World Bank. He contacted his friend, Professor Richard Eckaus, who happened to be my principal thesis adviser at MIT, informing him about a job opportunity at the World Bank in a department devoted to collecting, assembling, and analyzing statistical data pertaining to global economic development and growth – my specialty. Professor Eckaus suggested that I apply for the job. He was aware of Sanjay's need for medical care and thought that moving to Washington, DC would provide us with access to excellent doctors and hospitals, as well as good schools for both Sanjay and Gautam.

Professor Richard Eckaus, Vinod's PhD thesis advisor at MIT and a long-time mentor to Vinod. Picture taken in 2009.

The metropolitan location and the salary were enticing enough on their own, but the prestige of the World Bank (and its many perks, like paid home leave trips to India every two years, and first-class air travel on official missions) convinced me to apply. The World Bank's president was then Robert McNamara (1968-1981). After interviews with Hollis Chenery, Helen Hughes, and others, I was offered the position. Though Rhode Island offered the prospect of a happy and relaxed life, the World Bank beckoned and hence our lives would change once again. In accordance with the World Bank relocation policy, transitional arrangements for our stay were made in Northern Virginia. I would commute by car to work in D.C.

One day, I asked Sarla to bring our children to visit me at work, so I could show them my new office. She had acquired a driver's license by then, but in the excitement of this visit she had forgotten to put it in her purse. She drove them into the city without any incident but, as we were driving away from the Bank afterward, a taxicab hit our car as Sarla turned left from 18th Street NW onto Pennsylvania Avenue. I reported the incident to the police promptly, though the African cab driver simply wanted to exchange phone numbers and leave the scene. An African-American policeman arrived and gave Sarla a $5 ticket for failing to exhibit her driving permit. He then asked us to follow him to the police station around 23rd Street NW to file an official report. While at the station, Sarla went out to check on Gautam, who was only two, and Sanjay, who was ten, as they were waiting in our car alone. The police officer, furious that she left without permission, proceeded to arrest us! He gave us a $50 ticket in place of the original $5 ticket, which angered me. The cop and I got into a little scuffle during the process, after which he shut both of us in a closed room (while Sanjay and Gautam continued to wait for us alone in the car). Curious about why we were locked up, I inquired as to what had happened and was informed that a serious charge had been registered against me, that of assaulting a police officer on duty while on the premises of the police station. Apparently, after the scuffle, the African-American cop had blood on his hands and a senior white officer came in to make sure that the accusation was valid by inspecting my hands closely as well as the cop's hands and fingernails. It turned out the blood on the officer's hands was fake. We were immediately released and we returned home. Later, I had to appear in court, but that cop failed to appear,

Despite our eventual exoneration, this encounter with the police was one of the more harrowing experiences we faced while living in D.C.

enabling the judge to waive not only the $50 fine but also the $5 ticket. Despite our eventual exoneration, this encounter with the police was one of the more harrowing experiences we faced while living in D.C.

4.4: The World Bank – Some Recollections

My first official trip on behalf of the World Bank was a Basic Economic Mission to Indonesia during the summer of 1972. I was made Acting Division Chief during the second year of my tenure at the World Bank. I then resigned from the University of Rhode Island, from which I had been on official leave. In 1976, I led the first mission to South Korea, and later led missions to Malaysia, Indonesia, and the Philippines, where I met and negotiated with the country's top government officials responsible for planning and development. I was also appointed to the Bank's Task Force on Computerization in 1977 and designated a team leader for writing reports and leading missions.

Consistent with the Bank's policy to encourage using consultants from the developing world, as a project officer I visited the Indian Statistical Institute, Calcutta (my alma mater), and the Indian Institute of Management, Ahmedabad, during the late 1970s. My task was to invite a team of experts in industrialization and trade policy. But due to the lack of team spirit and inadequate expertise, I was compelled to hand over the project to an Australian team. A couple of years later, I visited India again, this time to study the adequacy of extension services for small-scale enterprises. For the comparative study, I chose Andhra Pradesh, Bihar, and Gujarat and was really impressed by the work culture in Gujarat.

In D.C., we met Adi Davar, a World Bank employee, and his wife Parveen, who helped us adjust to our new surroundings around Lake Barcroft, in Falls Church, Virginia. We lived in that neighborhood for a year, but we soon moved across the Potomac River to 8217 Hamilton Spring Court, in the Carderock Springs development of Bethesda, Maryland.

Our Home. Carderock Springs. Bethesda

Prakash family home in the Carderock Springs neighborhood of Bethesda, MD. The family resided there from 1972 through 1987.

We chose Maryland because it is a more liberal state than Virginia but still allowed me easy access to the Bank. The homes in our neighborhood were built in a contemporary style during the early 1960s, with many windows enabling us to view the beautiful wooded lots. At least a quarter of the neighborhood's residents were officials of the World Bank, the International Monetary Fund, and various embassies. Carderock Springs thus acquired the nickname "the International Ghetto."

The community was well-organized, cordial, and friendly. It had its own newsletter and a local directory of residents, with telephone numbers and the names and ages of children, which was helpful in organizing carpools and social activities. The area's schools were excellent, and the local public high school, Walt Whitman, is still one of the top-rated high schools in the country. The community also had its own swimming pool and tennis courts. One summer, we decided we should all learn to swim. And so, we did! During these summers, out in the sunshine and at the swimming pool, we mingled with our neighbors and enjoyed the comfort and joys of American suburban living. The only drawback of the area was its distance from the nearest Metro station which was six miles away. This caused some inconvenience when friends and relatives came to visit, but the difficulty was minimal compared to the advantages.

One unique and challenging experience we had was in 1973 during our family's Christmas vacation to Disney World. This was the time of the energy crisis, and I realized this only when I failed to fill up our gas tank before the trip, even after checking at five local gas stations. My family was disheartened. Fortunately, a friend advised me that if I changed all my reservations to stay at 8 Days Inn hotels throughout our travel, the Inn would fill our tank while checking out. That tip worked but with a snag, for the payments were to be made in cash only for which I was not well prepared. While returning from Orlando, all my travelers checks were exhausted, and I was in dire need of cash. So, in Atlanta I went to a bank to withdraw $100 with my personal check. The manager courteously declined even though I had a bank balance of over $3,000. However, my demeanor, along with my World Bank

ID, prompted him to give me $25 cash in accordance with state law, but this was not enough. So, I went to a nearby Sears store and tried to borrow against my store credit card, but there too I could only borrow $25, since I had never used their card.[45] We had to stay overnight on our way home, and the next morning missed our breakfast due to a shortage of cash. As soon as I could, I reached a bank where I had an account and withdrew some cash.

My colleagues at the World Bank were friendly and professional, but the institutional culture was a little intimidating. A typical bureaucratic hierarchy prevailed there. For example, I could see the Division Chief at any time, but I could not directly communicate with the Director unless given consent by the Division Chief. A significant challenge for me was navigating the subtle etiquette at the Bank which required a more sophisticated grasp of the English language than I possessed. I benefited from the Bank's employee English enrichment program. Not only was I keenly aware of my limitations in speaking and writing, I had been taught as a child to be direct and straightforward in my communication, which didn't quite mesh with the rhetorical finesse required at the international institution, where careful articulation and diplomacy reigned supreme. It might have been slow-going, but I eventually learned the nuances of the Bank's erudite culture.

4.5: Traveling for Work and Home Leave

Despite these initial issues with communication, I found the work both challenging and interesting. In those days, there was no digital or electronic database of statistics available to specialists, and so I was asked

---

[45]   Being an Indian of modest origins, I had developed a habit of living within our own means. I was not at all used to relying on credit cards. During our domestic and international travel, I used American Express Travelers' Checks which were available on the World Bank premises. In those days, American Express guaranteed their travelers' checks would be replaced if lost or stolen, making them safer to carry than cash and easy to use. Due to technological advancements, particularly the proliferation of debit and credit cards, travelers' checks are mostly a thing of the past.

to visit the United Nations and many of its agencies to meet with top experts in person.[46] I travelled the world in order to do so.

I recall meeting two people in particular who became lifelong friends. On the World Bank's Basic Economic Mission to Iran in 1973, I met an American woman, Ruth Tabrah, a renowned author and educational expert. We became close family friends over the ensuing years. She retired and moved to Hawaii after converting from Catholicism to Buddhism, and later traveled all the way to Washington, DC, to bless Gautam and his wife Anjali at their wedding in 1997. Basant Raj Bhandari, senior advisor at the International Trade Center in Geneva, another traveler whom I first met in the 1970s, also became our close friend, and we are still in touch with him to this day.

I met a variety of interesting people on flights and in the first-class lounges. Once, while relaxing in the Air India lounge at Heathrow Airport in London, I met the CEO of Wedgwood, the British makers of fine china, ceramics, porcelain, and luxury accessories founded in 1759. When I asked the CEO why he traveled by Air India instead of British Airways, he said that British Airways didn't provide him with the same care and respect as did Air India. That was lovely to hear. Back then Air India was true to its *"Maharaja"* (Sanskrit for "great ruler") slogan, which, alas, over the years has worn down.

In the early part of 1982, I was part of the World Bank's Basic Economic Mission to Zimbabwe where I met with Robert Mugabe, who was serving as Prime Minister at the time. On this trip, I purchased a large copper wall-hanging as a gift for my family. I was quite sad when, during the last leg of my flight back to Washington, this precious memento was stolen.

---

[46] These agencies included: UNSO (United Nations Statistical Office) in New York; UNIDO (United Nations Industrial Development Organization) in Vienna, Austria; UNESCO (United Nations Educational, Scientific and Cultural Organization) in Paris, France; the ITC (International Trade Centre) and UNCTAD (United Nations Conference on Trade and Development) in Geneva, Switzerland; FAO (Food and Agricultural Organization) in Rome, Italy; and some of the regional development banks and institutions in Asia.

In addition to my official travels for the World Bank, I traveled with my family to India every two years for home leave (one of the generous perks of working at the Bank was paid biennial family trips to one's homeland). On the way to India, we often stopped to see as much of the world as possible: we visited over 40 countries on our home leaves, including the United Kingdom, Germany, the Netherlands, Norway, Sweden, Austria, Denmark, France, Spain, Portugal, Italy, Greece, Yugoslavia, Egypt, the Philippines, Japan, Malaysia, Indonesia, Thailand, Taiwan, Hong Kong, Singapore, and Nepal.

I took my first home leave in 1972, for a period of five weeks, and the family traveled to India, where Sarla and the kids stayed for five additional weeks to attend the wedding of Sarla's niece. Sanjay's school permitted his long absence with the understanding that he would keep a diary about his visit and give a presentation to his class upon his return. Both his classmates and his teachers enjoyed hearing about the trip. This home leave was very special because it enabled me to bring to DC from India my household effects such as a steel *almirah* (cabinet), furniture and fixtures, kitchen stainless steel utensils, and a stone mortar. I shipped everything from Bombay (now Mumbai) and received it at Baltimore. No customs had to be paid because of my diplomatic G4 visa status.

Another enticing feature of the Bank's home leave policy was the opportunity to sail on a luxury cruise ship, the Queen Elizabeth II (QEII) from New York to Britain. We all experienced seasickness, but not Gautam! At just three years old, he was the only one who fully enjoyed the 5-day trip across the Atlantic. After disembarking at the port in South Hampton, we reached London by special train. As a vegetarian family, we had access to only steamed vegetables, salads, fruits and dairy products, unlike the myriad vegetarian options available today. We had another nerve-wracking experience in London, as we nearly missed our flight to India. We arrived late at the check-in counter because of traffic. The Air India agent insisted that the door to the plane was already closed and said that we could not board. Fortunately, a British agent heard my plea and quickly whisked us to the door of the aircraft by special car.

In India, the children loved all the new sights and sounds. While traveling by taxi from Delhi to Meerut, about a 2-hour journey, Gautam spotted various animals on the road – dogs, cows, buffaloes, camels, donkeys, and monkeys – all regular sights in the Indian countryside, but new to the American-born child. He jumped up from his seat shouting "Mummy, Mummy, we are in a zoo!" Later, some friendly villagers hoisted Gautam and Sanjay onto a bullock cart for a short ride, which was great fun for the kids, and just one of the highlights of our travels.

"Mummy, Mummy, we are in a zoo!"

Though we did take the children to visit some temples and pilgrimage sites, it was not our focus in India. Instead, we scheduled visits to village schools and new industrial plants, like the Bata Shoe Factory in Patna and the Hindustan Machine Tools and Hindustan Aeronautics plants, both in Bangalore (now Bengaluru). Even before the founding of the India Development and Relief Fund (IDRF) in 1988, we were committed to social justice and wanted our visits to be educational in all senses of the term. We especially wanted to make sure that our sons continued to feel a connection to India and were familiar with the ground realities there, despite their upbringing in the U.S.

Our home was burglarized and vandalized while we were away during our home leave trip in the summer of 1975. Apparently, such burglary was fun for local high school students roaming around during their summer vacation. They entered the house by breaking the skylight and stole some portable gadgets such as our stereo, TV, kitchen utensils, and alcoholic beverages.[47] Fortunately, my friend had our key, visited the house, and promptly locked it again after the incident. Upon our return I filed a home insurance claim. To my utter surprise, the policy was deemed to have been cancelled because of non-payment of the premium. It was to be paid by my bank upon the premium notice. The bank confirmed that it hadn't received any notice at all. I had to hire a

---

[47] Many years later we had another funny experience of being locked out of our house, while we waited for the locksmith for more than an hour, and it took only 20 seconds for him to open the lock. Lesson learnt: we immediately installed a latch lock and stopped relying exclusively on auto lock.

lawyer to proceed further. The insurance company agreed to pay but we faced hurdles in proving the value of each stolen item to the court. We had to arrange for the store managers to appear in court. The case was settled for 50 percent of the actual value. What an experience! On all subsequent home leave trips, we rented our home to European scientists visiting the National Institutes of Health for short visits, as a way to reduce the risk of a burglary.

We had an interesting travel experience when we visited Egypt in 1979, on our way to India, during one of our biennial home leave vacations. We had a wonderful trip, visited the pyramids, and were scheduled to head to Bombay (now Mumbai). When we reached Cairo airport, we found it an absolute jungle, overcrowded, and almost impossible to find the check-in counter. We missed our flight, and since there were no daily flights to Bombay, we had to rebook the hotel for another three days. Interestingly, however, as we were getting ready to leave the airport, we learned that the plane had not yet taken off – there was a man gesturing to us. Being a stranger in a foreign land, I could not figure out what he meant. Later, I realized that if I had bribed the man we might have got onto that India-bound flight! Given the fact that we did not have Egyptian Dinars left, and we had to stay in the hotel for an additional three days, we had to go in search of an American Express bank where we could exchange our travelers' checks. Not all was luxury and efficiency in the past, and air travel, especially to developing countries, was fraught with problems. But that did not deter us.

Later, I realized that if I had bribed the man we might have got onto that India-bound flight!

I recall some bad experiences, including one in Hong Kong, where Indian visitors were regularly cheated by the Chinese shopkeepers who looked down upon Indians. I bought a duty-free Japanese Minolta camera in Hong Kong. While talking to the hotel manager I learned that it was not uncommon practice in Hong Kong for shopkeepers to dupe customers, and Indian visitors were some of the more commonly duped. Indeed, when I returned to my hotel and examined the camera I had just purchased, I realized that while I paid for a Minolta SRT 102,

I was actually given the less expensive Minolta SRT 104, which had a smaller focal length. Prior to leaving Hong Kong, fortunately, I had time to revisit the shop and exchange it for the desired one. In contrast, I found Singapore shopkeepers to be much more trustworthy; plus, we found that the city was better organized and cleaner than Hong Kong. I did, however, have an overwhelmingly positive experience with Chinese custom tailoring and still wear the suits I had made in Hong Kong in the 1970s and 80s.

The other memorable trip was to Indonesia in 1988: we loved Yogyakarta (also called Jogjakarta) in Java and we also visited one of the largest 9th-century Mahayana Buddhist temples at Borobudur in central Java. We enjoyed our visit to the island of Bali, where Hindu ethos are retained to this day. We were even invited to enjoy a local wedding. I was busy in official meetings, and so Sarla attended the wedding and was pleasantly surprised as she observed many Hindu traditions and rituals that Indonesian Muslims followed at their weddings. During informal chats with Indonesian officials, I repeatedly heard from them that even though their ancestors converted from Hinduism to Islam, they succeeded in retaining their historic cultural values.[48]

I recall our visit to Germany, where we toured the Dachau concentration camp in Munich, in which nearly 41,500 Jews were massacred under Hitler's reign. Dachau epitomizes man's inhumanity to man. But the Germans have acknowledged their dark deeds and Germany has quickly re-emerged as a strong, healthy nation, committed to protecting human rights around the world. We also visited Stuttgart and the Mercedes-Benz headquarters and factory. We were escorted from the airport by the company and taken to the headquarters as guests because of my semi-diplomatic status (G4 Visa). Every time my family visited Germany, we had the privilege of ordering a new Mercedes-Benz. We were shown a memorable film about their manufacturing process and were able to see the factory floor as well.

---

[48] For instance, *Ramayana* ballet (cultural dance drama) is routinely played in Indonesian hotels. During Prime Minister Atal Bihari Vajpayee's government, an Indonesian ballet team of more than 100 performed a *Ramayana* dance drama in several cities of India.

The Prakash family in 1976 in front of their car. The World Bank provided diplomatic status which avoided taxes, so families could buy a foreign car, such as a Mercedes, and then sell it 2-3 years later for the same price!

I visited Malaysia on official business, along with my family, as I did to Indonesia and the Philippines. In Japan, we were awestruck by the cleanliness of houses and by their tiny size. We took the early morning bullet train from Tokyo to Nara, the ancient Japanese capital, now a UNESCO World Heritage site. We visited nearby Kyoto and were once again impressed by the Japanese mindfulness and attention to detail, as well as their courtesy and kindness.

I visited Johannesburg in South Africa, during the days of apartheid. From the hotel, I called an Indian, whose name was given by one of my Sangh Parivar (RSS) contacts in Canada. I was staying in that hotel just for a day. My Indian contact told me that if I had been in town longer, he would have insisted I stay at his home. He took me around Johannesburg, where I witnessed racial discrimination firsthand: Indians could buy homes and live only in "Lenasia," 20 miles away from Johannesburg.[49]

---

[49] Asians had a colony exclusively for them where they had schools, shopping, and temples and mosques, etc.

4.6: Indian / U.S. Citizenship

Sarla became a citizen of the United States in 1976 in order to become more closely involved in American society. She wanted to vote and exercise her rights as a full-fledged American. As required under U.S. law, two close friends, Margie Johnson and Carol Lowe (both US citizens), appeared in court as her witnesses and they still continue to be good friends even now after four decades.

Sarla with Carol Lowe and Margie Johnson

I, on the other hand, remain loyal to my Indian citizenship – I am a green card holder to this day. I was never very political and would not have actively participated as a citizen of the United States in public affairs, beyond voting periodically. What was most important to me, instead, was retaining my connection to India and my identity as an Indian. In particular, I was not willing to take the Naturalization Oath of Allegiance to the United States of America which requires that I "absolutely and entirely renounce and abjure all allegiance" to my home country.

> **What was most important to me, instead, was retaining my connection to India and my identity as an Indian.**

4.7: Hospitality to Friends and Relatives

For many years, we routinely housed various friends, relatives and social service volunteers for days, weeks or even months at a time. This was the Indian hospitality we had grown up with, but it was something our American friends found odd. Some examples follow.

For many years, we routinely housed various friends, relatives and social service volunteers for days, weeks or even months at a time.

It was an honor to sponsor my research assistant from ISI in Delhi, AP Narayana Paudwal, who joined the World Bank as my assistant upon my recommendation in 1972. He stayed with us for a month until he found an apartment. We also assisted our friend's niece, Achala Mittal, who had completed her MBBS in India. On December 22, 1976, when we were already in bed, we received a call from my childhood friend IB Gupta, who was Achala's maternal uncle, and her father, requesting sponsorship for her visa, so that she could receive her green card in India before she traveled to the U.S. I remember I cancelled our Christmas vacation to complete the paperwork and promised financial support – without consulting Sarla. Achala could receive a green card in India only if she was able to depart by January 10, 1977. My sponsorship enabled her to arrive at Dulles International Airport on January 5 with green card in hand. Fresh from school, Achala arrived at our home not knowing anything about cooking or about household chores. She stayed with us for five months, a gesture that surprised our American friends. Similarly, at our new home in 1988, we hosted Sarla's niece and her husband, Drs. Madhu and Anoop Goyal, along with their baby daughter Mansi, for five months helping them in making appropriate arrangements for their medical residency.

Two of my nephews traveled from India to the United States to pursue higher education on their own merit and I guided them. The first, Mahesh *bhaisaheb's* son, Abhay Indrayan, received his PhD in 1977 in biostatistics from the Ohio State University, and retired as the Head of the Department of Biostatistics and Medical Informatics at the Delhi University College of Medical Sciences in 2010. Secondly, Savitri *jiji's* son, Ashutosh Varshney, received his PhD in 1990 from MIT and now teaches at Brown University as the Sol Goldman Professor of Political Science; we even supported his college education in India. Sarla and I cherish our memories of Sharda *jiji* followed by Satya *bhaiya* and *bhabhi* while they visited us here. Their visit to Niagara Falls on the Canadian side was most memorable.

For two decades, 1984-2004, our home was a regular guest house for RSS leaders, which provided us the unique opportunity to closely interact with them. We also continued to keep in touch with and provide hospitality to other members of the family and particularly to IDRF volunteers. All credit goes to Sarla. Our adherence to the tenets of *Arya Samaj* helped us to act with generosity and promote the well-being of others.

4.8: Connecting to Indian Culture

We consider our Hindu faith more in spiritual than religious terms: we discard all caste, creed and ritualistic traditions. Instead of working toward a universal ideal, we are grounded in our Hindu upbringing and embrace humanity at large. Therefore, over the years, we were not active members of any Indian cultural group in DC, nor did we visit any temple regularly. We did occasionally attend a *katha* (sermon), including one by the spiritual leader Morari Bapu during his nine-day *katha* in 1984, and the lectures of Swami Chinmayananda's, as well as various *Diwali* and *Janmashtami* festivals. While Sanjay and Gautam were growing up, we regularly celebrated Christmas and Thanksgiving along with our Korean friends and neighbors, Dr. Jay and Sookie Lee, and allowed the boys the fun of having gifts under the tree. This tradition is followed by our sons and grandchildren.

> **We consider our Hindu faith more in spiritual than religious terms: we discard all caste, creed and ritualistic traditions.**

Thanksgiving at Sookie Lee's home. We spent many years celebrating both Thanksgiving and Christmas with the Lee family (Sookie, Jay and sons Erich and Brian). Erich is not in the picture as he is the photographer!

We supported *Natya Bharati*, an Indian theatre group in Washington, DC, which produces stage-plays in Hindi with the help of local talent. In addition, in 1974, Sarla was involved in the very early plans to establish The India School which is still dedicated to teaching Indian languages, fine arts, and culture in Bethesda, MD on Sundays.

India School teachers. Sarla is 2nd from right in the back row and to her right is Darshan Krishna who founded India School in 1974. The school continues even today. Sanjay and Gautam attended the school for many years while Sarla was teaching there.

Sarla taught Hindi and social studies at the school for two decades, but resigned when she sensed administrative hiccups, and was alleged to have been incorporating Hindu thought and philosophy into her lessons. One day a student brought in an *aarti* (Hindu religious ritual of worship) prayer from home. Sarla viewed this as an opportunity to expand the class' Hindi vocabulary, but Darshan Krishna, the administrator/founder, objected to even this tangential use of religion in the school. Sarla was basically asked to stop referring to the Vedas and to Indian epics and scriptures. Her strong belief that much of the Indian ethos and culture is rooted in these spiritual texts led her to dissociate herself from the school in 1994. However, we are happy that India School continues to serve the local community and we remain friendly with Darshan Krishna.

4.9: Travels to Cultural and Historical Sites in India

We feel privileged to have extensively travelled from Kashmir in the north to Kanyakumari in the south, starting in the 1970s for four decades until 2009 (the year before I became completely blind). We also endeavored to gain firsthand insight into India's cultural and historical heritage during our visits. We went to Dal Lake, Srinagar taking the *shikara* (houseboat) to the floating market and it was great fun. My sister Sarla jiji flew from Pondicherry and accompanied us on this trip. While there, we purchased a handmade Kashmiri silk rug that still adorns our front hallway.

While visiting Trivandrum and Kerala in 1979, we were keen to view the southernmost tip of India, Kanyakumari (Tamil Nadu). During this visit we also took a short trip by boat to the renowned Vivekananda Rock memorial, where Vivekananda attained enlightenment while he meditated for 3 days, December 25-27, 1892. Though only 29 years old, Vivekananda was subsequently sponsored to represent Hinduism by Raja Bhaskar Sethupathy of Ramnad, Madurai to attend the First Parliament of the World's Religions, held at Chicago, USA in September 1893. Our experience at Kanyakumari was so mesmerizing that it transformed our lives permanently; serving the marginalized and deprived in India has become our life's mission.

In 2009, we had an exciting visit to The Paradesi Jewish synagogue in Kerala. It was built in 1568 by the Jewish community in Kochi, composed mainly of Malabari Jews originating from the period of King Solomon (dating back to 970 BCE). A Sanskrit phrase that's embedded in the Indian tradition and culture reflects "Vasudhaiva Kutumbakam, which means "The World is One Family." There is a small Jewish community that has been left behind to hold the history and heritage after most Jews migrated to Israel upon its formation in 1968. Also in 1968, Indira Gandhi, the Indian Prime Minister, attended the 400th anniversary of the synagogue celebrations.

Although our travels were done over a decade ago, we continue to have vivid recollections of many sights and sounds. We visited the ancient Nalanda Buddhist Monastery, the world's earliest residential university (500 AD to 1200 AD), which is located just a few miles away from Sarla's hometown of Bihar Sharif. The university was destroyed by Muslim Turkic general Muhammad Bakhtiyar Khilji who massacred and burnt Buddhist monks and Brahmin scholars to ashes during his raids across the North Indian plains. The tremendous odor of the burnt relics was so strong that it is still experienced by us as tourists, many hundreds of years later. It is now a UNESCO World Heritage Site.

It was imperative that we visited Rajgir and Pawapuri, not only due to their proximity to Sarla's hometown but also due to their great historical and cultural significance. History of Rajgir dates back to 558 BCE for its association with Haryanka Dynasty as the capital city and is also famous for its hot water springs and hilly landscape. Even in the epic of *Mahabharat* it is called a Girivraja. We ended our trip by paying our respects to the 24th thirthankar Mahavir's place of nirvana. Both Mahavir and Buddha were contemporaries who denounced their royalty and dedicated their lives towards betterment of humanity. While in Bangalore, we made an overnight bus trip to visit Gommateshwara statue, in Shravanbelagola, the tallest monolithic statue in the world, carved out of a single block of granite which was dedicated to the Jain figure Bahubali. It was built around 983 BCE. This trip reinforced our faith in the Indian ethos.

We were fortunate to visit the Ram Janma Bhoomi, Ayodhya in 1990, prior to the demolition of Babri Masjid on December 6, 1992. Ayodhya is revered as the birthplace of Hindu deity Rama and was marked by a temple, which was plundered and destroyed by orders of the first Mughal emperor Babur (1526-30 AD) and a disputed mosque was erected in its place. The relics made it obvious for laymen like us to believe that there was ancient temple. It took a long time for independent India to resolve this matter amicably and legally. The final judgement in the Ayodhya dispute was declared by the Supreme Court of India on November 9, 2019. In accordance with its final verdict, the groundbreaking ceremony took place on August 5, 2020 to rebuild a temple.

Our 1990 India trip was very special to us since we visited Shri Kashi Vishwanath Temple, which is one the 12 Jyotirlingas, the holiest shrines among Shiva Temples. We still reminisce about this visit and the extremely congested roads and dilapidated surroundings. The last original structure of the Temple was demolished by Aurangzeb, who constructed the Gyanvapi Mosque on its site. The current structure was built on an adjacent site by the Maratha ruler, Ahilya Bai Holkar of Indore in 1780. Maharaja Ranjit Singh, First Sikh Maharaja, donated one ton of gold for the Flaming Temple's Dome. To facilitate the visits of numerous devotees and tourists, the government of India initiated a long-term development plan in the year 2020.

We enjoyed our hopping air flight to visit the Khajuraho Group of Monuments, comprised of Hindu and Jain temples in Chhatarpur district, Central India. They are famous for their Nagara-Style architectural symbolism and their erotic sculptures. Most Khajuraho temples were built between 950 AD and 1050 AD by the Chandela dynasty. These temples are a UNESCO World Heritage Site.

During our 2004 visit to Gujarat, we combined our trip to see earthquake rehabilitation work along with the Somnath Temple, Dwaraka (the ancient capital of Shri Krishna), and Porbandar, Mahatma Gandhi's birthplace. Somnath Temple is also one of the 12 Jyotirlingas and is believed to have been prehistoric. The destroyed temple was rebuilt by the Yadava kings around 649 AD. It was raided by several Muslim rulers, most prominent was in 1024, by Turkic Muslim ruler Mahmud of Ghazni. The present temple was reconstructed in 1950-51 by the orders of the Home Minister of India Sardar Vallabhbhai Patel. President Dr. Rajendra Prasad inaugurated the Somnath Temple, despite Prime Minister Nehru's reluctance. In our visit to Gandhi's home, we picked up a hand-painted photo frame of Gandhi and Lal Bahdur Shastri and other leaders during the Independence movement. This painting still adorns our entryway.

Though we are not religious, it was imperative for us to visit world famous south Indian Hindu temples which escaped Muslim invasions. The most prominent Hindu shrine in south India is the Venkateswara Temple in Tirupathi, Andhra Pradesh, believed to have been built around 300 AD in the style of Dravidian architecture. This shrine is visited by 50,000 to 100,000 pilgrims every day and for the *darshan*, there are two queues, one free and the other is paid, but for charity. Everyday *Prasadam* and *Annadanam* (free food) is offered to pilgrims. The devotees who contribute to the Annadanam believe that offering food (to the needy) without expecting anything in return is the purest form of devotion.

We had an opportunity to visit Meenakshi Temple in Madurai, which was invaded and looted in 13th century by Aladdin Khilji Muslim ruler. Late in the 16th century Vijayanagara kings restored and brought glory back to Meenakshi Temple. We also have been to Ramanathaswamy Temple, one of the 12 Jyotirlingas, in Rameshwaram, Tamil Nadu. According to Ramayana, an epic of ancient India, deity Rama worshiped Shiva at Rameshwaram prior to his fight with Ravana in Sri Lanka. He won the battle and brought his wife Sita back. It is believed that the couple crossed a 30-mile-long bridge (Rama-Setu), which is a chain of limestone shoals, between Pamban Island (also known as Rameshwaram Island) off the southeastern coast of India, and Gulf of Mannar Island, off the northwestern coast of Sri Lanka.

We flew from Bombay to Aurangabad and visited the Ajanta-Ellora rock-cut Buddhist cave monuments. These caves were carved from

2nd century BC to 5th century AD. The caves include paintings and sculptures described as among the finest surviving examples of ancient Indian art, particularly expressive paintings that present emotions through gesture, pose and form (a UNESCO World Heritage Site). Later, we learned that the scenic view of travel from Bombay to Goa by train would be eye-catching. So, we travelled by train instead of plane. The train had a deluxe Vista dome carriage, offering passengers supersized windows and a see-through canopy roof with spectacular view. This route crossed over 2000 bridges and ducked through 92 tunnels making it very memorable.

Our active involvement in IDRF's Orissa super cyclone relief and rehabilitation in 1999 provided us an opportunity to pay our respects to Shri Jaganadh temple, Puri. Thousands of pilgrims from all over India visit this temple. The reconstruction of the temple was completed in the early 13th century by the Ganga dynasty and Gajapati dynasty on the banks of eastern coast of India. We have a vivid memory of hundreds of poor people, particularly widows, sitting on the roadsides waiting for alms. This image is another reason for us to recommit ourselves to social service.

As a couple, the only city in India where we resided is Delhi. One of Delhi's most famous tourist destinations is the Red Fort. From the time India gained Independence on August 15, 1947, the occasion has been celebrated every year at the Red Fort. The celebratory light and sound show still mesmerizes us. The Red Fort was built by renowned Mughal Emperor Shah Jahan (1639-1648). The most significant among his architectural achievements is Taj Mahal, Agra, one of the Seven Wonders of the World. The construction of the Taj Mahal involved more than 20,000 artisans for a period of twenty-one years (1632-1653). As the most popular tourist site in India, the government has recently introduced a high speed (bullet) train from Delhi to Agra and back, similar to what we experienced in Japan.

Sanjay and Gautam at the Taj Mahal, Agra, India, 1981.

The Qutub Minar is a minaret and "victory tower" that forms part of the Qutub complex, another UNESCO World Heritage Site. It was built by commander Qutb-ud-din Aibak (1199-1220). We enjoyed climbing all the way up the 379 spiral stairs to see the entire city of Delhi, a spectacular view from some 236 feet high. Part of the Qutub complex is an iron pillar. This pillar was built by Chandra Gupta II. It is famous for the rust-resistant composition of the metals used in its construction (375-415 AD). We wonder how the pillar was moved hundreds of miles away from its original place, it being over six tons of weight and over 24-feet high. In our view, this pillar provides another example of looting by Muslim rulers/invaders in medieval India.

Republic Day is celebrated in New Delhi on January 26 every year since 1950. On this day, ceremonious parades are performed on Rajpath (formerly known as Kingsway) from Rashtrapathi Bhavan (Presidential Palace, formerly Viceroy's House) to India Gate as a tribute to India, its unity in diversity and rich cultural heritage. As frequent visitors to Delhi, we watched the progress of the tableaux that represent the history, heritage, and culture of India. Although the program is telecast throughout India and watched by millions, tens of thousands of people assemble around Janpath to watch this spectacular event live despite the typically very cold January weather. The Rashtrapathi Bhavan is built on 320 acres of land, with a 340-room main building that has the president's official residence, including reception halls, guest rooms, and offices. It is the largest residence of any head of state in the world, and so was the glory of the British Empire!

We planned our trip to Rashtrapathi Bhavan so that we could enjoy the beauty of its Mughal Garden in bloom, along with a small portion of the bhavan's complex that is accessible to tourists. Along with our children, we also visited the Parliament house when it was not in session. We visited many interesting sites in and around Delhi, such as Birla Mandir, ISKON Temple and BAPS, etc. While visiting the Birla Mandir, Sarla instantly recalled her visit as a child along with her Jijaji, wherein she had attended Gandhiji's prayer of "Ishwar Alah tero naam…." that still reverberates in her mind. It was inevitable for us to pay our respect to Gandhiji at Rajghat; all foreign dignitaries pay their tributes to him there.

We made a trip from Delhi to Jallianwala Bagh, Wagah Border and Golden Temple – all around Amritsar. Jallianwala Bagh is a historic garden and 'memorial of national importance,' to the massacre of freedom fighters that occurred there on April 13, 1919. Fifteen thousand peaceful patriots attended the gathering, of which over 2500 were inhumanely wounded or killed upon the orders of General Dyer of the British army, who opened fire here on unarmed people. It is thus an everlasting symbol of the non-violent and peaceful struggle for the freedom of India. Just 20 miles from Amritsar is the renowned Attari-Wagah Border (only 15 miles from Lahore in Pakistan), which is on the historic Grand Trunk Road connecting Peshawar (in northwest Pakistan) to Calcutta (in eastern India). The daily ceremony honoring and lowering of the national flags is held at the border as a military practice that the Border Security Force of Indian and Pakistani Rangers have jointly followed since 1959. As representatives of IDRF, an MLA of

Punjab accompanied us to witness the program from the VIP corridor. Attari Wagah Border is famous as an international trade route where traders not only from India and Pakistan but even from Afghanistan trade mainly dry fruits.

We have vivid and loving memories of paying our respects at the Golden Temple. We delightedly followed all the etiquette expected of visitors. The Golden Temple is also known as Harmandir Sahib, spiritually the most significant shrine in Sikhism. The Gurdwara was repeatedly rebuilt by the Sikhs after it became a target of persecution and was destroyed several times by the Mughal and invading Afghan armies. Maharaja Ranjit Singh after founding the Sikh Empire, rebuilt it in marble and copper in 1809 and overlaid the sanctum with gold foil in 1830. Harmandir Sahib Complex has a Langar, a community-run free kitchen and dining hall. Vegetarian food is served to all visitors and all people eat together as equals.

4.10: State of Emergency in India

Our family retained many connections to India during my time at the World Bank. We took special care to follow the news from India as closely as possible. Though there were no Indian newspapers or Indian TV programs available in the United States at the time, we learned of the significant events through mainstream American media. The event which most significantly impacted my life during this period was the imposition of Emergency by Prime Minister Indira Gandhi. The country had been in a state of political unrest for some time when, on June 12, 1975, the Allahabad High Court found Indira Gandhi guilty of electoral fraud and declared her 1971 election to the *Lok Sabha*, the Lower House of the Parliament of India, null and void. Though the Supreme Court later granted a stay allowing Indira Gandhi to remain a member of the *Lok Sabha*, she was restricted from voting in parliament's proceedings. Jayaprakash Narayan, the independence activist popularly known as JP, called for a peaceful Total Revolution and announced his plan for daily demonstrations throughout the country, beginning on June 25th and lasting until Indira Gandhi resigned.[50] In response to these events, Indira Gandhi issued the Declaration of Emergency on June 25, 1975, and it remained in place until March 21, 1977.

4.11: Support for IRF and Reconnection to RSS

During the Emergency, elections were postponed, newspapers were censored, and parliamentary proceedings were often replaced by Ordinances. Thousands of RSS *swayamsevaks* and other activists participating in JP's demonstrations were arrested and had their legal rights revoked. Among them was Yashomati *Jiji*'s son, Professor B.K. Rastogi, known as Suresh, who had socialist leanings even as a young man. Not long before the Emergency, he had won a college election in Bhopal, running as a socialist and defeating the Congress Party candidate. As soon as the Emergency was imposed, he was arrested. His older brother Sandesh traveled from Moradabad (in Uttar Pradesh) to Bhopal (in Madhya Pradesh) but was not given permission to visit Suresh in prison. His younger brother Ravindra, who was more politically savvy, successfully paid off the prison officials, who then allowed Suresh's wife and children to visit him and to supply him with homemade food on a weekly basis. Even during the Emergency, corruption in India functioned like a well-oiled machine.

Even during the Emergency, corruption in India functioned like a well-oiled machine.

Emergency also impacted the lives of many Indians in the United States, who responded strongly to the undemocratic act. I recall how Dr. Subramanian Swamy, one of the founding members of the Janata Party, successfully escaped arrest in 1976 by masquerading as a Sikh and fleeing to London via Colombo, Sri Lanka. This bold action earned him goodwill and support from many Indian expatriates. Various political groups were organized in the United States during

---

[50] It was also called *Sampoorna Kranti* (Total Revolution Movement). In 1999, *Lok Nayak* JP was posthumously awarded the Bharat Ratna, India's highest civilian award, in recognition of his social work.

this time, including the Friends of India Society International (FISI) and Indians for Democracy. I was active in both. I believe that the Emergency was a blessing in disguise, as it ignited patriotism amongst Indians who came to the U.S. primarily to enhance their careers. Many Indian-Americans and their supporters demonstrated in front of the Indian Embassy in Washington, DC and presented memoranda to T. N. Kaul and Kewal Singh, the Indian ambassadors to the U.S. during the Emergency. The activities of Indian-Americans like us in response to the Emergency were generally peaceful and drew some media attention, but they had little impact on politics in India.

I firmly believe that Indira Gandhi declared the internal Emergency not for any national security reason but simply for the sole purpose of perpetuating her leadership. I also feel that, though Indira Gandhi had badly misjudged the mood of the country by imposing Emergency, she was still a Nehruvian and a democrat at heart. This explains her willingness to call for new elections on March 24, 1977. The Janata Party, which was elected to power in the post-Emergency elections, was comprised of various political groups whose only common purpose had been to oppose Emergency and some of the policies adopted while it was in force. Though Indians were initially thrilled by the result of the elections, various factions within the party eventually came to loggerheads, and Prime Minister Morarji Desai resigned on July 28, 1979. That is how Indira Gandhi returned to power in 1980.

During Emergency, several activists, including Dr. Mahesh Mehta (recipient of the Pravasi Bharatiya Samman in 2017), a polymer scientist, started the India Relief Fund (IRF) as a public charity in the U.S., with the initial objective of assisting families of political prisoners arrested during Emergency. Once Emergency was revoked, I volunteered, in 1977, to take on a leadership position as President of IRF, while continuing with my work at the Bank. At this point, the Fund's focus shifted to development and disaster relief.

In August 1979, the Machchu-2 dam near the town of Morbi in Gujarat collapsed, causing massive floods, crop damage, and thousands of deaths. It is still considered the worst dam-burst in Indian history. I wanted to raise relief funds from the 300 or so fellow Indian staff members at the Bank. As a forerunner of fundraising for any disaster relief, I sought the help of M. Narasimham, Executive Director representing the Government of India, who in turn contacted the World Bank's Director of Personnel, Mr. Clarke, who gave me permission to use interdepartmental mail for my fundraising effort. However, many Bank staffers believed that the money I might be able to raise from individuals at the Bank would be 'a drop in the bucket' compared to what the World Bank could contribute, and I was unable to convince them about the importance of individual contributions in such situations.

4.12: Impact of the Raid on the Golden Temple at Amritsar

I remember working closely with Sikhs in June 1984, in the wake of Operation Blue Star, during which Indian soldiers stormed the Harmandir Sahib or Golden Temple, the most revered Sikh holy shrine in Amritsar, Punjab. Jarnail Singh Bhindranwale, a self-proclaimed Sikh leader intending to form Khalistan (a separate state for Sikhs in India), along with his militant cadre, occupied and fortified the shrine. Indira Gandhi had encouraged and supported Bhindranwale in an effort to split the Sikh-majority Akali Dal party, which opposed Gandhi's Congress party. Bhindranwale began to support violent actions and his militant cadre was involved in terrorist actions against the public and the government. It is reported that arms and ammunition used by his group were provided by Pakistan's Inter-Services Intelligence (ISI).

The government sent a team led by P.V. Narasimha Rao (who later became the Prime Minister of India in 1991-1996) to try and convince Bhindranwale to back out but he was adamant, and refused all efforts made by Mrs. Gandhi's administration to negotiate a settlement.[51] The negotiations failed and the law-and-order situation in Punjab continued

---

[51]   Bhindranwale was the head of an orthodox Sikh religious school, Damdami Taksa, and held the title of missionary "Sant." In the late 1970s Indira Gandhi's Congress party supported Bhindranwale in a bid to split the Sikh votes and weaken the Akali Dal, its chief rival in Punjab. Bhindranwale was responsible for launching Sikh militancy during the 1980s.

to deteriorate. Indira Gandhi tried to persuade the Akalis to support her in the arrest of Bhindranwale peacefully. These talks ended up being futile. In June 1984, Mrs. Gandhi ordered Operation Blue Star, an Indian Army operation carried out to remove Bhindranwale and his armed militants from the buildings of the Harmandir Sahib complex. He had made the sacred temple complex an armory and was killed in the operation which horrified Sikhs around the world and led to Indira Gandhi's assassination by two of her Sikh bodyguards on October 31, 1984. After her assassination, it is alleged that Congress Party leaders led a three-day massacre against Sikhs, mostly in North India, during which nearly 2,800 Sikhs were brutally massacred and more than a million were temporarily displaced. As an aftermath of these horrendous events, hundreds of children became orphans. IRF launched an annual support program for more than hundred orphaned children (both Sikhs and Hindus), to continue for as many years as needed.

In the wake of these events, I hoped to befriend and work with my Sikh colleagues at the World Bank. Emotions were running high and trust was low. In an attempt to restore goodwill between Sikhs and Hindus, I, together with IRF board members, Ram Gehani, Jatinder Kumar, and Satish Tamboli, organized an event at the University of Maryland campus celebrating the 520th birth anniversary of Guru Nanak Dev Ji, the fifteenth-century founder of Sikhism. Hinduism and Sikhism share common religious beliefs with spiritual philosophies and traditions. Sikhs and Hindus have intermarried for centuries and have traditionally gotten along very well. But in D.C. at that time, there was infighting among Sikhs between those who strongly supported the Khalistan movement and those who were disturbed by the violence inherent in that agenda.

A few days before our event, leaders of the *Gurudwara* (Sikh temple) in Silver Spring, Maryland issued an edict that no Sikh should attend the celebration, while scheduled Sikh speakers were instructed not to speak. Consequently, they withdrew. I was dumbfounded by these actions. I

In the wake of these events, I hoped to befriend and work with my Sikh colleagues at the World Bank. Emotions were running high and trust was low.

approached Hardayal Singh, a close Sikh friend from the World Bank, who immediately picked up the phone to seek support for the event. Meanwhile, I met with the top administrators of a *Gurudwara* in Burke, Virginia, and helped convince them to send speakers and audience to the event. In the end, the program was conducted with around 200 participants, split evenly between Sikhs and non-Sikhs. I spoke, along with ten other speakers, on topics centered on unity and brotherhood. The event was successful and was covered in the local print media.

4.13: India's Worst Industrial Disaster – Bhopal

On December 2-3, 1984, there was a large gas leak at the Union Carbide plant in Bhopal. This is still widely considered the world's worst industrial disaster, which resulted in 8,000 fatalities on the day of the disaster and more than 8,000 additional casualties from exposure. The cause of this disaster is still unclear. A court claim submitted in 2006 states that this leak caused over 550,000 injuries. In my efforts to raise money to bring relief to the victims of the tragedy, I worked closely with India Relief Fund team members across the U.S., many of whom had some background with the RSS, including Chicago's Dr. Mohan Jain, who would later found the India Development Coalition of America.

4.14: Embracing *Vanaprastha*

In 1987, after ten years of volunteering with the IRF, I realized that continuing in my time-consuming, high-pressure position at the World Bank was not conducive to the development work I was doing for IRF.[52] I knew what I wanted to do and I just had to break the news to my family. Immediately after our wedding in 1960, I had told Sarla that I planned to work for 25 years and then devote myself to full-time social

---

[52] I was already considering the possibilities beyond my current position when Barber Conable, then president of World Bank, effected a major reorganization within the institution. During this process, Bank staff members were asked to resign and reapply for their positions or apply for early retirement.

service. We discussed the fourfold age-based stages/*ashramas* of life. The four *ashramas* are: *Brahmacharya* (celibate student), *Grihastha* (householder), *Vanaprastha* (retired) and *Sannyasa* (renunciation).[53] She was therefore aware of my desire to embrace *Vanaprastha* (the third stage in life, a partial retirement from worldly life) after a quarter century at work. By god's grace I was 55 in 1987 and was eligible to avail

Immediately after our wedding in 1960, I had told Sarla that I planned to work for 25 years and then devote myself to full-time social service.

my retirement benefits. Though their mother was well aware of my heart's desire, our sons were surprised. Yet they were very supportive. The change significantly impacted our financial situation. We simply would not be able to maintain the same lifestyle that accompanied my World Bank position. Before my retirement, I drove a Mercedes Benz and was even able to acquire a new model every couple of years. The transition to an ordinary Toyota Camry may have felt strange, but in the end, I didn't mind the change, as long as it meant I would have more time and energy to pursue my larger dream of contributing to the welfare of those in need in India.

Sarla, who grew up immersed in the *Arya Samaji* family values of simple living and unwavering compassion, understood not just the need to provide developmental opportunities in India but also the responsibility of those who had prospered to give back to society. Our sons, too, understood the significance of our humanitarian impulse. On our many trips to India, we had taken them to visit and investigate service and community development projects at villages in remote and needy regions across the country. I found that we had taught our boys well – Sanjay (26 years old) and Gautam (18 years old) were more than willing to make the necessary sacrifices so I could focus on social service. It was a challenging period, but it allowed us to pause and take stock of the things we considered most important in life. In the end, our family felt that the work to be done for India's poor was much more urgent than our own need for a comfortable life.

---

[53] *Encyclopedia of Hinduism*, Volume A, page 464

4.15: Closing of IRF and Founding of IDRF

Having fully prepared for the next phase in our life it was imperative for me to wind up IRF and replace it with a new organization called India Development & Relief Fund. Hence, in November 1987, the organization was legally incorporated in Maryland as the India Development & Relief Fund, and it received its 501(c)(3) tax-exempt status effective January 1, 1988, at which point India Relief Fund was closed. Besides me, IDRF had three Board members: Satish Tamboli, Jatinder Kumar and Ram Gehani. More than 35 years later, IDRF's work is still going on at my home with my support as a full-time volunteer, as well as with a small, dedicated staff.

The best way to find yourself is to lose
yourself in the service of others.
Mahatma Gandhi

Ask not what your country can do for you
Ask what you can do for your country.
President John F. Kennedy

CHAPTER 5

Serving India: Nurturing IDRF (1988-2019)

5.1: An Inspiration for Giving Back

AS A YOUNG man, I was surrounded by Gandhian thoughts. I will never forget these words of Gandhiji's: "The world has enough for everyone's need but not for everyone's greed."

My vivid memories of the 1942 Quit-India Movement, when six members of my immediate family including my mother, were incarcerated for *satyagraha*, have been a constant reminder of the need to fight for

> **I will never forget these words of Gandhiji's: "The world has enough for everyone's need but not for everyone's greed."**

social justice. This experience led me to embrace Swami Vivekananda's philosophy of *Nar Seva, Narayan Seva* (service to humanity is service to God). Vivekananda was a strong influence on Mahatma Gandhi as well. My philosophy is so like Gandhiji's that, I am proud to say, a radio interviewer once interspersed my voice with Gandhiji's voice.[54]

I was also inspired by Dr. Rakesh Popli, a native of Delhi, who earned a PhD in nuclear physics from Purdue University in the US but returned to India to establish a non-governmental organization (NGO) engaged in rural development and aimed at innovation in technology. He played a critical role in the early stages of the *Ekal Vidyalaya* (one

---

[54] *A World of Possibilities*, a 2006 radio interview conducted at our home by Mark Sommer, an award-winning nationally syndicated public affairs radio host. Replay link: http://snd.sc/eGwwdH

teacher for every school) movement for the education of India's rural and tribal children, which is thriving today. In the early 1980's, Dr. Popli, Ashok Bhagat (Padma Shri, 2015) and three other courageous social activists founded Vikas Bharti in Jharkhand, for the purpose of developing self-sufficiency in rural areas.[55] Another person who inspired me was a socio-political stalwart, Nanaji Deshmukh (Padma Vibhushan, 1999), who was elected to the Rajya Sabha, the Upper House of Parliament.

Nanaji Deshmukh, one of Vinod's mentors, 1998. He was committed to seva his entire adult life and has been an inspiration to Vinod.

He left politics when he was 60 years old to dedicate the rest of his life exclusively to integrated social and economic development (*vikas*) in rural India. He urged all politicians to follow the same path when they reached the sixth decade of their lives. I was honored to meet Nanaji

---

[55] IDRF supported Vikas Bharti for almost 3 decades and it is now the largest NGO in Jharkhand, a state with a population of over 32 million.

several times in Delhi and Chitrakoot. When Nanaji visited the U.S., we were thrilled to be able to welcome him into our home. I was struck by the fact that the only sights he wanted to see on his trip were public libraries and public parks, from which he drew inspiration for India's development at the grassroots level.

In choosing to dedicate myself to IDRF for more than 30 years, I hoped to follow the examples set by these great men. I found their philosophy to be correct – the greatest pleasure I have known in my life has come from the good work I have been able to do through IDRF. Lives change in an instant, and so was it with me: when, on one of our first IDRF trips to rural India, I was wonderstruck to see villagers sharing their sleeping and living area with their cattle. I found myself heavy-hearted, fighting back tears. I resolved to focus on building IDRF to be a stalwart supporter of NGOs and their volunteers to serve the poorest of the poor with missionary zeal and spirit. This was a turning point for me; I was inspired and uplifted by their spirit to serve the downtrodden. By 1999, the transition was complete – as evidenced by our cheeky letter to our family and friends:

> **The greatest pleasure I have known in my life has come from the good work I have been able to do through IDRF.**

As we approach the new millennium, we think it's only appropriate to tell you a deep, dark secret of our past.... Yes, Sarla and I have a secret third child. This boy is now a teenager and has grown so rapidly in recent years that we had no choice but to cancel our usual annual pilgrimage to India and steer the teenager towards a more mature stage. The child's name is IDRF and his growth has not been painless and has led to stresses and strains in our family life. Yet when we are ...helping thousands of beneficiaries in India, we feel that life is worth living.

5.2: Overview of IDRF's Contributions

IDRF's goal is to put power, not charity, into the hands of India's impoverished, through multifaceted development programs implemented by reliable, local NGOs. Since its inception, IDRF has been committed to long-term, sustainable, grassroots development in India, and recently extended to Nepal and Sri Lanka. IDRF receives donations in the U.S. and gives grants to NGOs in South Asia that have approval under India's Foreign Contribution Regulation Act (FCRA) to receive international contributions. In the past 30+ years (1988 – 2022), IDRF has raised $49.3 million, of which $8.1 million has been disbursed for disaster relief and rehabilitation programs, and $35.3 million for sustainable

> **IDRF's goal is to put power, not charity, into the hands of India's impoverished, through multifaceted development programs implemented by reliable, local NGOs.**

development grants to empower the downtrodden people.[56] IDRF's administrative plus fundraising expenses have been exceptionally low – approximately 96 cents of every dollar we raise go directly to the people who need it. I feel privileged that Sarla and I traveled to India at our own cost, and never used IDRF funds for our travels.

5.3: Disaster Relief and Rehabilitation

IDRF has a long-standing commitment to rebuilding communities in the aftermath of various natural and other disasters. Some of these calamities devastated communities that were already living in extreme poverty and deprivation. Rather than focusing on transitional relief, IDRF gives priority to long-term rehabilitation, with the goal of turning disasters into opportunities for new sustainable development. To date, grants for relief and rehabilitation programs have amounted to $8.1 million. For example:

- On October 20, 1991, a 6.8 magnitude earthquake struck Uttarkashi (Garhwal region), causing an avalanche and other destruction. We visited the disaster site, and IDRF started a relief program in collaboration with Uttaranchal-based *Daivi*

---

[56]   Detailed data are provided in: Appendix 8 (Grants for Disaster Relief and Rehabilitation) and Appendix 9 (IDRF's Finances: 1988-2022).

Apda Peedit Sahayata Samiti, followed by the reconstruction of a vocational training facility.

- On September 30, 1993, a 7.4 magnitude earthquake struck the Latur district of Maharashtra, causing 8,000 casualties and injuring 30,000 people. This devastating event prompted me to visit the affected areas and gain firsthand insight to the dire situation. IDRF immediately launched a special campaign, sending grants of $303,000 which established IDRF as a premier Indian-American community organization in relief efforts. The American Embassy in India, with the help of the Indian Embassy in D.C., set up an interview for IDRF with the U.S. Information Service (USIS), which was broadcast throughout Asia. The interviewer seemed astonished to learn that I was not a native of Maharashtra and yet I was doing all this charitable work as a full-time unpaid volunteer without any paid staff. My only passion was to serve my motherland, India. IDRF's popularity led to my first appearance on the local television channel *'Darshan'*, thanks to the courtesy of Dr. Suresh Gupta, who continues to be a strong supporter of IDRF.

- November 4-7, 1996, a cyclone (hurricane) struck the coastal areas of Andhra Pradesh, then an IDRF grant to a local NGO enabled the affected families to rebuild their homes.

- In October 1999, communities in Orissa (now Odisha) were devastated by the strongest tropical super-cyclone ever recorded in the Indian Ocean. IDRF sent grants of $620,075 for relief and rehabilitation programs. A video link, "A ray of hope," is posted about IDRF's contributions on its YouTube channel.[57]

- After a catastrophic, 7.7-magnitude earthquake hit Kutch, Gujarat on January 26, 2001, India's Republic Day, IDRF sent grants of over $3 million, far beyond anyone's expectation. The emotional and financial support from the public at large as well as U.S. corporate entities was overwhelming. In fact, I felt as if donation checks were falling from the sky. I must express my

---

[57] https://www.youtube.com/watch?v=0tYuYLUCx-w

deep gratitude to scores of volunteers all around the U.S. whose instantaneous involvement made this outcome possible. As a development economist, I took a strategic decision to release 3 percent of funds raised by IDRF for relief work and around 97 percent for long-term **I felt as if donation checks were falling from the sky.** rehabilitation and development. A video link "Sparsh" is posted about IDRF's contributions on its YouTube channel.[58] We visited the affected areas many times and witnessed the devastated schools, roads, bridges, hospitals, and even entire villages. I will never forget meeting families of female entrepreneurs – some with four generations of women producing world-class handicraft work – despite their disadvantaged backgrounds.

Sarla and Vinod visiting an IDRF project in Kutch following the January 2001 earthquake. This particular project established a girls' hostel at a residential school.

- IDRF sent grants of $1.14 million for relief and rehabilitation work after the tsunami which slammed into South Asia on December 26, 2004. The tsunami was caused by a 9.1

---

[58] https://www.youtube.com/watch?v=RakpAWu5p7o

magnitude earthquake in the Indian Ocean. Moreover, IDRF worked closely with the United Nations Foundation. The very nature of this disaster required IDRF to go beyond Indian borders to support Sri Lanka, Indonesia, and Thailand.[59]

- On April 25, 2015, an 8.1 magnitude earthquake in Nepal provided another opportunity to go beyond India's borders. IDRF supported both relief and rehabilitation programs and sent grants of $107,000 for earthquake victims.

- On February 3, 2016, an avalanche hit an Indian military base in northern Siachen Glacier under the Line of Control region, trapping and killing 10 soldiers under deep snow. IDRF helped the affected families.

- In March 2020, with India under complete lockdown to prevent the spread of Coronavirus (COVID-19), IDRF immediately started working with its partner NGOs in Gujarat, Maharashtra, Odisha, Rajasthan, Utter Pradesh, and West Bengal to support 6,500 daily-wage migrant laborers, who had lost their livelihood as the local economy shut down, by providing relief kits with food and essentials to save them and their families from starvation. Though this was an emergency measure, IDRF still worked to ensure $137,000 of the donor funds would be used efficiently and effectively. In 2021, when India was battling the second wave of coronavirus, IDRF provided $1.4 million for various relief and rehabilitation measures. In addition, IDRF sent $25,000 to the Kathmandu Model Hospital, Nepal to provide financial help for hospital staff (laid off or had work hours reduced), equipment for the care of in-patients, and emergency supplies for the coronavirus control and containment measures. More than $12,000 were sent to Sri Lanka Centre for Development Facilitation to provide livelihood support to poor families suffering during the pandemic.

---

[59] http://www.idrf.org/wp/wp-content/uploads/2012/09/IDRF_Tsunami_Report_113005.pdf

- During exceptional emergencies in the United States, IDRF has also partnered with local organizations to help those in distress. For instance, after the terrorist attacks on September 11, 2001, IDRF had promptly provided relief to the families of the first responders in New York and was honored as an "Angel Donor" for contributing $12,000 out of $100,000 raised for that purpose in the DC metro area. The COVID-19 pandemic is another such situation where IDRF once again provided help to the families hit hardest by the coronavirus in the US. IDRF joined hands with the Indian-American community and 20 organizations local to Washington, DC to provide groceries at 36 Grab & Go free distribution events, helping a total of 15,500 struggling families between May and November 2020[60].

- Post-flood support including Surat-Gujarat, (2006), Bihar (2009), Karnataka (2010), Uttarakhand (2013), Jammu and Kashmir (2014), Chennai-Tamil Nadu (2015), Bihar, Gujarat, Uttar Pradesh and West Bengal floods (2017), Kerala floods (2018-2019), Bihar flood (2019), Odisha cyclone (2019), West Bengal floods (2021), and Telangana floods (2022). Altogether IDRF's grants amounted to more than $600,000 to support the flood victims.

- Besides the victims of natural disasters, IDRF has also lent substantial support to the war heroes throughout India. For example, in 1999, IDRF was confronted with another challenge – of raising funds in support of Kargil War heroes. Of the total grant of $313,000, a significant portion of it was raised during Morari Bapu's Ram Katha[61] in Houston. IDRF's check of INR

---

[60] VP of the Montgomery County Council (Maryland), Tom Hucker, awarded citations to IDRF on August 15th, 2020- India's 74th Independence Day, for its commendable relief work done to serve the multicultural and diverse communities in the Washington DC Metropolitan Area during these challenging times.

[61] Morari Bapu is a world-renowned Hindu spiritual leader who narrates the epic poem *Ramcharithamanas* by Tulsidas in Hindi and Gujarati. He depicts the epic, the story of *Rama*, in a unique way by comparing its morals to modern day's lifestyle. His storytelling is enjoyed by the entire audience with pin drop silence. He doesn't

51 lakhs ($125,000) was presented to Indian Prime Minister Atal Bihari Vajpayee in support of the 'Army Welfare Fund' on February 6, 2000 in Delhi. This check was presented by an IDRF volunteer from Houston as I was preoccupied with the Orissa (now Odisha) super-cyclone work. It was very gracious of Prime Minister Vajpayee to thank me personally at Blair House during his September 2000 visit to the White House.

Ceremony at Blair House with Prime Minister Atal Bihari Vajpayee thanking Vinod and IDRF for its contribution to the Kargil War heroes.

5.4: Development and Economic Self-Reliance

I feel blessed when I think of IDRF's contributions ($35+ million) towards the development work over the past three decades. The preparation of a comprehensive list of accomplishments over such a long period is an onerous task and therefore, not attempted. However, here are a few illustrations:

- IDRF's support to 2,130 thriving Women's Self-Help Groups in 333 villages of Haryana, Maharashtra, and West Bengal

charge for his narration, but the organizers collect donations for the specific cause for which they have organized his *katha*.

- 10,000 women farmers from Maharashtra and other states trained in eco-friendly farming techniques
- 2,500 private toilets constructed for rural poor in Gujarat, West Bengal, and Tamil Nadu;
- 14,000 patients cared for annually through Mobile Clinics in Arunachal Pradesh and Assam
- IDRF prevented seasonal migration of people from 105 villages in Gujarat by constructing 130 check dams/ponds and 150 wells. Also, IDRF helped in improving education, health, and economic sustainability for 250,000 people
- 10,000+ poor students helped in schools and affection homes (known in the West as orphanages) in nine states across India
- Thousands of *Ekal Vidyalayas* (one-teacher schools) established in many states of India
- IDRF's tribal girls' hostel accommodates up to 100 tribal girls each year, from Northeastern states, for free, holistic education, lodging, and boarding
- 303 unemployed youth (71 girls) provided vocational skills training, of whom 245 were placed in jobs (51 girls)
- 225 children with special needs were provided education in Gujarat, Punjab, and Telangana 27,000 students in 400 schools across 12 cities in India trained to be responsible citizens
- 48 *Gram Panchayats* in 10 districts of Bihar and Jharkhand trained to access government programs and benefits, as well as combat corruption
- 1.84 million citizen complaints raised and resolved through a mobile app called 'I Change My City.'

Although IDRF has been enormously successful in implementing various development programs since its inception in 1988, the road has been long and arduous. We have faced some significant challenges along the way, including a public attack that sometimes felt personal as well as political. At one point, ironically, IDRF was nearly

At one point, ironically, IDRF was nearly destroyed by its largest individual donor.

destroyed by its largest individual donor, who attempted to use IDRF to hide a donation he was unable to make legally. The story of how it all began, and some of the details of how we weathered the obstacles in IDRF's path, is mentioned in sections 5.9 to 5.11.

5.5: Formative Years

IDRF's initial Board members were chosen from a local circle of my Indian-American friends. We were drawn together by our commitment to protecting democracy during the Emergency period. Most of the work was done manually, a time-consuming process. As a statistician with a penchant for details, I made sure that all accounts were meticulously maintained in large, bound ledgers, which still adorn the shelves of the IDRF office in our home. Sarla and the children helped with endless organizing, filing, and storing of documents, while I was able to make copies on the World Bank's huge Xerox photo copier machines.[62]

In 1988, its first year of operation, IDRF raised only $16,000, but by 2017, its thirtieth year, it raised $2.1 million (more than 125 times the initial amount). While IDRF has become one of the largest nonprofits focused on the Indian subcontinent, our beginnings were humble, without a grand vision. As a developmental economist, I had only a bit of fundraising experience. For example, on the occasion of the birth centenary of Dr. K.B. Hedgewar, the pioneering social activist and founder of RSS,[63] I raised $46,000 for *seva* (social service). Until 2005, I was also a *Seva Pramukh* (head of social services) with the *Hindu Swayamsevak Sangh*, U.S.A., an offshoot of the RSS. Later, I found that my fundraising experience on behalf of IDRF gave me credibility among RSS *swayamsevaks* (volunteers) in the U.S. who were drawn to

---

[62] Komala Ghosh, my former secretary at the World Bank, typed up IDRF's appeals and annual reports during its initial years. Later this work was done *pro bono* at a Board member's corporate office, and eventually IDRF hired a professional, a wheelchair-bound American lady, as a typist.

[63] For more information on the RSS, see Appendix 4.

the philosophy of IDRF. Many began donating and volunteering for the organization.

I also raised money from family, friends, and colleagues, while continuing to deepen my network amongst RSS *swayamsevaks* in India through my annual trips where I attended various meetings such as the *Vishwa Sangh Shivir* (VSS), a worldwide conference organized by the RSS every five years.

Sarla and Vinod attended VSS in December 2001 where India's
Prime Minister Narendra Modi, who was Chief Minister
of Gujarat at the time, addressed the attendees.

Many members of the IDRF team developed innovative ways to raise funds. For instance, Adesh Jain in Virginia took charge of distributing an annual calendar; Suresh Deopura in California took care of two programs – grocery coupons (where IDRF received 5% of gross proceeds) and IDRF's credit card (where IDRF received 1%); Shyam Gokal Gandhi in California collected monthly pledges from donors and got donor checks printed and deposited every month into IDRF's account; and Abhay Balambe in Massachusetts organized cricket tournaments to raise money. With the help of Vijay Pallod in Texas who was in charge of media and public relations, IDRF also reached out to a variety of Indian-American community groups outside of the

Sangh Parivar. For instance, in 1992, IDRF helped in planning Indian Independence Day celebrations with the India Cultural Coordination Committee (ICCC) in the Washington, DC metro region.

We strongly felt that unless we engaged the next generation of Indian-Americans in the development of India, IDRF's efforts would peter out over time. So Sarla and I got involved in some of these efforts, such as the D.C.-based *Natya Bharati* theatre group, founded in 1984 by Dr. T. Srikantiah, a World Bank colleague, which produces Hindi plays every year. After being involved with the group, I expressed my concern whether Indian-American children would be interested in Hindi plays since many of them do not follow the language as they grow up in the U.S. Prompted by me, Srikantiah, Suma Muralidhar, and associates from *Natya Bharati* started a tax-exempt organization, *Sahara Inc.*, to perform plays in English annually about social themes of contemporary India. IDRF's collaboration with them, initiated in 1993, continued throughout its operations until its closure in 2018.

5.6: Challenges in Managing Volunteer Network

The vital role of volunteers in the relief and development efforts of IDRF cannot be overstated. Even IDRF's website, established in 1998, was designed and managed by volunteers until 2009, with my minimal involvement. Vijay Mellampati was very resourceful in helping us get the website unveiled by Chandrababu Naidu – then Chief Minister of Andhra Pradesh. In turn, IDRF gifted 100 bicycles to village girls for going to school. Chetan Gandhi hosted the first-ever annual meeting of IDRF volunteers in 2000 in Los Angeles. Many of the male volunteers spent so much time on IDRF work, in addition to their careers, that they had little free time to spend with their families. At IDRF's second annual meeting, held in September 2002, and hosted in Boston by Abhay Belambe, Sarla insisted that volunteers

The vital role of volunteers in the relief and development efforts of IDRF cannot be overstated.

change their approach so that they could devote more time and energy to their personal and family lives.

Local IDRF volunteers – without the active support of such individuals in the DC metro area, it would not have been possible for IDRF to send out thousands of mailings and raise over $50 million at a bare minimum overhead rate, almost unheard of in the non-profit world.

Focused on *seva* (service) as the volunteers were, challenges did emerge. Virtually all of the volunteers were skilled in engineering or information technology (IT), but few had experience with social development. IDRF had minimal compliance standards until 2003, and there were few written internal rules for project evaluation and grant giving. Many enthusiastic volunteers wanted IDRF to fund projects simply on the grounds of their trust in the NGOs – without regard to whether they had submitted proper documentation or not. Unfortunately, many NGOs continued to ask for funds without completing the necessary paperwork. I explained that IDRF needed complete documentation to be accountable to its donors and to comply with U.S. and Indian laws. In an effort to standardize accounting and grant-giving procedures in 2003, I hired Sharad Agarwal to draft a project management manual, as Sharad was an Indian-chartered accountant with experience in audits of international organizations in

Asia and Africa. I sent this manual to key volunteers, but no one showed any interest to read it. This was a dismaying experience for me.

5.7: Streamlining Operations

Accounting at IDRF was complicated due to its regional bank accounts, which were autonomously maintained. Thus, there was no consistency about the paperwork involved, and there were no rules for minimum grant amounts. Shyam Gokal Gandhi, in particular, did an excellent job in fundraising and managing the California account which was the most active and prominent among the regional accounts. I was maintaining two separate bank accounts, one for receiving donations at Chevy Chase Bank (Rockville, MD) and the other for sending grants through the State Bank of India (SBI), New Delhi.

In July 2004, after the Government of India began to investigate violations of the Foreign Contributions Regulation Act (FCRA). The Reserve Bank of India, the country's central banking institution, notified IDRF, along with all others, that they were no longer allowed to transfer funds to their bank accounts in India. In response to the new rule, I opened a new account with the State Bank of India, New York, for IDRF grants. This gave IDRF an impetus to close its regional bank accounts in 2006, so that we could adopt uniformity and move towards meeting the higher compliance standards. From then on, IDRF electronically transferred each grant directly to the recipient NGO's FCRA bank account.

I was manually maintaining all the accounts meticulously and always submitted annual tax returns to the U.S. Internal Revenue Service (IRS), even though I was not a trained accountant. By 2001, before the U.S. government had adopted stricter regulations, I had started having some concerns about IDRF's complicated financial structure. I hired a CPA, Agnelo Gonzalves, (courtesy of V.S. Raghavanji) to prepare formal accounts and lay the groundwork for independent audits in the future. The task was challenging, since he had to make accounts for 2000 and 2001 auditable, so that beginning from 2002 IDRF accounts could be audited by an independent professional company. Since 2002,

IDRF's accounts have been audited in a timely manner by Desai and Shah, P.C. CPAs. Audited financial statements and tax returns for recent years are now posted on IDRF's website.

5.8: Smear Campaign

While I was making these improvements to IDRF's practices, a group called the Forum of Indian Leftists (FOIL), along with Sabrang Communications,[64] launched a smear campaign portraying IDRF as a sponsor of hatred against non-Hindus in India. I believe this campaign was triggered by a tragic event that occurred on February 27, 2002, in Godhra, Gujarat. A train carrying Hindu pilgrims returning from *Ram Janma Bhoomi*, Ayodhya, was set afire by a group of extremist Muslims. 59 pilgrims were killed in this violent act, inciting riots across Gujarat that led to the deaths of an additional 1,000 people, according to official reports. Rumors began to emerge that the violence was abetted by the state government, then-Chief Minister Narendra Modi, his political party (the BJP), and the RSS.

The first major attack on IDRF came on July 22, 2002, when the weekly *Outlook India* printed an article by Ashish Kumar Sen, a freelance journalist and maverick.[65] The article, titled "Deflections to the Right," referred to IDRF as a "front for radical Hindu organizations in India," among other accusations. Sen contacted me through Vijay Pallod, who was IDRF's media coordinator at the time. I agreed to an interview but was unaware of the journalist's intentions. Sen also obtained a photograph from Vijay, in which I am handing a copy of an IDRF check of INR 51 *lakhs* (about $125,000), made out to the Army Central Welfare Fund, to the then-Prime Minister Atal Bihari

---

[64] Sabrang Communications, founded by Javed Anand and Teesta Setalvad in the early 1990s, published *Communalism Combat*. More recently, the organization was mired in controversy as a report in The Pioneer found that significant amounts of money donated to the Sabrang Trust to help riot victims had been diverted to the bank accounts of the two founders. *Source: Wikipedia*

[65] http://www.outlookindia.com/article.aspx?216550

Vajpayee. This check represented funds donated by non-resident Indians specifically to aid the families of Indian soldiers, Hindu or not, who had been killed or seriously wounded in the 1999 Kargil War (this photo is at the end of Section 5.3.) However, the caption for the photo in Sen's article read: "Prime Minister Vajpayee and Vinod Prakash: Funny Money." In my view, Sen's distortion of the facts infuriated me.

Things went from bad to worse. On November 20, 2002, at the Press Club of India in New Delhi, Sabrang Communications and Forum of Indian Leftists (FOIL) released a report titled, "The Foreign Exchange of Hate: IDRF and the American Funding of Hindutva."[66] It alleged that IDRF had been funneling money from the U.S. to RSS-affiliated organizations for the promotion of communal violence and other hateful activities. FOIL and its sympathizers in the media and academia also asked the U.S. government to investigate IDRF and terminate its 501(c) (3) tax-exempt status. This report was distributed to the U.S. Congress, Department of State, and the Internal Revenue Service (IRS) but no U.S. government officials contacted IDRF. IDRF immediately began reviewing the audits of NGOs named in the report to confirm that funds had only been used for intended development or rehabilitation projects. From this point on, IDRF was caught in the crossfire between *Sangh* organizations and those who opposed any activity related to the RSS. Though its programs had consistently benefited Indians of all faiths, IDRF was depicted as a nefarious and sectarian organization. The most popular Indian-American newspaper, *India Abroad* (Aziz Hanifa reporting), and *The Baltimore Sun* (Scott Shane reporting) published reports giving more balanced perspectives.[67]

Things went from bad to worse.

Without a professional media team or strong support from academics, it was left to IDRF volunteers and a rag-tag group of supporters to dispel the allegations. The

It was left to IDRF volunteers and a rag-tag group of supporters to dispel the allegations.

---

[66]   2002, Sabrang Communications & Publishing Pvt. Ltd, Mumbai, India, and the South Asia Citizens Web, France. http://www.sacw.net/2002/FEHi/FEH/

[67]   https://www.baltimoresun.com/news/bs-xpm-2002-12-04-0212040225-story.html

---

volunteer team created a response website called "Let India Develop. Org." This site was maintained by Rajesh Gooty, an old-time IDRF supporter and volunteer. The website succeeded in securing more than 7,000 signatures on a petition in support of IDRF, whereas the FOIL managers could not secure half that number.[68]

In response to the allegations, a team of six Indian-American academics and activists, led by Dr. Ramesh Rao, conducted a thorough investigation and concluded that IDRF was not, in fact, supporting violence or furthering any hateful ideology at all. Their final report was published in 2003 in the U.S. as "IDRF: Let the Facts Speak."[69] Sarla and I met the Indian Home Minister, Lal Krishna Advaniji, and furnished him detailed information about IDRF's grants to various NGOs in India. A few months later, I was informed by his office that there was no evidence of any violation by IDRF of Indian law.

Vinod and Sarla with Home Minister LK Advaniji and Chamanlalji in Dec 2002.

---

[68] Surprisingly and disappointingly, one of the earliest FOIL signatories was my nephew, a professor at a prestigious U.S. university, who did not have even the minimum courtesy to contact me as to what was going on prior to signing the FOIL petition.

[69] https://www.amazon.com/IDRF-Facts-Speak-Ramesh-Rao/dp/1540640779/ref=sr_1_1?keywords=IDRF+let+the+facts+speak&qid=1581781540&s=books&sr=1-1

http://www.idrf.org/wp-content/uploads/Let-the-Facts-Speak-IDRF_Defence_Final.pdf

---

5.9: Enticing Donation Received

In December 2000, a $2 million donation was given to IDRF by a donor, a very successful businessman, who is also renowned in our community. The donor furnished a promissory note prepared by an American law firm on his behalf, payable in three years, compounded daily at 9% annual interest, with no stipulations for the use of the funds.[70] The interest rate was precisely the same as that of the donor's multi-million-dollar line-of-credit. By the end of 2001, the bank interest rate fell significantly and therefore the interest rate on the donor's line of credit also fell from 9% to 7%. Hence, it was logical for him to pay off the entire Promissory Note to IDRF. He did so by December 2001, depositing the entire sum in the IDRF bank account with full interest. As per U.S. law, IDRF was permitted to use the funds at its discretion. All of these transactions were in full compliance with state and federal laws.

A few months later, the donor proposed to borrow money from IDRF and pay it back with 7% interest according to the ongoing rate. Seeing an opportunity to increase donations by generating an attractive rate of return on our cash balances as compared to the interest rate our bank paid us, IDRF agreed, and a loan agreement was signed for $4 million.[71] He paid off the entire amount with full interest by December 2002. The same thing happened in 2003, and a similar arrangement was made in 2004 as well, but the funds for 2004 were not paid off on time. This led to a court battle, where IDRF ultimately prevailed, as described in the following two sections.

---

[70] The promissory note structure enabled the donor to take his $2 million charitable tax deduction in 2000 while holding onto the cash until a later date when he would pay it along with the stipulated interest.

[71] IDRF had raised more than $3 million following the Gujarat earthquake. Given IDRF's policy of allocating only a minimal amount to relief and vast majority to rehabilitation, IDRF was holding onto 97% of those funds, which were going to be disbursed over several years. That is how we could spare $4 million.

5.10: Standing up for the IDRF Charter

Later in 2004, the donor requested IDRF to send INR 10 million, culled from the interest he had paid on the 2004 loan, to Ekal Vidyalaya Foundation (EVF), India; this request was rejected because IDRF's interest income could not be considered as 'donor advised fund' since IDRF maintained rights over its own interest income in terms of determining which NGOs to support with those funds. The donor then asked IDRF to redirect his entire donation to Hindu University of America (HUA) in Florida, now known as International Vedic Hindu University. IDRF's grant to a Hindu university in the U.S. was not appropriate, as it was inconsistent with IDRF's charter of helping marginalized people of all faiths in India. Moreover, under U.S. law, he was not allowed to donate funds through a promissory note to HUA as he was a member of its board of trustees. Hence, this request was also declined. (Though in our private lives, we supported HUA and even gave a donation of $5,000 out of our personal account.) My role as a president of a public charity precluded approving such a grant.

In December 2004, IDRF's law firm, Trister, Ross, Schadler & Gold, advised me to recover any outstanding money from the donor, and in future to follow loan documentation practices that the law firm had outlined. Hence, I asked the donor to pay back the 2004 loan. Though there was an exchange of letters, the loan was not paid off. I then sought help from senior RSS/HSS leaders (popularly known as *Hindu Swayamsevak Sangh*) in the U.S. to intervene but, to my utter dismay, it was all in vain.

In January 2005, a U.S.-based *Sangh* leader asked me to hand over all IDRF responsibilities, enabling him to oversee IDRF. He and other *Sangh* leaders had no practical – let alone formal – role in running IDRF, but they felt that it should follow the *Sangh's* directives. I explained through an email that IDRF is an independent 501(c)(3) public charity and refused to hand it over to them. I then approached IDRF's law firm to issue a demand letter to the donor. In brief, the other two board members, being *Sangh* volunteers, refused to approach the law firm, and as a result the firm declined to represent IDRF because of the split among the Board members.

In the spring, as advised by the auditors of IDRF, I went to another law firm for a demand letter, but the other two board members thwarted these efforts again and even threatened to sue the firm. They again insisted that IDRF should negotiate with the donor. This law firm responded to the conflict in the same way as the earlier one, by cancelling their retainer agreement. The other two board members went to the extent of threatening IDRF's auditors, claiming that an audit was unnecessary and that if they continued, they would not be paid. Pointing to Maryland law and the Board's own resolution requiring audits, the auditors continued their work as usual. Thereby, IDRF's audit of 2004 was delayed by more than a year.

In August 2006, the Maryland state government instructed IDRF to suspend any fund raising until the 2004 audit was submitted. At this juncture, Jyotish Parekh of VHP America agreed to assist and he succeeded in persuading the donor to confirm the loan amount which had been the bottleneck to completing the 2004 audit. Thereby, IDRF's state tax-exempt status was restored by November 2006. Given the long delay, it was futile to expect another loan confirmation for December 2005 over the next few months.

5.11: Adherence to Compliance Impels Filing a Court Case

I had therefore no choice but to file a loan default case in court by November 2007 due to the three-year statute of limitations – even though I was well aware that my decision would mean losing the support of virtually all IDRF volunteers owing to their *Sangh* affiliation. I had an arduous task of saving IDRF from dissolution under the provisions of Maryland state law. The only option left for me was to search for a law firm that would be willing to take my case. So, I hired Julian

I was well aware that my decision would mean losing the support of virtually all IDRF volunteers owing to their *Sangh* affiliation.

Spirer, a corporate lawyer and a specialist in tax-exempt organizations. Having no support from the Board, I had to pay a personal deposit of $20,000 to his firm so that he could take up the case. He issued a notice to the two board members as well as the donor, but all in vain. A case was filed at the Montgomery County Court, Maryland in November 2007. I was the only plaintiff in the case and the donor was the defendant, along with the two other board members as "nominal defendants."

Ultimately, Jatinder Kumar, one of the other two board members, realized the gravity of this situation and supported me. In fact, this court case could have been avoided if the donor had accepted Jatinder's plea, supported by his personal financial guarantee in early October 2007. The U.S. legal system allows time for the parties to negotiate before the court intervenes in civil cases. I did not believe that the donor would push it all the way to a trial, given how untenable his demand that IDRF transfer funds to HUA. The donor's counsel, Steven Barley of Hogan and Hartson LLP, was a celebrated litigator. Lawyers on both sides entered negotiations but unfortunately failed to reach an agreement.

So, the next step was to explore the prospects of a court-mediated settlement in June 2008. The donor was interested in settling since he knew that his demand to donate to HUA was not allowed per the loan agreement, so he agreed that the funds would be sent to mutually-agreed NGOs and causes in India (which IDRF terms as 'advisements'). Moreover, IDRF consented to give him credit for his three donations made to Ekal Vidyalaya Foundation USA (for onward transmittal to Ekal Foundation India). According to the settlement, the entire loan was to be paid back in three installments – $1 million in July, $1 million in September and the remainder by the end of December 2008. However, this schedule was not followed and IDRF received only $2 million by December. IDRF agreed to delay the balance payment by a couple of months due to the stock market crash in 2008.

In all earnestness, IDRF tried to receive adequate documentation from Ekal Foundation USA to confirm if they had received three donations from the donor totaling approximately $900,000 on IDRF's behalf. The Ekal Foundation USA declined to confirm the above. While disregarding the ground realities, the donor sued IDRF for a breach of settlement in February 2009, which was an utter shock to me. The court date was fixed for September 2009. In between, both parties had to submit detailed depositions involving considerable time and effort. At this crucial stage, intervention by a mutual friend, Virendra Parikh, a CPA, helped in resolving this matter. He convinced the donor that IDRF was not to be blamed because its account books could not be matched with those of Ekal Foundation USA. At Parikh's insistence, Ekal Foundation USA asked the donor to provide an affidavit certifying that he had not availed of any tax benefit for the above. It turned out that he had already received tax benefits for the first donation of $300,000. Hence, he could claim tax benefits only for the remaining two donations and with a spirit of compromise, IDRF honored it. The donor was served a notice to pay off the remaining balance in one month prior to the court date. Eventually, with all these arduous trials-and-tribulations, I finally succeeded in receiving the entire loan amount by August 2009, thus barely meeting the deadline set by the court.

My struggles were not over yet. Another court case was still pending because the donor had not completed his advisements acceptable to IDRF. In response to the court's intervention in the spring of 2010, I had to persuade IDRF's lawyer to fix a date by which the donor must act. At that point, the donor had no choice but to meet the deadline once again. IDRF had to follow its grant-giving process involving due diligence and to ensure that its compliance standards were met. As soon as his advisements enabled me to complete the disbursements, this case formally closed in November 2010.

With an immune system compromised due to the stress of this lawsuit, I later contracted a virus that led to the loss of my eyesight in 2010. In retrospect, I feel this trauma was nothing short of a 'crucifixion' for me. Still, throughout the long ordeal with the donor, I retained my passion for India's development

This trauma was nothing short of a 'crucifixion' for me.

and my commitment to making a difference in the lives of the underprivileged. In return, I have won the gift of tremendous inner joy, or *aatma santushti,* which helps me cope with any external stress. The story would not be complete without appreciating the positive contribution of IDRF's auditors – Raman Desai and Rakesh Shah. Also, the personal attention of my asthma specialist and family friend, Dr. Sudhir Sekhsaria, was highly commendable. This is how my excruciating saga of the ill-fated "Enticing Donation" ended.

5.12: Sarla's Ardent Support

Sarla has done a great deal for IDRF, especially as reflected in her constant endeavors to interest her friends in IDRF's work. She made sure that our home was always open to IDRF's staff and volunteers, and she always insisted that visitors enjoy a home-cooked meal before they left. She went even further by welcoming them to stay with us, often for several weeks and even months at a time. I know the volunteers enjoyed her hospitality when they came to assemble hundreds of copies of IDRF's annual reports and fundraising appeals. I would then carry these in a huge plastic bag for mailing at the local post office.

Vinod mails the IDRF annual report and fundraising appeal, before email became commonplace.

On one of our annual visits to India in the 1990s, Sarla's childhood friend, Kukum Jalan, introduced us to the Oral School for Deaf Children in Calcutta (now Kolkata), which had no funds to take on any additional students from its long waiting list. Upon her return to the U.S., Sarla decided to open our kitchen for an annual fundraiser for the school. She invited 20-25 people (mostly Americans) to a formal luncheon, during which she and her friends demonstrated their cooking techniques and made gourmet dishes that encompassed a variety of Indian (Bengali, Gujarati, Maharashtrian, Parsi, Punjabi, Sindhi, Rajasthani and other cuisines) and international cuisines. Each guest donated at least $25, which IDRF matched. This program raised around $1,500 annually for the school over a decade. When the principal of this school visited us, IDRF made a video called "Sarla's Kitchen," to demonstrate how homemakers could make a difference in the lives of the underprivileged. Specifically, I would like to express our deep gratitude to Yo Chacko, from whom Sarla learned Chinese cooking and was motivated to launch this program.

One of the "Sarla's Kitchen" fund-raisers for The Oral School for Deaf Children in Calcutta. From L to R: Yo Chacko, Sujeet Singh, Mrs. Mukerjee (principal of the school), Sarla, Betty Parker, Sookie Lee, Betty's friend, Jim Parker, Mridula Tamboli.

5.13: Choosing Whom to Help

We traveled to India nearly every year to check on the progress of IDRF's projects and to scout for new opportunities to serve.[72] We witnessed poverty, ignorance, illiteracy, and also incredible hospitality, gratitude, and perseverance by the local NGOs and ultimate beneficiaries, alike. Often, what we learned and experienced helped us identify new recipients for IDRF's grants. Here are a few illustrations of IDRF's development work:

> **We witnessed poverty, ignorance, illiteracy, and also incredible hospitality, gratitude, and perseverance by the local NGOs and ultimate beneficiaries, alike.**

- We have been the forerunners of the *Ekal Vidyalaya* movement going back to 1989-90. We travelled to Calcutta (now Kolkata) to meet the founders of the *Ekal* movement in India. Initially, IDRF supported the Friends of Tribal Society and subsequently different NGOs in Jharkhand, Madhya Pradesh, Tamil Nadu, and Uttarakhand, etc. Later, IDRF transferred the responsibility to Ekal Vidyalaya Foundation, USA, as soon as it was established in 2001-2002. However, over the years, IDRF continued supporting the *Ekal* movement in parallel by sending donor-advised funds to Ekal Vidyalaya Foundation, India.

- In the early 1990s, we also visited Akhil Bharatiya Vanvasi Kalyan Ashram in Jashpurnagar, Chhattisgarh. We were privileged to meet its founder Balasaheb Deshpandey. This meeting was followed by a field trip, which led to our life-long support for their tribal welfare programs. Similarly, in Patna, Bihar, we visited a rehabilitation center for young widows who were shunned by their families (both maternal and in-laws) after the death of their young husbands, because of the persistent superstitious belief that 'it was the daughter-in-law who brought

---

[72] We are grateful to Jaiprakash *ji* and Surya Foundation for graciously inviting us to stay at their guest house in Delhi when we came to visit IDRF projects, as well as having Sarla and me as dinner guests in his home.

the bad luck which killed their sons at a tender age.' IDRF subsequently partnered with the local Rotary Club president, and with a Rotarian who was a family friend, to provide sewing machines and a temporary workspace for these widows.

- In Bihar (now Jharkhand), we saw four men carrying a sick person on a cot because there was no ambulance to transport the patient to a hospital. This motivated us to initiate a Mobile Clinics program at an affordable cost with the help of Birsa Seva Prakalp, Hazaribaugh. Initially, the clinic was not serving the Maoist (Naxalites) villages due to the threat of violence. But because of the clinic's effectiveness, the Maoists approached us to include their villages while assuring complete safety of the clinic and its staff. Eventually, the Maoists became social volunteers with us and productive citizens in society. What a transformation!

- India is confronted with problems like population explosion and gender inequality. IDRF initiated a family planning program in 12 villages of Haryana with the help of Arpana Research and Charities Trust, Karnal. Believe it or not, the natural growth rate in these villages declined in just five years from 33:1,000 to 23:1,000 (and population stabilizes at 21:1,000). What an amazing result of our hard work. We then expanded our program to 40 villages and included gender parity therein. Subsequently, this program was extended to 165 villages, including micro-credit and micro savings through women's self-help groups. Through today, over 11,500 women have become entrepreneurs – and are leading their lives with dignity.

- In December 2000, we visited an orphanage managed by Vatsalya Trust, Kanjur Marg, Mumbai. This visit led to our continued support, helping them in expanding their programs such as a separate *Balikashram* (girls' orphanage), patient assistance program, and *'Aakar'* (early intervention center for special needs children).

Besides our India visits, my close interaction with the NRI (non-resident Indian) community in the U.S. has led to many initiatives and successful stories as well. Just a few examples of those are given below:

- Nearly three decades ago, I met Jaipal Rathi, a New Jersey-based NRI, and was spellbound when he shared his dream to build a school in his village Nagauri[73] in Meerut district, UP. He was the first highly educated person from that village who had earned a PhD and was working in a prestigious U.S. corporation. We immediately developed a close bond, and I wanted to help him realize his dream. I contacted Vidya Bharati – the largest private network of schools in India – and succeeded in establishing a school in his village. Initially, the school faced tremendous opposition from the villagers who believed once the children got educated, they would leave the village. The school had a modest start with just two rooms, two teachers, a hand-pump and no electricity. It provided free education to the children. Today, around 1,000 students from 30 villages are brought by five buses to attend the school – enabling them to receive education from kindergarten through 12th grade. These students also perform better in the state board exams compared to other schools in the region. Moreover, the operational costs of the school are now met by the same villagers who first opposed the idea of having a school in their village. Finally, the school is now managed by its alumni and many others, who are leading a successful life in India or abroad.
- More than a decade ago, I met Dr. Vibha Gupta, graduate of IIT Delhi and Chairperson of Magan Sangrahalaya Samiti in Maharashtra, during her visit to the United States. She was engaged in the emancipation of poor people living in the rural areas of the state through developing indigenous artistic skills. We joined hands right away with her organization. To date, IDRF has supported over 10 projects and has brought the

---

[73]   https://www.youtube.com/watch?v=SJnW32q924Y&t=80s

organization to a level of sustainability where it has become a hub of women's empowerment in the region.

5.14: Overhauling Governance and Management

In hindsight, I feel that if I had done a little more homework on the organizational aspects of IDRF, its independence, integrity, and sustainability might have been unassailable and the complex ordeal with the aforesaid donor might have been avoided. However, the court case and the FOIL attack allowed me to reevaluate IDRF's methods, after which IDRF evolved into a more professional and independent organization. Although it was painful to lose so many volunteers, IDRF now runs more efficiently with a small paid staff and a revived Board.

In August 2011, upon receiving advice from IDRF's legal advisor, I decided to reconstitute the IDRF board by inviting four long-term donors to serve on it. At that time, Dr. Neelam Chitre, Ms. Malati Gopal, Dr. Jaipal Rathi, and Dr. G.R. Verma were willing to join the Board. Since December 2002, IDRF had only three board members: me as president, and Jatinder Kumar and Ram Gehani as members. To include new board members, approval was needed by the majority. This was not an easy task. Eventually, I sought the advice of my friend and strategist, Shekhar Tiwari, a *Sangh* volunteer, whose plan ultimately enabled me to obtain Jatinder's consent. Thereafter, the board resolution was passed two to one and the above four donors joined the IDRF Board. In 2012, both Jatinder Kumar and Ram Gehani finally resigned from the board.

The new board members were aware of the earlier troubles and were committed to IDRF's values and integrity.[74] With a rich variety of

---

[74] Dr. Sasala Challa, Dr. Raghu Korrapati, Hemant Shah, and Dileep Thatté joined the board in 2013. Subsequently, Dr. Prem Garg (2014), Reena Goyal (2016) and Mohinder Gulati (2017) joined the board. In between, Hemant Shah (2014), Dr. Jaipal Rathi (2015), Malati Gopal (2017), Dr. Neelam Chitre (2017) and Dr. Raghu Korrapati (2017) resigned from the board. As of July 2023, the Board consists of Dr. Suresh C. Gupta (Vice President), Dr. Prem Garg (Treasurer), Shubhra Garg (Secretary), Mohinder Gulati, Nisha Narayanan, Adesh Jain, Bharathi Mallampati, Manu Anand and Dr. G.R. Verma (Emeritus).

experience in management, fundraising, and international development, IDRF's board is now poised to lead the organization to greater heights. Recently, as part of succession planning, the board created a new paid position of Executive Director and appointed Rajeev Jain in that role to carry forward IDRF's mission.

Since the closing of its regional bank accounts in 2006-07 that were managed by respective regional IDRF vice presidents, IDRF's bookkeeping has vastly improved and funding has become more tightly controlled. All partner NGOs must now communicate by email, leading to virtually paperless management. NGOs are now required to complete the 'Basic Information Form' when applying for a grant. This form is designed to make sure that the NGO meets all the compliance standards required by governments of both the U.S. and host countries (India, Nepal and Sri Lanka). Since 2012, IDRF has gradually increased its minimum grant amount from $1,000 to $7,500 to keep administrative work more manageable. The staff now manages its accounts on QuickBooks software, so they can now generate any report with just a few clicks. IDRF also now applies special standards to ensure that its prospective partner NGOs are accountable, honest, and effective (beyond verifying their compliance with FCRA rules). Under current procedures, each NGO must provide feedback and progress reports along with a detailed funds utilization summary.[75]

In order to get wider outreach to the Indian business community, US Corporations, Indian and American philanthropists, the Board of Directors discussed the possibility of forming an Advisory Council. The Advisory Council would bring the perspective of the business community and philanthropists to the Board's deliberations, advise outreach strategy, align the programs with the interests of the large donors and be a bridge between IDRF and the large donors. As of July 2023, the Council consists of Dr. Madhu Mohan, Dr. Nilima Bhirud, Nitu Gupta, Rajesh Gooty and Dr. Sudhir Sekhsaria.

[75] I needed additional hands for streamlining IDRF's accounts and administration. Fortunately, during the initial stages, IDRF headquarters was blessed by dedicated volunteers such as Sonia Bhatnagar, Shivaram Sitaram, Umesh Rohatgi, Harish Pant, Savita Srivastava, Manju Joshi, Anurodh Agarwal, Rajesh Gooty, Rajeev Jain, Sudha Jain, Capital Infotech Inc,. In recent years, IDRF had to rely on paid staff – Dharmesh Naik, Sarika Srivastava, Dharma Naik, Pooja Sadani, Pooja Varma,

5.15: Modernization of IDRF

Since 2012, IDRF has been a member of the Combined Federal Campaign (CFC), USA's largest workplace campaign for giving, which allows federal employees and retirees to contribute to a network of vetted organizations. In 2013, after careful examination, the World Bank added IDRF to its Community Connections Fund. Bank staff and retirees can now donate to IDRF through payroll deductions and direct gifts. Starting in 2014, the World Bank even began matching up to 100 percent of their gifts.[76]

In celebration of its 25th anniversary in 2012, IDRF launched a new user-friendly website (www.idrf.org) thanks to Rajita Majumdar, a skilled communications consultant, and Rajat Arya, my grand-nephew and an experienced software engineer. This new website also has a secure online donation facility – thus giving even more options for donating to different partner NGOs. In 2013, IDRF also released its first-ever full-length illustrated annual report, which was sent to hundreds of donors.[77] IDRF has entered the realm of social media as well, with over 6,000 Facebook followers, Twitter and LinkedIn accounts, and its own YouTube channel. We also fully overhauled our website in 2023.

5.16: IDRF's Recognitions and Awards

IDRF's practice of close collaboration with the Indian-American community is evidenced by the many awards it has received since 1994.

Sareesh Rawat, Melissa Rice, Nahal Jalali, Ritu Chowdhry, Dr. Niti Duggal, Vandana Matravadia, Banu Ramakrishnan and Rajeev Jain. IDRF's present volunteer team includes Durgeshnandini Gupta, Navin Prasad (India), and Rajesh Sinha (India), besides many donor coordinators.

[76]   Until 2018, World Bank matched 50 percent of employee gifts until 55 percent of the staff had participated in giving. Once that threshold was met, a 100 percent match was provided to all staff and retiree gifts. From 2019 on, World Bank matches 100 percent of gifts, up to $25,000 per donor.

[77]   http://www.idrf.org/wp/wp-content/uploads/2013/05/Annual-Report-Final-Online-Release.pdf

However, even the recognition IDRF received has not been without controversy and surprise. For instance, the Association of Indians in America (AIA) awarded me with the 1994 Community Service Award for outstanding fundraising for the 1993 Latur Earthquake – but this led some to attack me for my personal beliefs and support for the *Ram Janma Bhumi* Movement. Thanks to Dr. Govind Kapadia, ultimately the AIA board was fully convinced that IDRF funds were awarded without regard to caste or religion.

I have been privileged to receive 22 *seva* awards (1994-2023) for IDRF, as detailed in Appendix 10. It is especially noteworthy that in 2012, the Hindu American Foundation (HAF), renowned for its advocacy work on interfaith engagement, recognized my service to Indians of all faiths with its *"Dharma Seva* (Social Service) Award."* This was a real surprise, at least for me, given the strong feelings that IDRF's legal battle with the large donor (as mentioned in sections 5.9, 5.10 and 5.11) engendered in the Hindu community. Furthermore, the National Federation of Indian American Associations (NFIAA), whose regional office had balked in 2004 at giving IDRF an award during the FOIL smear-campaign, awarded me the Social Service Award in 2013 – thanks to Harihar Singh – which was another pleasant surprise.

Awards ceremony with Indian Deputy Ambassador T.P. Sreenivasan,
standing to Vinod's left, presenting Vinod with a seva award.

In 2013, for the first time in two decades, I was interviewed by a renowned community activist, Dr. Satish Misra, for the Capital Forum show on Global TV (GTV), a program aimed at Indian-Americans in the Washington, DC metro area.[78] I was interviewed once again by GTV in 2015. In 2014, when Narendra Modiji became the Prime Minister of India, an article written by Dr. Ashok Sinha about IDRF, "Development Mantra" was published in Hindu Vishwa USA. This article was followed by other articles as mentioned on the IDRF website. In 2021, I was interviewed for "Frankly Speaking with Vibhuti Jha", telecasted on ITV Gold (a South Asian TV station). In this interview I talked about how IDRF has empowered the marginalized for over three decades

As I will explain later, I lost my eyesight in June 2010 due to medical negligence. Yet, my passion to serve the downtrodden in India not only remains intact but has, in fact, grown stronger. While I can no longer visit India, I have concentrated on strengthening IDRF. For instance, in 2010 IDRF was a bronze-level participant in Guidestar.org, the world's largest source of information on nonprofit organizations, and received just one star by Charity Navigator, the premier nonprofit rating agency in the U.S. But, by December 2021, IDRF has become a platinum-level participant in GuideStar for the last six years and has received the highest 4-star rating for eight consecutive years by Charity Navigator for demonstrating strong financial health and a commitment to accountability and transparency. Only seven percent of recipient public charities have been able to retain 4-star ratings for eight consecutive years! Finally, until September 2013, IDRF had no reviews on Greatnonprofits.org, but now IDRF is considered a top-rated charity with 5-star ratings based on over 125 independent reviews. These reviews were written by volunteers, supporters, clients, and donors reflecting upon their experiences with IDRF.

---

[78]   Part1:http://youtu.be/MFC4zT5GITU, Part 2: http://youtu.be/9EavioWcboE

To put the world in order, we must first put the nation in order; to put the nation in order, we must first put the family in order; to put the family in order; we must first cultivate our personal life; we must first set our hearts right.

Confucius

The happiest moments of my life have been the few which I have passed at home in the bosom of my family.

Thomas Jefferson

CHAPTER 6

Family Life

6.1: Joy of Living in a New Home *(Grihasth Jeevan)*

MY FAMILY LIFE has been through a huge transformation involving many challenges and uncertainties. Yet, I feel blessed by divine guidance to have successfully faced them. Leaving a top-notch position in India and making a life-changing decision to emigrate to the United States is stark evidence of the value I place on family. By 1987, I had ensured that my family could live in a brand-new home in close proximity to the DC Metro system and shopping malls. Moreover, this community provided outdoor swimming pools and tennis courts within a two-minute walk. Given the high frequency of visitors and guests, we opted for a furnished, walk-out basement from the builder. We were astonished to see the construction of a new house which was very different from that of India, as the house is primarily made of wooden frames and dry wall, while concrete blocks were laid for the basement. The front side of our house is built with multi-colored stones and has a huge stone mailbox. The backyard of our house was densely wooded which we cleared to have a nice garden and large lawn.[79] It was not only fun but a learning experience to visit our home construction site from time to time. I feel that I fulfilled my dream of living in a house in a society that values transparency. The payments made for my house were recorded accurately up to the last penny (no corruption at all, unlike India!). Even the annual property tax that I pay to Montgomery County is a figure accessible to the public.

---

[79] We also had a stone patio built by an immigrant from Chile whose son continues to take care of our lawn today.

We had duly considered the situations and aspirations of each family member as we thought about moving to a new home. We wanted more space, we wanted to be closer to the Metro, and Sarla especially wanted a kitchen on the first floor. In our Carderock home, the kitchen was upstairs, which was always a frustration for her. Our new home was also nearer to Sarla's workplace and provided her ample time for her daily chores as well. When we moved, Sanjay had completed his CPA and was ready to go for his master's degree at Pace University in New York. Gautam had completed high school and was ready to go to Yale University for his undergraduate studies. The location of our new home also facilitated both children's visits to their respective work and university destinations.[80]

The present Prakash family home in Rockville, MD which Vinod and Sarla moved into in 1987 in order to be closer to the metro station and other conveniences.

6.2: Sanjay's Medical Complications, Education and Career

Sanjay had a difficult childhood and youth. He had spent a part of his childhood in India, between 1962 and 1968, the last year in Pondicherry (now Puducherry) with his aunt who lived as a devotee at

[80] Sincere thanks go to my former World Bank colleague Hari Agarwal for drawing my attention to this new housing development in his back yard.

the Sri Aurobindo Ashram. His doctors had warned us about what he might have to face in life because of his disabilities. Still, we were shocked when Sanjay had his first epileptic seizure while we were in Moradabad, U.P., visiting my sister during our 1975 home leave. We immediately rushed back to Delhi because the local doctor could not explain what was happening. Sanjay recovered, but in February 1976, when he was at Pyle Junior High School back home in Bethesda, Sarla received a call from the school informing her that he had been taken to the Emergency Room at nearby Bethesda Suburban Hospital. He had suffered a seizure in the classroom. Subsequently, he was precluded by the school administration to attend science labs, shutting the door to what are known today as STEM classes. From that point on, Sanjay needed perpetual treatment for seizures, and he faced an extremely challenging life. He could not easily develop hobbies or participate in sports. He did learn how to swim. He was industrious and hard-working, despite his disabilities. He attended secondary school with other neighborhood children, including

He was industrious and hard-working, despite his disabilities.

Walt Whitman High School (considered at the time to be the best public high school in the DC region). While we contemplated private school for Sanjay, we felt that his social life would be more manageable at Walt Whitman because of his reserved nature.

Sanjay, after graduating from high school in 1979, was admitted to Drexel University in Philadelphia and was keen to attend there. We also felt it would be good if he joined Drexel because it had a work-study program that would allow Sanjay to gain real-world work experience. But Sanjay's neurologist, Dr. Schuline at Georgetown University Hospital, dissuaded us from sending him away from home for college given his disabilities. That led Sanjay to pursue his undergraduate degree at American University and live at home. He was not yet driving, so Sarla dropped him off at classes quite often. He returned by bus and had long walks to reach our Carderock home.

In his second year of college, Sanjay, seeking greater independence, moved into a college dorm. At the first dorm that he stayed in that fall semester, he found it difficult to deal with students drinking and carousing. When he moved into another dorm for the spring semester, he could not stand the students bringing in their girlfriends to their rooms and doing more than carousing. He moved back home after these two semesters of "real-life" experience.

In his third year of college, he learned to drive, succeeding in doing so with the use of just one hand. After he graduated with his BA degree in 1983, Sanjay prepared himself for the CPA (Certified Public Accountant) exams. Given his somewhat limited career options, he rightly chose accounting and passed his CPA exams – demonstrating that he could work hard and accomplish his goals. He started his career initially at the U.S. Department of Agriculture, and then moved to the Department of Treasury. His industrious work habits enabled him to attain promotions from time to time. Accounting could have been a good field for him, but he did not like taxation, so he joined an MBA program at Pace University in New York and graduated successfully in 1993. He later joined the Environmental Protection Agency (EPA) as internal auditor and moved from Washington, DC to New York, and later to Boston to lead a family life.

Sanjay's graduation from Pace University with his MBA in May 1993.

For many years, Sanjay was on an anti-seizure medication known as Dilantin.[81] The doctors did not clearly indicate to him or to us that Sanjay should never miss his morning or evening dose of the medicine. Because of some lapses in taking the medication, Sanjay again suffered a seizure while Sarla was driving and Sanjay was sitting next to her in the front seat. They were driving to the World Bank to pick me up from work. Fortunately, at the very moment of the seizure Sarla had already stopped in front of the World Bank. She instantly put her finger into his mouth so that he would not bite his tongue, as was recommended by the medical establishment at the time. Her motherly love and instinct to protect her son did not hinder from hurting herself. In that process, Sanjay bit Sarla's finger and she had to get a tetanus shot to prevent harm to her health.

This was just one of a series of medical mishaps that made it difficult for Sanjay to get better command over his health. Simultaneously, the Dilantin medicine was adversely affecting Sanjay's brain, though it was very effective in controlling seizures. Neurologists in Washington, DC, New York, and Boston continued to prescribe this potent but deadly medicine to Sanjay over a period of some 30 years. The neurologists failed to inform Sanjay about the nature of the medicine and its long-term side effects. Surely, there must have been medical literature indicating the effects of Dilantin. The doctors should

The neurologists failed to inform Sanjay about the nature of the medicine and its long-term side effects.

have prescribed brain magnetic resonance imaging (MRI) to check on these side effects. His brain neurons were being damaged, and that began to affect his work. He started making mistakes, which he himself noticed, as did his managers. Sanjay went to see a neuro-psychoanalyst who took hours to evaluate him. From that analysis, it became abundantly clear what was happening to his brain. Luckily, he had completed 15 years of federal government service and was therefore eligible for early retirement on disability in 2008. Naturally, he had to find another neurologist who would prescribe a different medicine.

---

[81]   http://www.drugs.com/dilantin.html

Once again, Sanjay had to face detrimental side effects of the new medication, but the enduring perseverance and affection of his wife Renu enabled them to find another efficient neurologist who prescribed yet another medicine whose side effects were, thankfully, acceptable. This has allowed him to lead a normal life for the last decade.

6.3: Gautam's Early Life, Education and Career

We moved to Rhode Island in August 1968, where I began my career as a faculty member at the University of Rhode Island. Our son Gautam was born in May 1969, a healthy baby. He grew up to be a curious, intelligent, and sometimes naughty, boy. When Gautam was about three or four years old, I recall that he took out all the record albums from their sleeves and spread them around the living room floor of our Carderock Springs home (back when people listened to music on vinyl records!). Sarla admonished him and warned him that she would throw him off the balcony if he did it again. Sanjay, believing that his mother would actually do so, begged her not to. Sanjay was always very protective of his little brother. They continue to get along well in their adult years.

Gautam was so active, even seemingly hyperactive, and therefore somewhat inattentive, that Margie Johnson, a family friend, wondered if the little fellow had some learning disability. Gautam first began attending the Concord St. Andrews Co-op Preschool and then was enrolled in Primary Day School, later at the elite Sidwell Friends School (where the daughters of Presidents Clinton and Obama would later attend). Now his son Rahul and daughter Tara also attend this school. I was pleased that, as a World Bank employee, I was able to support Gautam's education at Sidwell Friends. Gautam was strong academically, and was a happy, socially well-adjusted boy. Sarla and I remember fondly that when Gautam was in tenth grade, he, like other American boys, earned pocket money by mowing lawns of neighbors in Carderock Springs. We had no idea how seriously he would take his first job, as we promised him that we would double whatever he earned. He would return home perspiring, his face and arms almost black from sunburn, but he was determined to earn a fat sum that summer. He was so good at it that he earned nearly $1,800 by the time school began. When we expressed concern that perhaps it was too much work and too much money for a young man, he responded, "Don't tell me how much I should earn. They pay me and I accept." That enterprising nature and hard work later made it possible for him to found Monsoon Capital, a successful India-focused hedge fund.

He would return home perspiring, his face and arms almost black from sunburn, but he was determined to earn a fat sum that summer.

With his good grades and hard work, Gautam was admitted to Yale University, but we were initially reluctant to have him so far from home. We wanted him to attend a nearby school, like Johns Hopkins in Baltimore (where he also got admission), that was close enough to home to allow him to easily visit us. Gautam was also accepted at Princeton and MIT, but he chose Yale because he wanted to pursue a degree in medicine. It was almost *de rigueur* among the educated, first-generation Indian families that their children become professionals, but especially doctors, because doctors were some of the most affluent professionals. Yale had a great medical program, and we were happy with his decision. Gautam declared Molecular Biology as his major, but fate and natural inclination intended differently. In his Economics 101 class, he had a great teacher, and he took other economics classes. In the end, Gautam graduated with a B.S. degree in Molecular Biophysics & Biochemistry and a B.A. degree in Economics, *summa cum laude*.

Gautam's graduation from Yale University in May 1991.

Gautam straightaway joined the analyst program at McKinsey in New York, the most prestigious management consultancy company. During his two years as an analyst, he learned enough to author a book titled, *The Insider's Guide to Management Consulting: Opportunities for Undergraduates*, which was published by Wet Feet Press in 1995. While in New York, Gautam studied for both the MCAT exam (for medical school) and the GMAT exam (for business school). He fortunately scored highly on both exams and ended up getting admission to a number of schools, including Stanford, Yale, and University of Pennsylvania for medical school and Stanford, Harvard, and Wharton for business school. He accepted a joint 6-year MD/MBA at Stanford and we were over-the-moon excited for him.

However, just a few months before moving out to Stanford for this joint degree in summer 1993, he received an offer to join Bessemer Venture Partners in Boston. He wanted to try out venture capital for a couple of years to get more work experience before his MD/MBA, but we were concerned about this delay and worried about what had happened to his dream of becoming a doctor. Stanford willingly granted Gautam a two-year deferral for medical and business schools, so they told him he could work at Bessemer for two years and then matriculate at Stanford in 1995.

However, Gautam really struggled with the decision about whether to go to medical school or not. He told us an interesting story of what helped him make his decision. A friend of his at Harvard Medical School had introduced him to one of the young and upcoming cardio-thoracic surgeons at Harvard who invited Gautam to scrub in and watch a couple of open-heart surgeries. As Gautam was watching the surgeries, literally standing just inches from the patient, he started dozing off! He felt that if watching this type of high-tech surgery wasn't exciting, then perhaps medicine was not the field for him.

> **As Gautam was watching the surgeries, literally standing just inches from the patient, he started dozing off!**

At the same time, he was also struggling with whether to go to business school since he was getting such great real-world business experience as a venture capitalist. He went back-and-forth on this decision but ultimately decided to forego both Stanford and Harvard business schools since he didn't want to give up his partner-track position in the VC industry. He told us that students who joined an MBA program mainly learned good networking skills, and since he had already been in the business of consultancy and VC for more than five years, he had established a strong enough network of business professionals and friends. Given the priority we place on education, Sarla and I really did not understand Gautam's decision to forgo such excellent schools as Stanford and Harvard, and we worried about his future with just a bachelor's degree, but there was little we could do as he was quite determined with his decision.

6.4: Sanjay's Wedding

Education and career are important, and once those challenges are figured out it is time to enter the period of *gruhasthashram* (the life of a householder, according to Hindu and Indian tradition). Marriage, children, and all the joys and challenges of managing and maintaining a household are part of this *samsar* (world), and domestic life is generally considered an important and necessary step on the path to ultimate realization of one's destiny. Marriage of one's children is a basic concern for all parents, and it is especially a difficult challenge for those of us who have a child with disabilities. I advertised for Sanjay in the matrimonial ads section of *India Abroad*, and received proposals, but nothing materialized. Then, during our 1994 visit to India, while we were at the Delhi home of my nephew Shishir (Satya *bhaisaheb's* youngest son), there was a conversation about Sanjay's marriage. Shishir knew a girl, Dr. Renu Bansal, who he thought might be a good match for Sanjay. Shishir invited Renu to meet with us. Not knowing that it might be a potential match she came over, wearing jeans and a shirt, not the traditional *sari* or *salwar-kameez* (loose pajama-like trousers tapered at the ankles with a long or short tunic worn on top). Renu was a graduate of Lady Hardinge Medical College in Delhi. Sanjay and Renu met every day while he was in Delhi. Sanjay was his honest and straightforward self, and Renu said yes. This was in late November 1994.

Sanjay made sure that he met Renu's sister Meenaxi and her husband Nalin, son of Shishir's *mamaji*, in Bangalore (now Bengaluru). Upon reaching Bangalore, our families discussed the proposal and at about 11 p.m. we called Renu's mother Sharda *ji* at home to confirm the marriage proposal. We had planned to visit Sarla *jiji* in Pondicherry (now Puducherry). From Pondicherry I called Shravan *ji*, my most trusted friend in Delhi, shared the good news, and asked him to make arrangements for the engagement ceremony. Before we returned to the U.S. the engagement ceremony was quickly performed. To this day, Shravan *ji's* family is as close as our own.

The engagement ceremony took place in Delhi, and true to my principles and values, there was no talk of giving or accepting dowry. After all, when I married Sarla, all I had accepted was a silver coin and *kum-kum teeka* on my forehead. While in India, Sarla and I, along with Sanjay and Renu, had visited Seva Bharti's Seva Dham Vidya Mandir, the residential higher secondary school for underprivileged boys on the outskirts of Delhi. Sanjay and Renu found that many students were sharing the same textbook, so they decided to forgo personal wedding gifts and donated the entire $8,000 they received as gifts to Seva Bharti through IDRF. Sarla and I were touched by their decision.

A new challenge arose when Sharda *ji* insisted that the marriage be performed immediately on our return to the U.S. and also that we accompany Renu on her journey. Sarla asked to have more time to prepare for the wedding and to hold it in May 1995, but Sharda *ji* insisted that January 1st was an auspicious day for the wedding. In fact, Renu had already planned to visit the U.S. to take the U.S. Medical Licensing Exam (USMLE), having been sponsored by her *chachaji* in Hawaii. Since Indian doctors were migrating to the U.S. at a fast pace, the Government of India had banned taking the USMLE in India. USMLE is a prerequisite for foreign doctors in the U.S. We planned to return to the U.S. on December 19th, and coincidentally on the same date, Renu was to fly to Hawaii. Upon our return, we wanted to perform their wedding at Gandhi Memorial Center, but it was not available. Instead, we decided on Sri Siva Vishnu Temple in Lanham, Maryland, on January 1, 1995.

E-mail was not yet common then, so communication was by telephone. What about drafting and printing the invitation cards and sending them out to friends and family in the U.S., we wondered. Who would take care of the various arrangements for food and a hundred other matters involved in organizing a wedding on less than two weeks' notice? I spoke to Rameshwar *ji*, a dear friend who was deeply touched by the young couple's decision not to accept personal gifts. He readily designed and printed the wedding invitations for us. The wedding ceremony was held as scheduled, and our close friend from South Korea, Jay Lee, jokingly remarked that "the wedding seemed to be some kind of organized chaos." There was no quiet or serenity, children ran all over the place, some were crying, and people chattered all around.

> **Who would take care of the various arrangements for food and a hundred other matters involved in organizing a wedding on less than two weeks' notice?**

Sanjay and Renu's wedding, January 1, 1995.

6.5: Gautam's Wedding

Gautam had made it clear to us that we not tell him "what clothes he should wear, who he should marry, or which career he should pursue." He was just a teenager when he made these things clear to us. Yet, we still discussed with our friends and wondered what was in store. Gautam met Anjali in January 1993 when he was making a presentation at a South Asian

> **Gautam had made it clear to us that we not tell him "what clothes he should wear, who he should marry, or which career he should pursue."**

student's conference. We first met her in 1994 in Rhode Island. We were thrilled that Anjali was able to attend Sanjay's wedding to Renu.

We all agreed to Gautam and Anjali's wedding plans. They had given themselves a full year to prepare for the wedding on May 24, 1997. Gautam, true to his business management credentials, had prepared a detailed spreadsheet as to what would be done when, by whom, where, how, the cost and with what consequences. I was in charge of getting the wedding invitations ready. I went to a graphic designer in Delhi who designed a beautiful card. I am grateful to my friend Jaiprakash *ji* (Padma Shri, 2020 and Surya Foundation) for introducing me to a reputed artist for designing the wedding cards. About 500 people were to be invited. Anjali and Gautam had visited several hotels in the Washington, DC area, as they wanted the wedding at a central location for friends and family from around the country. They looked at the facilities, sampled the food, and finally decided on the McLean Hilton which employed an Indian chef unlike the other venues they visited. The hall capacity was about 350, so the additional 150 guests were invited to a Sunday reception in the backyard of our home, rather than to the wedding itself.

Gautam and Anjali's wedding, May 24, 1997. Credit: Robert Issacson

Most of our local friends were invited for the Sunday reception. Our large backyard could accommodate those guests and we arranged large garden umbrellas under which tables and chairs were set. Catering and other arrangements had been made – it would be a grand party. As the guests began to arrive it started to rain heavily. Guests had to scamper inside, and our house quickly became overcrowded. The caterers had to move all the cooking and organizing inside the garage instead of the open driveway. But, because of the flexible Indian approach to life, all this was done without too much heartburn or anxiety.

We also had a grand wedding reception at the India Habitat Center in Delhi in 1998, where the young couple was blessed by several dignitaries, including L.K. Advani *ji*, Minister of Home Affairs, and Arun Shourie *ji*, Minister of Communications and Information Technology. Thanks go to the courtesy of Dr. S.P. Gupta, my World Bank colleague, for reserving the facility and making it available to our family. Jaiprakash *ji* took care of the arrangements at the venue. The program was attended by more than 80 guests in the end, and the couple were personally blessed by Rajju Bhaiya, the RSS *Sarsanghchalak* at the *Sangh Karyalay* (Head Office), Keshav Kunj, Delhi. During this visit, I ensured that Anjali and Gautam themselves visit impoverished areas, which they did graciously. They also visited Dr. Hegdewar Hospital, Aurangabad, Maharashtra, a rare institution reflecting a blend of professionalism and social values. During their stay in Aurangabad, they were also blessed by Anjali's *nanaji*.

6.6: Unique Tradition for Wedding Gifts

Overriding the American wedding registry tradition and inspired by Sanjay and Renu, Gautam and Anjali also arranged to donate their wedding gifts, which exceeded $30,000. I was overwhelmed, and with tears of joy blessed them at their reception for their benevolence. I still have the list of guests who agreed to this idea and made their checks payable to IDRF. Others felt that weddings need not be the venue or occasion for such donations. The couple also donated all the cash and checks they received as gifts to IDRF. *The Washington Post Magazine* covered their wedding celebration, because it was a unique gesture to share funds with the needy, rather than accept personal wedding gifts. Seven or eight other young couples

The Washington Post Magazine covered their wedding celebration, because it was a unique gesture to share funds with the needy, rather than accept personal wedding gifts.

embraced our children's gesture and donated their wedding gifts as well to IDRF, enabling us to purchase ambulances and mobile medical vans that were needed desperately by NGOs.

One fun activity that Sarla engaged in ahead of Gautam and Anjali's wedding was to prepare a recipe book for the newlyweds by asking our friends to share their favorite family recipes. This book, *Food for Thought*, ended up being a compilation of 40 international recipes with photos and short biographies of all the contributors, so both Anjali and Gautam would know more about our closest friends. This unique feature was enjoyed by all who contributed.

Photograph of the contributors to "Food for Thought". In this photo are 44 families which are among the closest friends of the Prakash family where some friendships date back over 50 years. Back row (l-r): Adi Davar, Pradeep Rohatgi, Thomas Tabrah, Hemant Joglekar, Helene Tabrah, Bharati Mitra, Brian Lee, Peter Lowe. Fourth row (l-r): Moneik Jonkman, (unknown), Jay Lee, Rana Batra, Jenny Lowe, Irene Jonkman, Soma Mitra, Joram Piatigorsky. Third row (l-r): Dorothy Grayson, Malini Joglekar, Shanta Agarwal, Ashi Rastogi, Neelam Chitre, Mohini Gehani, Carol Lowe, Connie Michel, Krishna Agarwal, Rukmini Verma, Amita Sarin, Lona Piatigorsky, Jim Parker. Second row (l-r): Pervin Davar, Uma Arya, Jugnu Jain, Sudha Garg, Betty Parker. Front row (l-r) Ruth Tabrah, Sookie Lee, Sarla Prakash, Neeru Agarwal, Rama Paul, Kusum Batra, Jean Jenkins, Andrea Haber. Credit: Robert Issacson

During the ceremony, Anjali and Gautam received blessings from three close friends of ours, with whom we have shared a special friendship. I first met Ruth Tabrah, a fellow traveler, on a trip to Iran in 1973. She became a very close friend. She visited us and we visited her in Hawaii where she lived. Second to bless the happy couple was Connie Michel, wife of my colleague at the University of Rhode Island, who has also remained a devoted friend. The third person who gave his blessings was Dr. Har Swarup Rohatgi, Sarla's uncle.

Vinod and Sarla with both sons and daughters-in-law, early 2000s.

6.7: Joyful Life as Grandparents

The next phase in family life was the birth of our grandchildren. On August 7, 2002, Sanjay and Renu became proud parents of their daughter, Anisha. Some months later, Gautam and Anjali followed them and became parents of their son Rahul, born on March 13, 2003. Our third grandchild is their daughter Tara, born on June 7, 2006. When a child is born, life changes in dramatic ways, which we could only comprehend later. Likewise, grandchildren indeed change the perspective of grandparents in many subtle ways: there is a harking back to tradition, a consultation of almanacs and experienced friends, and some anxiety that your children have also become parents.

As she was born very early in the morning, Renu and Sanjay chose to name her Anisha, which means "continuum," "perpetual," "everlasting," or "eternal." It is also one of the names of Goddess Lakshmi (the goddess of wealth).[82] The process of taking care of baby Anisha was simplified because by that time Renu's mother was living with Renu and Sanjay in Massachusetts. Sharda *ji* had emigrated to the U.S. through Renu's sponsorship. Moreover, it was comforting to have Renu's elder sister, Meenaxi, and her family close by, as she lived in Connecticut and already had two children. Anisha was fortunate to have her *nani* around during her childhood, though Sharda *ji* did return to India prior to her death in 2005.

Sarla and Vinod presiding over havan (fire worship) in honor of Anisha's birth in August 2002. Photo taken at Sanjay and Renu's home with family (including their niece, Tanya, and nephew, Tushar).

We arranged for the *annaprashan* (first feeding of grain-based food, other than just milk) ceremony for Anisha in our backyard.[83] Neeta *ji* and Satyapal Khera *ji*, the *Arya Samaj* activist, majestically performed

---

82 http://en.wikipedia.org/wiki/Lakshmi
83 http://en.wikipedia.org/wiki/Annaprashana

the relevant *sanskars* (rites, rituals) for the newborn.[84] All the gifts received on this auspicious occasion were donated to IDRF in support of the children's dorm, "Jeevan Prabhat" in Gandhi Dham, Gujarat. I fondly remember a photo of one-year-old Anisha doing *namaste* that day, wonderfully captured by my good friend and great photographer Rajan Devdas (Padma Shri, 2002).

Anisha learning her Indian greeting of Namaste!

Since Gautam was named after Gautam Buddha, and Rahul is the name of Lord Buddha's son, it seemed an appropriate choice for Gautam and Anjali to choose Rahul as the name for their son. A short, two- syllable name was also fitting for the American context as well.

---

84   http://en.wikipedia.org/wiki/Sa%E1%B9%83sk%C4%81ra

Family gathering at Anjali and Gautam's home in Cambridge, MA for Rahul and Anisha's naming ceremony, June 2003. Includes Prakash family and Anjali's parents.

When it was time to name Tara, they looked up the book of baby names that Maneka Gandhi had published.[85] Tara was an appropriate and symbolic name because Anjali's grandmother's name was Tara, and it was also the name of the mother of Gautam Buddha. Tara means "star," as well as "rescuer," and it has many other powerful, tantric meanings, both in Hindu and Buddhist traditions.[86] Innocent 3-year-old Rahul was awestruck when his mummy came home with his baby sister. Sarla and I had innumerable joyous and unforgettable moments during the early years with Rahul and Tara. Even though they have grown up and are teenagers now, we still enjoy their frequent visits.

With God's blessings all three grandchildren are not only excelling in their academic pursuits but are also playing leading roles in extracurricular activities. For instance, Anisha has represented her school at the Model UN program in New York and won an award. She also participated in a concert as a violinist at the prestigious Carnegie Hall in New York. She graduated from high school in June 2020, in the midst of the COVID-19 pandemic, and is now attending Barnard

---

[85]   http://www.amazon.com/Penguin-Book-Hindu-Names-Reprint/dp/0140128417
[86]   http://en.wikipedia.org/wiki/Tara_(Devi); http://en.wikipedia.org/wiki/Tara_(Buddhism)

College in New York. Rahul played tennis at a high level throughout high school as the #2 varsity player on a team that was ranked 6th in the nation among private schools. He graduated from high school in June 2022 and is now attending Rice University in Houston. Tara's innate feelings of empathy and compassion, along with her talent as a prolific creative writer and journalist, is reflected in her book, "The Hunting Season" which she self-published in 2016 and is available on Amazon and her poems, flash fiction and creative non-fiction pieces, several of which have won national awards and have been published. She is also an enthusiastic athlete and loves soccer, basketball and track.

Sanjay and Gautam had both settled down in Boston after their weddings and we visited them frequently until I lost my eyesight in 2010. In 2006, Gautam and Anjali elected to return to the Washington area, shortly before Tara was born. They bought a home in Chevy Chase, walking distance from Gautam's company, Monsoon Capital, and about 20 minutes from us. Renu and Sanjay decided not to follow because allergens and pollen affected Anisha to the extent that she had to use a nebulizer as a young child.

Full family portrait, July 2012.

6.8: Engaging with a Vibrant Network of Friends

We made friends easily and feel lucky that many of our friends from the days when we first arrived in the U.S. in 1960 remain our friends to this day. Our group of friends began to form when we met Margie Johnson, who was instrumental in introducing us to Carderock Springs. Sarla and Margie hit it off immediately, and they began to attract others to become part of their social life. We started a gourmet dinner group, which continued for four decades, despite all the members retiring from their professional careers. We would meet six to eight times per year in each other's homes and prepare one dish that the hostess would suggest. These evenings were very enjoyable – filled as they were with good food, good wine, and the company of our good friends. Some of the members continue to live in Carderock Springs, while others have relocated.

Sarla and Vinod participated in a monthly Gourmet Club starting in 1974 which continued for several decades. Many of the couples have been part of this club since the beginning. From L to R: Kathy O'Brien, Henry Beenhaaker, Jay and Sookie Lee, Ray and Isabella Van Raalte, Stefano and Meta O'Rourke, Sarla, Caroline Beenhaaker, Steve O'Brien and Vinod.

Another social group, joined by Sarla in 1981, was the Asian-American Forum (AAF) which focused on building greater understanding of the Asian-American experience. It met monthly with focus on films, books, museum visits, small discussion groups and so forth. Upon my retirement, I began to attend their plenary sessions, which were held nine times a year. This group provided opportunities for intellectual discourse and the exchange of ideas like no other social group to which we belonged. AAF was a friendly group of about 200 members, all well-traveled, warm, and highly accomplished people.

Asian American Forum, a friendship group focused on Asian American understanding.

We loved to sit down with our friends to share food and conversation, to discuss world events, and the latest exhibition at the Smithsonian. We celebrated Sarla's 60th birthday by reserving Tiffin Restaurant in Silver Spring for our guests. We invited old friends from Rhode Island and Boston, and many attended. Once again, we refused to accept personal gifts. All gifts were contributed to IDRF. My 75th birthday was celebrated in 2008 at Gautam's home. By then guests were aware of where their gifts should be sent!

*August 2008, family celebration for Vinod's 75ᵗʰ
birthday at Anjali and Gautam's home.*

For many years, we hosted small monthly dinner parties with friends and sat at our round dining table (which is more than 40 years old). True to her organizing skills and interest in the world, Sarla took time to prepare some quizzes and games. Before or after dinner we shared some fun times testing each other's knowledge. We were devoted fans of Bill Moyers on PBS, who was highly acclaimed for his fierce independence and in-depth journalism. PBS News Hour continues to be routine TV watching at dinner time in our home. We also watch Fareed Zakaria on CNN and 60 Minutes on CBS on Sundays, and we have a variety of such programs on videotapes on our library shelves. Sarla has invested time and money listening to authors and scholars at *Politics and Prose*, a popular local bookstore. We have both enjoyed attending presentations by international writers, scholars, and experts. Washington, DC, being one of the most powerful and cosmopolitan cities in the world, has attracted its fair share of these speakers.

We have often hosted guests, taking them to museums, monuments, and libraries. The city is full of museums, and the public ones are free. The Holocaust Museum is a powerful reminder of what happens to people or a culture if they are demonized. Margit Meissner, our former neighbor, remained a docent at the Holocaust Museum into her 90s.

She once told us that as a Jew and a refugee she distinguishes between "forgiving and forgetting."[87] "If you forget, you are fooling yourself, because history can repeat; but if you do not forgive you are only hurting yourself," she told us. We should pay heed to these words, I feel.

We have hosted visitors from India including: Jagmohan *ji*, former Governor of the Indian State of Jammu and Kashmir; Professor Rajendra Singh (known as Rajju Bhaiya), *sarsanghchalak* (all-India chief) of the RSS; Ashok Singhal *ji*, International President of the Vishwa Hindu Parishad; K. S. Sudarshan *ji*, *sarsanghchalak* of the RSS; H. V. Sheshadri *ji*, *sarkaryawah* (all-India general secretary) of the RSS; K. Suryanarayana Rao *ji*, *Akhil Bharatiya seva pramukh* (all-India director of service programs); Dr. Shankar Tatwawadi *ji*, *Vishwa Vibhag Pramukh* (worldwide director of RSS volunteers); Dattopant Bapurao Thengadi *ji*, founder of the Swadeshi Jagaran Manch, Bharatiya Mazdoor Sangh (Indian labor organization) and the Bharatiya Kisan Sangh (Indian farmers' union); and Sikander Bakht *ji*, vice president of BJP.[88] Walter Andersen, a close friend of mine from Johns Hopkins' School of Advanced International Studies (SAIS), has interviewed most of these people at our home.

We have lived a full life, you may say, and indeed we have, receiving with gratitude what life has offered us, and carrying on with conviction, bravely, when life has posed challenges. We have had wonderful friends, we have traveled many places, and we have hosted men and women of accomplishment, talent, and achievement.

---

[87]   https://www.ushmm.org

[88]   http://en.wikipedia.org/wiki/Jagmohan,
http://en.wikipedia.org/wiki/Rajendra_Singh_(RSS),
http://vhp.org/news/media-watch/%E2%80%98dharmashree%E2%80%99-title-conferred-ashok-singhal,
http://en.wikipedia.org/wiki/K._S._Sudarshan,
http://hindubooks.org/whr/the_concept_of_hindu_rashtra/page1.htm

---

However we may receive blows, and however knocked about we may be, the Soul is there and is never injured. We are that Infinite.
Swami Vivekananda

Let us, then, be up and doing, with a heart for any fate; still achieving, still pursuing, learn to labor and to wait.
Henry Wadsworth Longfellow

CHAPTER 7

World Gone Dark: The Harsh Hand of Fate (2010-Present)

7.1: Cataract Surgeries

DESPITE OUR BEST efforts and good deeds, sometimes life betrays us. What I did not foresee, as I struggled to put the IDRF house in order, was that I would be let down by my own doctors, or to put it more correctly, that I would be robbed of my eyesight by expert physicians and surgeons in whose care and expertise I had put my trust. But this is precisely what happened.

Despite our best efforts and good deeds, sometimes life betrays us.

Since 1997, I had been consulting a suburban Maryland ophthalmology group that has been in practice for more than 60 years. Initially, I had cataract surgery in October 1997, which is one of the most common eye surgeries. Before that surgery, the same ophthalmologist had suggested that I should consult a glaucoma specialist from this same group. The suggestion was absolutely correct, as I did have glaucoma, and it required regular monitoring. Thus, I became a patient of one of only 69 glaucoma specialists nationwide included in the publication "Best Doctors in America." I had to visit him every three or four months.

I had a second cataract surgery the following year, after which I began to notice something else. Because the aqueous fluid humor pressure in my left eye was above the normal range and in my right eye below the normal range, I used eye-drops in the left eye to maintain normal pressure. I told my glaucoma specialist, in the spring of 2009, that I felt that my right eye, which had the low pressure, was weakening. He suggested that I consult a cornea specialist and a retina specialist, also in the same ophthalmology group, which I did. Both examined me and they gave me a clean bill of health. In the spring of 2010, I complained that the same condition was recurring. The retina specialist found nothing wrong, but the cornea specialist suggested a corneal transplant in the right eye because, she said, the inner tissues were dying. She proposed using the DSAEK (Descernet's Stripping and Automated Endothelial Keratoplasty) corneal transplant procedure. She did not explain why, but she said that the earlier the surgery was performed, the better it would be.

7.2: Corneal Transplant: Ophthalmologists' Blunders

The surgery was scheduled for June 1, 2010 so that my glaucoma specialist could attend. He came by to wish me well, we shook hands, and then the cornea specialist did the corneal transplant. So, until May 31st, I had perfect sight in my left eye but weakening sight in my right eye.

On June 2nd, following the eye-surgery, the patch over my operated right eye was removed. I could not see with my right eye, but the cornea surgeon claimed everything was fine. She gave me an appointment for June 10th as my progress required monitoring and a follow-up examination. On that date, my left eye had normal vision and I drove myself to her clinic. She recommended that the surgery should be repeated and performed a repeat surgery on June 16th, the earliest date that she had available. At that time, she told me that there was a 25 to 30 percent failure rate with the transplant. Although a fairly new technique, she told me the DSAEK procedure was technically far superior to the older method of surgery.

I began to worry when I did not recover eyesight in my right eye even after the second surgery. I also found that I had lost my appetite. Three days after the second surgery, on Saturday, June 19, 2010, at around 6 p.m., as we were getting ready to attend a wedding reception of our family friend and former World Bank colleague, Prem Garg's son Nikhil, I started vomiting. The vomiting was so fierce that Sarla immediately called 911, and the ambulance that arrived transported me to the nearest hospital.

7.3: Medical Catastrophe

When I was admitted to the hospital, Sarla and I repeatedly told the Emergency Room doctors that I had undergone eye surgery twice since June 1st and that I had a severe headache on the right side, accompanied by fierce vomiting. What the ER physician recorded in his notes is not clear, and I was treated for vomiting only, and remained in the hospital for three nights. On Sunday morning, June 20th, Sarla had called my

I had a severe headache on the right side, accompanied by fierce vomiting.

cornea surgeon and reported my emergency situation. She was not there to respond, but the on-call physician of the medical group took the call. Sarla called again on Monday, and on Tuesday, but the cornea surgeon never called back, nor did she call the hospital or visit me at the hospital. I was released from the hospital on Tuesday afternoon, June 22nd. No ophthalmologist had come to see me, and since every day a new doctor made the routine rounds there seemed little continuity or careful monitoring of my condition. I was treated for severe dehydration, with the vomiting attributed to a stomach virus. By this time, I was noticing some problems with my left eye, too, mostly blurriness. Unfortunately, my right eye had never regained sight after the June 1st surgery.

Since I already had a follow-up appointment scheduled with my cornea surgeon for Wednesday, June 23rd, I went to see her. She checked, and at that time my left eye had 20/20 vision, though there was a loss of peripheral vision. Not bothering to perform a thorough check-up, she scheduled the next appointment for Friday, June 25th. This visit was with the same retina specialist, who prescribed a CT scan and diagnosed a hemorrhage in my eye. On the next visit with the cornea surgeon on

Monday June 28th, she performed a computerized test and it was obvious that there was a loss of peripheral vision in my good left eye. At that time, my left eye vision was 20/40. At an appointment the following day, the CT scan of my neck revealed that there was a blood clot in an artery of my neck. The retina specialist told me that if the clot had been discovered within 12 hours of the hemorrhage, it could have been surgically treated, but now there was nothing that could be done, because the hemorrhage had occurred around June 19th. Vision in my left eye began to deteriorate rapidly: initially it was 20/20, then 20/40, and then 20/60. I consulted and met with the retina specialist two or three times until July 1st, as I did with the cornea specialist. Since I trusted my glaucoma doctor, I met with him once too. Apparently, none of my doctors could correctly diagnose or fathom exactly what was going on. They allowed my left eye to deteriorate, relying

None of my doctors could correctly diagnose or fathom exactly what was going on.

blindly, as it were, on the efficacy of their own clinical instruments. They completely ignored the relationship between the two eyes, and of the eyes to the brain. As a result of their total negligence and overconfidence, they did not bother to refer me to a neuro-ophthalmologist or an appropriate ocular immunologist.

7.4: Treatment at Johns Hopkins Hospital

During my next appointment, on July 6th, the cornea specialist discovered debris in the retina of my left eye and she once again took me to the retina doctor, a substitute retina specialist, since the one who had previously checked my eyes was on vacation. The new doctor found the debris, and in consultation with other ophthalmologists in the group, referred me to the experts at The Wilmer Eye Institute at Johns Hopkins Hospital in Baltimore. Anjali and Sarla quickly took me to Johns Hopkins, but in the busy emergency department my turn didn't come until close to midnight, when the emergency room ophthalmologist did a quick check-up and realized the seriousness of my case. Not being able to figure out what was going on, the ER called Dr. David Barañano, the on-call retina specialist, at his home and he came to see me at about 1 a.m. He checked me and suggested a Foscarnet antiviral injection to be given directly into my left eye to stop spread of infection. It would give the doctors some time to do more tests to figure out what exactly was happening. Sarla called Gautam, since he was away in Europe for work, to check if he would agree to what Dr. Barañano was suggesting. Gautam agreed, and all of us realized that this was a last effort to save my eyesight.

Anjali worked her magic and was able to get a room for me. At around 5 a.m., I was formally admitted to the hospital. Sarla and Anjali returned home and awaited the doctors' reports. At around 9 a.m., a brain MRI was performed and by 1 p.m. they had the results: I had been stricken with the Herpes Simplex Virus (HSV). The doctors performed further examinations to rule out any other infections and problems. They did a brain scan and a lumbar puncture and other tests. They confirmed that it was HSV and started treatment promptly. The infection might have started during any one of the surgeries performed over the previous month.

I had excellent care at the Johns Hopkins main hospital. After four days of thorough checkup and treatments, the John Hopkins' medical assistance van transported me to Bethesda Health and Rehabilitation Center where I stayed for three weeks, so that I could continue my treatment including 24/7 intravenous therapy. After that stay, I visited and was checked by an infectious disease expert, as well as by my retina and cornea specialists.

Later in August, we consulted a locally renowned neuro-ophthalmologist at Johns Hopkins. Sanjay and Renu were visiting at that time and were able to accompany us. I recall that my cornea surgeon spoke with the neuro-ophthalmologist for 45 minutes or so, and God knows what transpired. According to him it was too late to correct the damage already done to the optic nerve. At this point, I had no idea that I could lose sight in my left eye too, because no one seemed to know or speculate on the status of my left eye.

7.5: Retina Surgery Reveals the Inconceivable Truth

More doctor visits and checkups followed. In the second week of October, the retina specialist recommended additional surgery for my left eye because the debris had spread. That surgery was performed on a Saturday in mid-October. I got better post-surgical care from the retina specialist than I ever got from my cornea specialist, but my confidence in this retina specialist was misplaced. The recovery from that surgery took three to four months, during which I was required to sleep on my back, and not turn left or right during sleep. The objective was to clear the left eye of debris, and to make sure the retina did not detach, and to stop further damage to the left retina, as well as to prevent pain in the eye and headaches.

Meanwhile, my family was not told (or the doctors did not know) that the optic nerve was damaged irreparably. I don't believe they were hiding this information; rather, it was not certain whether the damaged optic nerve would take 5 percent or 50 percent or 100 percent of the sight in my left eye. In February 2011, I recall that the retina specialist at the nearby hospital was so shocked at this finding that he could hardly speak and whispered that my optic nerve was pale (instead of thick pink, which indicates circulating blood). The optic nerve is viewed through the retina, and the debris had made it difficult to see it clearly before this time.[89] He said that I may not ever be able to see again.

He said that I may not ever be able to see again.

This harsh reality was unbearable for my family. Hence, we visited other specialists at Johns Hopkins Hospital, including another

---

[89]   Ironically, the first audiobook that we purchased following my blindness, *Self-Healing: My Vision and Life* by Meir Schneider, begins by stating that the most important visual organ is the brain. Ordinarily, we simply think we see through the eyes, but the reality is that it is the optic nerve in the brain that is the most important conduit for converting and relaying visual (real) images in nanoseconds. I was totally ignorant about this connectivity between the eyes and the brain. I strongly recommend that during or prior to college education, every student should take a basic course in human anatomy and physiology. Our children learn more about the outside world than they do about their own brains!

neuro-ophthalmologist, cornea specialist, and low-vision specialist, to seek second opinions during the spring of 2011. These specialists could not think of any solution in the foreseeable future, for what seemed to be a hopeless case. In accordance with the research protocol however, they entered my medical record in a database, in case a magical cure could be found in the next few years, perhaps through stem cell research going on around the world. So, by mid-2011, it was clear that I had completely lost sight in both eyes. My world had gone absolutely dark. What a cruel fate, and how much my family should bear!

My world had gone absolutely dark.

Sanjay and I are both victims of gross medical negligence, and our lives can never be the same as before. Yet we are victorious in leading our lives with dignity, and I am proud to be serving humanity at large through IDRF.

7.6: Confronting a New Reality: Blindness

My cornea specialist advised us to contact Columbia Lighthouse for the Blind in Silver Spring, MD, which is an organization in the D.C. Metro area that began one hundred years ago.[90] I am indeed grateful to the Lighthouse for easing my transition to manage my daily routine, specifically in mobility training; assistance in use of computers; and help in reading.

After my discharge from the rehabilitation center, I received physical therapy at our home. Thanks to the physiotherapist's invaluable service over many sessions, I have been greatly helped to get on track with my new life, enabling me to walk around, and restart using the treadmill. He pasted velcro on the treadmill settings with soft and hard bristles without which it is impossible for me to use. Interestingly, Medicare

---

[90] On May 17, 1900, the Columbia Polytechnic Institute for the Blind was incorporated by two blind men from Connecticut, Francis R. Cleveland, an attorney, and H. R. W. Miles, a graduate of the Perkins Institute for the Blind. Its overall mission is to help people of all ages overcome the challenges of blindness or vision loss and enable them to remain independent, active, and productive in society.

also provided for the services of an occupational therapist who came to our home with all the paperwork and told me that I could use his services for up to eight home visits. I did not need such help, but the therapist insisted that he could bill for his services and I need not do anything. This was not acceptable to me. It is an interesting and ironic commentary on the U.S. healthcare system that an enormous number of rules are written regarding medical benefits, making it easy for those who provide the benefits to bill Medicare for services that are sometimes not even required or warranted.

One of the most important challenges for the blind is *mobility*. I had five or six lessons from an instructor who was a part-time volunteer and he gifted me a walking stick and taught me how to use it. Sarla and Gautam also attended some of these sessions, as it was important for the family to get used to the new rules and roles, the new demands, opportunities, and challenges.

In order to maintain my sanity, it was necessary for me to relearn the use of a computer so that I could continue my passion to care for and do the necessary work to keep IDRF fully functioning. This process involved repeated visits to Columbia Lighthouse for the Blind. I learned how to use a computer and what kind of new software and hardware were necessary given my blindness. They provided JAWS (Job Access with Speech) software that was most appropriate among several others.[91] We installed JAWS on my computer, which could read aloud anything on the computer. It also enabled me to write online with a special keyboard and no mouse. I realized that my instructor from Lighthouse was a 64-year-old man, himself blind from birth and a national celebrity, who had memorized everything – but what was easy for him was much more challenging for me to learn. Despite having the most updated version of JAWS, I found that it was cumbersome software, with constant verbal reminders and pronouncements about where there was a comma, a semi-colon, or a period. It's no fun to ask JAWS to read. I hope someone will come up with more adept software.

---

[91]   http://en.wikipedia.org/wiki/JAWS_(screen_reader)

Lighthouse maintains a roster of volunteers interested in helping blind people. Triguna Ghosh volunteered to help me cope with my routine chores which depend upon my reading articles and mail. Obviously, such help was essential but naturally inadequate. He was just the right person who would read out accounting and billing papers, explaining to Sarla so that she could take care of them. As and when time permitted, he read to me from books, newspapers and magazines. Later, we advertised in our community's newsletter in search of additional readers. I was fortunate to have high school students from our neighborhood for a couple of years. I also relied on friends and caregivers to take me for walks.

The Maryland State government does have a program to help newly blind persons like me. A therapist, Beverly Kolb, visited a few times and provided suggestions and advice. She showed some tricks that one can use to do simple household chores like using the microwave, figuring out which CD to put in the player, and so on. There are other such devices available to ease the lives of the blind, but they go only so far to compensate for what is one of the most significant aspects of life, *sight*.

I also faced a challenge in figuring out the time of the day as I don't have any light perception at all. Gautam bought a talking wristwatch and a talking table clock. Time is a most important bearing for me, one I need to organize my daily schedule.

I also faced a challenge in figuring out the time of the day as I don't have any light perception at all.

The other connection to the world was the telephone, which became important because I needed to speak with IDRF donors, volunteers, and board members, talk to my family and friends, and keep in touch with the outside world. Again, Gautam stepped in to find the latest and the safest systems and technologies available for use on the landline. Unfortunately, the system had voice activation that was difficult to use because of my strong Indian accent and the technology's own limitations. Gautam had diligently put in a list of forty names and telephone numbers. The telephone was supposed to respond to my verbal commands rather than have me use the keypad. Alas, not even half the numbers responded correctly to my voice.

7.7: Combating Social Isolation

My social isolation now is a harsh reality. Throughout my life I have travelled extensively, across all six continents, enjoying

My social isolation now is a harsh reality.

numerous tours and making new friends. But due to my blindness and dependence on others, I have left Washington, DC only once since 2010. This final trip took place in 2016, when Sarla's grandniece, Alisha, graduated from high school in Ohio. Most of the extended family located in the US gathered to celebrate, turning the occasion into a family reunion. Sarla and I joined Gautam and his family for the drive to Ohio. Though it was a moment of great joy for everyone else, I had only tears in my eyes from all the emotions of being unable to participate fully. It was painful for me to visit an unfamiliar place where the independence I usually enjoy at my home was completely lost. My pain was so intense that I declined a second trip to Ohio in May 2019 for the wedding celebration of Anshuli, Alisha's older sister. Naturally, Sarla was also deprived by my inability to attend.

Given the technological advancement in communications, virtually everyone is now using smartphones that provide information like news, emails, videos, Facetime videocalls, Facebook, Instagram, Twitter, WhatsApp, GPS, and so on at one's fingertips. I also tried using an iPhone 4S, but it came with its own challenges and difficulties. At that time, there was no way that I could use an iPhone or any other smartphone for that matter, because just holding it and not inadvertently touching some parts of it became a challenge, even with the Siri application.

Even the normal cell phone that I had before I became blind would not work without sight. Gautam instead procured a popular device specifically for seniors called the Jitterbug. While a live operator responded to place calls, it did not work well for me because the system was limited to fifty phone numbers only. For nearly a decade, I used a Samsung Haven flip phone which has the capacity to save 500 numbers (cell, home, and work phone per person, or 166 contacts for me). Velcro is pasted on the phone keyboard so that I can use it accordingly because touch is the only way I can distinguish the various buttons. Making a call is quite a drill, but I'm satisfied with this phone because it reads out the contact names loudly. Still, I cannot independently manage all parts of it. My caregiver, Taylor Augustine, who has been Gautam and Anjali's nanny since 2007 and has become like family to us, has been instrumental in saving and updating all the contacts on my phone.

Despite these limitations, the phone remains the only way I can interact with people on a regular basis. There is no other means of communication for me to directly interact through any social media platforms. My long-time friends, Femma and Gerald Lo, helped me visit the office of the National Federation of the Blind in Baltimore and their technology center in order to gather more information about devices that could help me navigate my new world a little more nimbly, but I was unable to take full advantage of the technology available there because of my preoccupation with IDRF. Recently, I tried upgrading to a newer flip phone, but it wasn't possible because the old phone's data could not be completely transferred. I had to go back and use my same old 2010 model phone. But now Verizon is phasing out the outdated 3G platform, forcing me to upgrade, whether or not I want to learn how to use a new phone.

> **The phone remains the only way I can interact with people on a regular basis.**

Not only this, I'm confined to the four walls of my home, walls that are decorated with numerous artifacts that were collected over the four decades of our international travel, which alas I can no longer see and reflect back to our good old days.[92] Is it too much to expect friends and family members to close their eyes for five minutes and contemplate the impact of complete visual impairment? My isolation was so intense that I could

> **My isolation was so intense that I could only cry at first, but that is not the way I lead my life today, ten years later. Notwithstanding these extreme limitations, I continue to devote my days to the well-being of humanity.**

---

[92]   The drastic change in my life during the past decade is virtually inconceivable. I am now totally dependent on someone, to navigate me outside of my home. On rare occasions, however, I am able to attend or participate in community programs, World Bank seminars, and so on.

only cry at first, but that is not the way I lead my life today, ten years later. Notwithstanding these extreme limitations, I continue to devote my days to the well-being of humanity. There is a belief that God tests his believers, so I am determined to please the Almighty.

In my endeavor to face my social isolation, the unique facility of the U.S. Library of Congress came in very handy. It provides free audio books online for the blind, along with the requisite digital player. It is a digital library that provides thousands of books for the blind in a format that can be downloaded onto USBs and played with a special player that I learned to use. I began listening, and one book that inspired me is President Carter's "Beyond the White House."[93] After listening to that book, I feel it was a blessing for the world that President Carter did not win a second term. He would not have been able to contribute much in office, given the vagaries of the U.S. political system, whereas he and his wife have made an enormous difference in the lives of millions of people throughout the world with his post-White House work. "Beyond Religion: Ethics for a Whole World," by the Dalai Lama, is another inspirational book to which I have listened more than once without growing tired of it. I have become a careful reviewer of books that have caught the popular imagination and the attention of readers worldwide. One of those books was Walter Isaacson's biography of Steve Jobs, the legendary co-founder of Apple. I have mixed feelings about the life and work of Jobs. I do agree that Steve Jobs was among a handful of innovators and visionaries who transformed the world in the 21st century, however I am somewhat uncomfortable with the character and persona of Jobs – arrogant and obnoxious to his colleagues, and willing to manipulate the world of business and technology as he saw fit.

7.8: Split Thoughts on the Legal Battle

In March 2012, Gautam sent a letter to the nearby hospital where I had been treated, requesting a peer review of my treatment in the ER in 2010. All I received in return, after three months, was a short letter

---

[93] Please see Appendix 6 for a list of my favorite books.

that began with "we are sorry that our medical services did not meet your expectations." It is not the patient's expectations but their own standards for medical practice they had not maintained. These formal, legalistic responses, crafted by lawyers, make it exceedingly difficult for patients to know the truth. Is it not an irony and is this not a cover up?

This was no ordinary or simple mistake a doctor had made. This was a series of blunders, bad treatment, poor diagnoses, and irresponsible behavior by doctors and a hospital that led to one of the most severe losses an individual can suffer – the total loss of eyesight. I also feel that the doctors were negligent or careless because I was a 75+ year-old man and not a younger person earning an income.

This was a series of blunders, bad treatment, poor diagnoses, and irresponsible behavior by doctors and a hospital that led to one of the most severe losses an individual can suffer – the total loss of eyesight.

In the American legal system, a doctor sued for malpractice has to pay heavily if the patient is young and in the prime income-producing years. In brief, the so-called peer review system of hospitals in Maryland turned out to be a farce and cruel joke so far as my ophthalmic care at this nearby hospital is concerned. My family and I concluded that it was futile to move forward as far as my horrible experience at this hospital, and that we did not have the energy to wage another long, legal battle.

How would anyone respond to such culpability and negligence? Couldn't I at least have the satisfaction of the medical system compensating me a little for my enormous loss? We realized that this was a very, very complex issue. Just a few years earlier, we had faced a similar dilemma concerning the medical treatment Sanjay had received as his doctors had failed to consider the long-term side effects of his seizure medicine, Dilantin, and recommend better alternatives that had received FDA approval in the years since Dilantin was approved in the 1950s. In the end, our Indian cultural instincts prevailed, and we chose not to pursue any legal course of action in Sanjay's case. We believe in *bhagya* (fate). Does this mean we should believe whatever happened to us was simply *prarabdh* (God's will)? This was inevitably an undercurrent in our thinking about how to respond to these life-shattering experiences.

We knew that even if we took the doctors to court, my eyesight was not going to return. Plus, we had to consider the costs, in time and energy, that would be required to bring legal action. We had just come out of a long, arduous, and very draining IDRF battle with our influential Indian-American donor. We debated whether we should enter into another expensive, long drawn-out legal battle. We also considered the fact that I am now totally dependent on Sarla who would be facing new challenges from this unexpected and unfortunate turn in our lives. In turn, Sarla and I are dependent on Gautam and Anjali, and there are limits to how much time they could afford to spend to resolve this issue.

Finally, we met my ophthalmologists and hoped that they would at least admit their fault, to prevent such a horrible outcome for their future patients. Alas, we could not have even this much solace. Probably their response or lack of it was due to the fear of jeopardizing their malpractice insurance. We were left with no choice but to consider legal proceedings.

7.9: Medical Malpractice System is a Mockery!

We were persuaded that having lived in America for such a long time, we ought to fall in line with the American system. The dilemma was resolved, and we started contacting malpractice law firms but with no luck. It was quite a cumbersome task for us to find a medical malpractice law firm. Normally, such cases are taken on a contingency basis, implying that the law firm would initially incur expenses which they would recover only if they win the case. My case turned out to be unattractive because of my age as well as my fulltime volunteer work – meaning that my "economic value" was less than if I were younger with high income. In brief, we could hardly blame law firms as they are keen on earning money.

Fortunately, the compassion and empathy of one of my doctors helped us to secure the services of a prestigious malpractice attorney, Mr. Patrick Regan, from Regan Zambri & Long, a personal injury law firm in Washington, DC. Pat believed in our case, but we were nearing the expiration of the statute of limitations. Fortunately, Pat was able to file our case in state court against the ophthalmology group just days before the deadline. As is standard in these cases, the ophthalmology group turned the lawsuit over to their medical malpractice insurance company.

What followed was a long and arduous process of taking depositions for both plaintiff and defendants, along with those for witnesses to support their respective cases. Sarla and I were both deposed in a torturous process that required us to answer questions under oath for the entire day, with everything being video and audio recorded. After over 15 months of collecting evidence, taking defendants' depositions, preparing my family for our own depositions, researching our case to compile all of the areas of medical negligence, and responding to defendants' subpoenas for our own records, the trial date was set for the first two weeks of November 2014.

My attorney had succeeded in arranging a star witness. The key witness, an academic ophthalmologist at the University of California, Berkeley, was scheduled to appear on Friday of the first week of the trial. His earlier deposition was very powerful, mentioning that a basic, standard practice of care was overlooked by my doctors. On Monday of that first week of testimony, prior to jury selection, the judge met the two attorneys privately and told them that he was not available on Friday, due to some prior official engagement. My attorney called our key witness to reschedule his visit to DC, but that was not possible, due to other commitments he had. Hence, the only option left was a mistrial. I had a legal right to file for a mistrial on this basis, but the insurance company's attorney, Neal Brown of Waranch & Brown, emphasized that, were this to occur, they would exercise their right to appeal, should I win the case. Due to my advanced age, it seemed unwise to draw out the case for 7-8 months by opting for a mistrial, and even several years more in case of appeal. If I died during the appeals process, this case would be closed without a resolution. My attorney also informed us that he would then have no way to reclaim any legal fees which were contingent on winning the case.

Ultimately, I had no choice but to settle the matter out-of-court with our attorney negotiating the highest settlement payment that he felt he could get. Since the date of trial had been set months ago, I found it difficult to believe that the judge did not know of his lack of availability prior to trial. This kind of settlement serves the interest of protecting the reputation of doctors and discouraging malpractice lawsuits. This experience made a mockery of the judicial system and any rights that patients supposedly have. Anyone can guess what went on behind the scenes.

Besides this, we had a very interesting learning experience concerning the U.S. judicial system that relies on a jury. Present in the courtroom on the day of jury selection were the honorable judge, the attorneys representing the plaintiff (us) and the defendants' team, plus a group of about 80-90 randomly selected U.S. citizens from which the jury would be chosen. The jury selection process aims to identify common people who would be unbiased in their verdict. The jury would be comprised of nine people out of which three each were selected by the two attorneys and the remaining three were selected jointly by them. Each attorney made an opening statement. The opening statement of our attorney was very sharp and convincing. This was followed by the doctor's attorney who mentioned that my case was a "one in a million" adverse consequence in surgery. Later the judge adjourned the court, since attorneys were engaged in serious negotiations in the settlement of the case. The legal system prohibits me from disclosing anything about the settlement. I wish the system was more transparent and fairer.

7.10: Discovering Avenues of Learning and Sustenance

The past decade surely has tested my inner strength, my convictions, and even my faith in a higher power. How does one deal with something so catastrophic? The biggest challenge I face, beyond the physical challenges of being totally blind, is my total social isolation. I deeply miss our annual visits to India for they brought

> **The past decade surely has tested my inner strength, my convictions, and even my faith in a higher power. How does one deal with something so catastrophic?**

me tremendous joy, and as I saw how lives had been changed there through the work and support of IDRF. I also miss our socially active lifestyle here in DC. I am sad not to be able to use the latest, 21st-century technologies. My inability to do so has left me in almost total isolation.

I believe that launching IDRF more than thirty years ago has been a great blessing. Without this work, I would have been – and would today be – deeply depressed and bitter about life. I am lucky to have strong family support, financial security, and the comforts of modern life like television, audiobooks and music recordings. It is my deep involvement with IDRF that has made me able to get up each morning, go through the chores of getting ready, and look forward to something practical, noble, deserving, and fulfilling. People, including my doctors, are surprised that I am not taking any medication for depression.

> I believe that launching IDRF more than thirty years ago has been a great blessing. Without this work, I would have been – and would today be – deeply depressed and bitter about life.

In mathematics, in order to prove a theorem, one must satisfy both the necessary conditions and the sufficient conditions. I consider strong support and financial resources of my family as the necessary condition of my life, while my work with IDRF is the sufficient condition, my true purpose in life. I believe that being able to sustain my volunteer work after becoming blind is truly a blessing. What still drives and motivates me is *seva*. Despite what fate and the gods have thrown at me, I am dedicated to the cause of helping my fellow human beings. I firmly believe in the adage, *Nara seva Narayana seva* (service to humanity is service to God).

It is painful to me that I cannot help Sarla around the house to the extent to which I was accustomed before my blindness. The simple things that husbands and wives do together and in tandem to ensure the smooth flow of their daily lives all fall on Sarla's shoulders now – driving to the grocery store or to visit friends, keeping

> The simple things that husbands and wives do together and in tandem to ensure the smooth flow of their daily lives all fall on Sarla's shoulders now.

up with the yardwork and basic household maintenance, sharing the cleaning duties, taking turns cooking meals. Our relationship, to a large extent, has become that of a giver and a recipient, and that can change both subtly and glaringly the power, love, and affection equation. It takes physical and emotional energy from both of us to navigate this new world. Certainly, there is no dearth of love from her to me or the care she gives me. She is tireless. My daily medications must be carefully placed in a pill organizer, as I cannot tell the bottles apart. We also have an interesting early morning habit of drinking a cup of warm water with honey and lemon. We drink this concoction to keep our digestive systems clean by expelling the toxins from our bodies. Sarla guides me throughout the day, from preparing our honey-lemon water before breakfast and making my daily coffee and tea, to arranging the food on the table and doing the paperwork and chores for which I was previously responsible.

Gautam and Anjali moved to the DC area in 2006 and, in many ways, they have been able to provide the kind of immediate support that is invaluable. The energetic, multi-tasking professional he is, Gautam has been able to offer the kind of expertise, advice, and direction that would have otherwise been both slow and expensive from someone else. It is indeed a very busy life for Gautam and Anjali as parents of two energetic children and having both parents and in-laws in town. Bringing up children is a more complex affair than it was fifty years ago. Given the increasingly competitive nature of modern American society, the onus is on parents to provide their children the "very best" – which means time, energy, and support far in excess of what children of previous generations received from their parents. It is indeed demanding for Gautam to manage his work and to juggle a busy domestic life with all of things he does for us. He faces these challenges elegantly.

Our family at the grand ceremony in 2007 to open the new office for Monsoon Capital, Gautam's India-focused investment firm. We were happy to celebrate with Gautam's family and his in-laws, Indira and Girish Parekh.

Over the past years, my life has changed in major and in subtle ways. I am entirely dependent upon others to manage my life. Sarla and Gautam are now the two major pillars in my life, supporting me and helping me manage and maneuver both the physical and psychological challenges I now confront. I don't think I could conceive of any life without their strong support. If not for them, I may have become vegetative, and I suspect I would have been confined in a nursing home, where I surely would have died a quick death. Their support and care are absolutely critical to my survival, and I am more grateful to them than I can express in words.

I am not always easy to care for. Sometimes, I assume Sarla is still in the same room with me, but she might have left the room to attend to her chores. I cannot find out what she is doing or what she is feeling unless she tells me. Communication, after these many years of marriage, cannot happen now through the usual exchange of glances. Everything has to be verbalized. As we all know, sometimes verbalizing can increase one's frustrations or exasperation. But it is also an opportunity to improve communication: talking through everything as we now must do, has brought new insight and greater understanding.

I am not always easy to care for.

7.11: Unavoidable Accident

I follow my old routine of going up and down the stairs, and since I became blind, I have done so thousands of times. However, while I was going down the stairs to have my lunch on December 20, 2017, I encountered another consequence owing to both blindness and loss of some control over my legs due to spinal stenosis.[94] Despite holding onto the railing and careful use of my walking stick, I missed a step going down the stairs and fell, causing my walking stick to fly from my hand into the air and break the hanging chandelier. Thanks to the instant availability of both Sarla and my caregiver, Micaela, I was rushed to the hospital where I received prompt attention. Results of four x-rays and three CT scans led to my hospitalization and I remained at nearby Bethesda Suburban Hospital for six days. I went through unendurable pain due to several broken ribs and other injuries. My care at Suburban was professional and I was satisfied with the experience; the ER staff took good care of me and gave me heavy doses of morphine for my pain promptly. Another factor was the doctor who did the daily rounds happened to be my family friend's son, Dr. Atul Rohatgi. However, my experience in the rehab center this time (unlike 2010 after my blindness) was quite degrading and upsetting.

7.12: Impact on Relationship with Grandchildren

The impact of the loss of eyesight is absolutely immeasurable. I have lost three main senses: I cannot see motion; I cannot see shape; and I cannot see color. When my grandchildren visit, I cannot see how they have changed or the expressions on their faces. I

When my grandchildren visit, I cannot see how they have changed or the expressions on their faces.

---

[94] I was diagnosed with stenosis in 2016 and my pain initially responded well to pain injections. However, when the symptoms returned in 2017, I was unable to find a satisfactory way to manage the pain, despite visits to many doctors and physical therapists. I will have to live with this constant pain the rest of my life.

cannot gauge the passing of time by watching the seasons change, and the flowers bloom and die in the garden at home. I accept these losses as inevitable, but at times I feel both anxiety as well as humiliation, because I have to rely on someone else for even the simplest of things. It may be beyond comprehension for others to realize how I feel, confined to the four walls of my home. Even within my house, walking and talking cannot be done at the same time, since with my walking stick, I have to concentrate 100 percent on walking. With the slightest diversion of my attention, I feel lost. It must be difficult for those with sight to imagine how much I miss the simplest activities – like watching my favorite television programs with Sarla.

It may be beyond comprehension for others to realize how I feel, confined to the four walls of my home.

I miss our semi-annual visits to Anisha, our granddaughter in Boston. During the past decade she has grown up to be a young adult, but I could not be there for her presentation at the Model UN program in New York City or to see an orchestra performance at the Boston Conservatory. In 2014, I attended Rahul's graduation ceremony from lower school (4th grade) at Sidwell Friends School. While everyone was enjoying the ceremony, I began, silently, to cry. I was, of course, unable to attend Anisha's middle school (8th grade) graduation in 2016 in Boston. But in June 2017, I attended Tara's lower school (4th grade) graduation ceremony along with her other grandparents, but once again I experienced intense deprivation. I was overwhelmed to be present there, yet tears rolled down my face because I could not control my emotions.

Vinod playing with his older grandchildren, Anisha and Rahul, at his 75th
birthday party in August 2008. Those were happier times, as just two years later,
Vinod would go completely blind, unable to ever see his grandchildren again.

When Anisha graduated in May 2020, amid the COVID-19 pandemic, her high school held a virtual graduation ceremony which Sarla and I were able to watch from the comfort of our home in Maryland. During the 75-minute ceremony, we were able to see Anisha, as well as Renu and Sanjay, for about thirty seconds. Sarla was overjoyed to be able to see their expressions as Anisha reached this milestone. In the fall of 2020, Anisha was able to begin her college experience at Barnard College. However, this was affected by the pandemic as well; she and her roommates lived on campus while taking classes virtually. These experiences were one bright spot in the COVID-19 crisis.

7.13: Silent Cry and Tenacity

What enables me to reconcile this tremendous loss and sustain the determination not just to live but to contribute, especially to IDRF, and to try to change the fate of so many in India? What has enabled me to approach life steadfastly but not grimly? I believe that we have to go back to my childhood, my family's commitment to gaining India's freedom, despite their own modest circumstances. My family instilled in me strong ethical principles and a deep commitment to social justice, later enhanced through my connection with the RSS, and their ideals. Despite some terrifying moments of anxiety and fear, I have been able to sustain myself because of these deep, lifelong convictions.

Despite some terrifying moments of anxiety and fear, I have been able to sustain myself because of these deep, lifelong convictions.

Vinod with RSS leader, Rajju Bhaiya, on September 2, 1997 in Ujjan, Madhya Pradesh.

I have tried to be disciplined in my approach to dealing with my loss. I do *pranayam* (deep breathing) twice every day. I also begin my day with forty minutes of yoga (including *suryanamaskar* and *sarvangasana*). If I have not completed my eight hours of sleep, I complete my sleep soon after my yoga by lying down on my recliner chair with is foot stool.

I used to enjoy walking and jogging outdoors regularly, three to four miles a day; my home is so well-located that I was able to walk all seven days using a different route, including trails. Enjoying independent walks in the fresh air for my physical fitness and mental relaxation is a pleasure gone forever. For fitness, I bought an exercise bike and gained the confidence of my family that I could be left alone to use it in the basement. I then ventured onto the treadmill that I had used in my earlier days. For the first few months someone had to supervise me so I wouldn't injure myself. With a lot of willpower and commitment to focusing and keeping my hands firmly on the handlebar, I can now walk on the treadmill daily, even when no one is watching over me. The ability to concentrate fully on my exercise comes with practice. Letting my mind wander, even for a second, could potentially cause a serious accident. The physical routines I have maintained for the past 30 years now stand me in good stead. I remember visiting my cardiologist, Dr. Edward Bodurian, on May 24, 2010, just one week before my eye surgery. He expressed amazement that my heart was in such good condition. My hardcore discipline and embedded motivation have enabled me to take care of my daily chores.

I sorely miss the inner joy I felt on our field trips to India, to see how our donors' hard-earned money was being used, seeing the sparkle in the eyes of the children and the smiles on their faces, the joy on the faces of women empowered by IDRF's projects, and the enthusiasm of the staff of NGOs in India supported by IDRF. I do believe, however, that one benefit to IDRF of my loss of mobility is that I was able to bring IDRF's compliance standards to much higher levels than ever before. These high standards resulted in top ratings for IDRF on Charity Navigator, GuideStar, and Great Nonprofits. Consequently, IDRF has been receiving substantial donations from mainstream Americans as well. During the eleven years since I went blind in 2010, IDRF has raised

IDRF is not only helping the deprived in India but more importantly, it is providing me *aatma santushti* (intense inner joy) – the secret of keeping good health and my sustenance!

$18.3 million (out of $39 million in 32 years) and has sent grants amounting to $16.9 million (out of $37 million in 32 years). Believe it or not, IDRF is not only helping the deprived in India but more importantly, it is providing me *aatma santushti* (intense inner joy) – the secret of keeping good health and my sustenance! None of this would have been possible without the specific support of Vandana Matravadia and Niti Duggal.

It is said that people who lose the use of a particular sense organ make up for it by fine-tuning other sense organs. The senses of taste, touch, smell, and hearing need to compensate for the loss of sight. Alas, for the past four decades I have had some hearing loss in my right ear. Doctors had advised me to wear a hearing aid, but I felt I could manage well without it, and had not bothered to use one. Once I lost my eyesight, I became more conscious about the loss of hearing as well, because there was a total imbalance between the right and left ears. I tried a hearing aid, with many trips to the audiologist in an attempt to remedy the loss but, ultimately, I had to give up when there was no noticeable improvement.

Now it is all about touch, for it counts the most. It is my sense of touch that enables me to put on and enjoy the ironed clothes each morning, though I must now forego color coordination. It is touch that helps me shave, care for my teeth, use the toilet, and take a shower without assistance. In addition, I have learned a new language as my food is served on my plate as follows: salad at 3 o'clock, fruit at 6 o'clock, and so on, though the majority of my food is served mixed together in one bowl. I do miss being able to relish the taste and anticipate the sight of each individual part of the entrée. It is touch that enables me to efficiently unload the dishwasher and arrange the dishes back in place with high spirits. I try to be helpful to Sarla in daily chores. I have become adept at doing all those chores, after several years of practice. I have to "feel" my way around the house, and so I use the walking cane to touch and tap my way up and down the stairs, across the hallway, into the dining room, and to the bathroom. Like on the treadmill, navigating my way through the house requires absolute concentration. Despite living in the same home for three decades, I still have difficulty finding my way around without bumping into corners or getting confused about exactly where I am in the room. Again, I feel confined as I cannot even step out to check the mail without my cane and my cell phone, just in case I lose my way down the driveway.

Seven deadly sins
—wealth without work
—pleasure without conscience
—science without humanity
—knowledge without character
—politics without principle
—commerce without morality
—worship without sacrifice
Mahatma Gandhi

We must never doubt that a small group of
thoughtful, committed citizens can change the world.
Indeed, it is the only thing that ever has.
Margaret Mead

CHAPTER 8

Reflections on My Life

8.1: Looking Back

I WAS BORN in Meerut, India on March 9, 1933 and turned 90 this year (2023). It has been a long journey from those childhood games of *gilli-danda* in the little back-alleys of dusty Meerut during the time of the British Raj. I have traveled the world, and now live in a fine home in a pleasant neighborhood in suburban Maryland, close to the action in Washington, DC. No one can escape looking back, even the busiest person. What one sees in the rearview mirror of life can shape one's mood at any passing moment. However, those who dwell too much on the past could find the present too sour, and regret actions taken, rude words spoken, and rue opportunities missed. Whether we believe in the Hindu paradigm of *karma, prarabdha* (portion of the karma responsible for the present body), or *bhagya* (destiny), or in the Western/Christian concept of accountability and salvation or paradise, we do begin to look back more often as we get older. We begin to wonder what we could have done better.

Am I bitter about life, you may ask, after hearing my story? Do I wish I had pursued a different career in a different place with a different outcome? Not at all. But I do think I could have done some things better. I am certain, for example, that I should have paid more attention to acquiring tools and skills that would have made me a more proficient father and husband, employee of the World Bank, and founder of IDRF. I believe my success would have been enhanced if I had better English language skills. Specifically, I wish I had paid more attention to improving my writing in English, and in tweaking or changing my accent.

Living and working in the U.S., I could not pay much attention to our children or lend as much of a hand to Sarla as I would have liked to. So great were the demands on my time and on my energies, first at MIT, then for a short while at the slightly slower-paced University of Rhode Island, and then for almost twenty years at my demanding job at the World Bank. Life was also different then, even among American families, without as much close involvement with children's lives that is common now with soccer moms, helicopter parents, a surfeit of digital technology, and a faster-paced life.

8.2: Reflections on Career

As a small-town boy from North India, whose family was of limited means, I had a lot to learn. For many reasons, I seemed never to have the time I needed to focus on becoming a more proficient communicator. I had to make the transition from the small town to the cosmopolitan city, from the local to the international, and from the familiar to the foreign. The pursuit of my PhD in Economics at MIT took a heavy toll on my time and energy. I wonder sometimes what would have happened if I had not left India for higher studies and had continued at the Indian Statistical Institute and Planning Commission. I might have retired as a top technocrat with all the material goods and

I wonder sometimes what would have happened if I had not left India for higher studies.

power that come with such positions, including maids and servants at one's beck and call, but also the stresses and strains of pandering to the political class. I took a different fork in the road. The world I entered enabled me to participate in the grand commencement ceremony at MIT, when I graduated with a PhD in 1970. I still recall with pleasure that the "March No. 1" classic graduation music which played at my MIT convocation was computer generated. I had never attended a graduation ceremony in India because my family could not afford for my travel to Agra to receive my bachelor's and master's degrees from Agra University where the convocations were held.

*Vinod, Sarla and Sanjay at Vinod's doctoral graduation
ceremony at MIT in Cambridge, MA in 1970.*

At the World Bank, I became conscious of the unspoken standards of communication in interpersonal interactions, and of the behavior patterns and attitudes necessary for an elite institution led by American and European technocrats. My adaptation to the American cultural milieu happened a bit more easily at the World Bank, with its vast army of international staff, but it was still a challenge. None of my Indian colleagues at the World Bank were from an upbringing similar to mine. They were more established in their aspirations and careers, because of their family and educational backgrounds. For example, most of the other Indian employees had learned English during their schooling in India, while I attended English as a Second Language (ESL) classes with other new World Bank employees from countries where English was not the primary language. Still, I was confident in my professional abilities and did not suffer from an inferiority complex, which helped me to succeed. That confidence was my core. But my veneer – my presentation skills – had to be refined.

8.3: Inheritance of Ethical Values

In India or here in the U.S., class and caste can influence and shape our lives and our careers. Self-confidence, interpersonal skills, and communication abilities are much harder to acquire for someone from a rural, lower-caste, and lower-class background in India, as it is in the U.S. for someone from a rural family, a person of color, or one without higher education. Indian students who have come to the U.S. from upper-middle-class families and families that are already well established in India, tend to do well simply because they come with the confidence and requisite skills needed to succeed. Those who prosper quickly can build on their prosperity, while those who must overcome the initial challenges of lack of wealth and educational opportunities have to wage a harder struggle to establish themselves. My family was much different from many traditional patriarchal families in North India; my mother, sisters, and sisters-in-law were all involved in the struggle for the nation's freedom and in their pursuit of higher education. We were all committed to the *Arya Samaj's* ideal of service, and to Gandhian principles of simple living and high thinking. But we were not very well off financially.

Sarla's family, as I have noted elsewhere, was far better off economically. Three of her brothers and a sister studied and worked abroad. Om *bhaiya*, Dharam *bhaiya*, Vishu, and Sharada *jiji* were all established in the UK (Vishu had also been to Sweden and Switzerland). I was the only one in my social circle to travel beyond Meerut – from Calcutta (now Kolkata) and Delhi and then beyond Indian shores to earn my PhD degree, and settle in the U.S. I was the first in my family to be able to travel the world. Sitting in my family's shop, I decided **I must have a bit of the pioneer in me.** that life as a small-town shopkeeper was not for me, and in a sense, ran away from that life and sought refuge in academia and in an international career. I must have a bit of the pioneer in me. My risk paid off and allowed me to have no regrets in the area of giving, whether money or time.[95]

---

[95] In 2012, I was recognized by MIT for donations made by me to my alma

8.4: Reflections as an Indian American

We have been living in the US for over six decades and it may be appropriate to reflect back. It would be hard for our grandchildren to believe that we arrived in America with just two suitcases of which one had nothing but Indian groceries because they were just not available anywhere in the US back in those days. Whereas today there are dozens of Indian grocery stores all around our area. There was a time when mangoes were scarce in the US! But a dramatic change took place when President George W. Bush visited India in March 2006. Alphonso mangoes from India were allowed to be imported to USA after this Presidential visit. Subsequently mangoes have become available in the majority of grocery stores and have become a staple food in the American diet.

The influence of the Indian American community is also reflected by the celebration of India's most prestigious festival Diwali at the White House since 2003. Due the sustained efforts of Indian Americans, a Diwali Forever stamp was unveiled by the United States Postal Service in October 2016. Indian Americans are considered an affluent and educated community and are valued members of different businesses in the United States. Indians here excel as forerunners in technology and medicine as well as academics. Our young adults are well-known for being National Spelling Bee champions. Overall, in the past few decades, the prestige of India throughout the world has been significantly enhanced, yoga has become a household word, and Indian IT professionals are working in virtually every country.

8.5: Reflections on Sarla's Role

Sarla has been a steadfast partner and a rock in my life, bringing her own enthusiasm, energy, drive, and vision to family matters (see Chapter 9). With two Masters' degrees under her belt, she could have found a

---

mater: "You have given to MIT not only five-plus years in a row, but also every year since your graduation." I received an Infinite Circle identification pin from them in recognition of my inner desire.

very satisfying career in the Washington, DC area. Given her interests in politics, international affairs, culture, and the arts, she could have been an "India star" influencing and shaping Indo-American cultural and political dynamics. Ultimately, Sarla felt that her children, especially Sanjay, needed her attention and support and she did her best, as an outstanding mother and caregiver, to make them self-confident, strong, and steadfast. In her little spare time, she volunteered and then worked for the Jewish Foundation for Group Homes (JFGH), caring for adults with disabilities, an area that was close to her heart given Sanjay's own disabilities.

The World Bank allowed sponsorship of maids and domestic help for the staff. I wish I had taken advantage of that to enable Sarla to spend time out of the house and pursue her own career. Having grown up in a family where women were doing only household chores or, at the most, teaching in school, my values and vision vis-à-vis family life were different than Sarla's based on her own upbringing. None of my brothers' wives had a professional career, so in thinking of what married life would be like, I did not envision a wife who would have a professional career. In retrospect, I could have been more forward thinking in my decision making.

Sarla and Vinod sharing an embrace.

8.6: Values Inherited by Children and Grandchildren

I am especially proud that Sanjay, with impressive determination, passed the CPA exams and then graduated with an MBA degree. More so, I am proud that Sanjay and Renu, as well as Gautam and Anjali, did not accept wedding gifts but initiated the practice of donating all their wedding gifts to NGOs in India engaged in the empowerment of the under-privileged. I feel honored that the spirit of volunteerism has been inculcated in both Sanjay and Gautam. For instance, Sanjay volunteered at the Esther Sanger Center for Compassion, and volunteered for the "Rides for Vets" program. And Gautam served for eight years on the Board of Trustees at The Sidwell Friends School, his alma mater, and volunteered as President of the Boston chapter of The Indus Entrepreneurs (TiE).

I want my grandchildren, from a very early age, to have a similar community orientation and love for their fellow human beings. Sharing and caring should balance our academic, professional, and family lives. The Indian educational system virtually denies children the opportunity and ability to learn such values. I want my grandchildren to be good American citizens, but I hope that they will never forget the land of their ancestors and heritage. They should take pride not only in

> **I want my grandchildren to be good American citizens, but I hope that they will never forget the land of their ancestors and heritage.**

what India was, but work and help towards a great Indian future. While the U.S. is their *karma bhumi* (land of action), it is Bharat that is their *punya bhumi* (sacred land).

8.7: Reflections on IDRF

I believe in the principle and philosophy of *nishkaama karma* taught by the Gita (performing one's duty without any attachment to, or even any expectation of, the fruit thereof). I do, however, recall with great pleasure the many instances when IDRF's good work has been recognized both in India and in the U.S. I did not seek publicity or press coverage for IDRF, but word spread of the good work being done. For example, IDRF has been recognized by the largest circulated Indian-American weekly, *India Abroad*, with reports by its senior writers, like Aziz Haniffa and Arthur Pais. The relief work funded by IDRF following the Latur earthquake in 1993 was telecast throughout Asia by the United States Information Service (USIS). In terms of global reach, a radio interview broadcast, *A World of Possibilities*, was done at our home in 2006. It was included with an interview of a World Bank Vice President, and I was given pride of place. In the segment containing my remarks, the producers included a fitting audio excerpt from Mahatma Gandhi. What an honor this was for me!

It is likewise an honor to have my children and grandchildren follow in my footsteps with regards to giving, both in the U.S. and in India.

Vinod, Sanjay and Gautam proudly wearing their matching IDRF t-shirts!

I am delighted that Gautam is taking more interest in Indian-American political affairs now, as well as being a generous contributor to IDRF. Around the time he was starting Monsoon Capital in 2004, Gautam led a delegation of U.S. venture capitalists to India to expose them to the opportunities in India and he was able to arrange a private audience with the President of India, Dr. APJ Abdul Kalam (Bharat Ratna 1997).

*Gautam meeting with the President of India, Dr. Kalam,
in 2004 when he led a delegation of VCs to India.*

Gautam's business interests have since taken him to India often. He supports the good work of organizations like the Hindu American Foundation (HAF) which is led by Indian-American professionals of his generation. These philanthropic values were reinforced by his Quaker education, so he and Anjali have decided to pass them along to their children by enrolling them at the same Sidwell Friends School of which their father is an active alumnus. The children have inspired their parents as well: at our 2014 family Diwali celebration, Rahul and Tara surprised Anjali's parents with a decision to donate major portions of their pocket money savings to IDRF, continuing this family tradition. I posted a photo of the kids making this donation on the IDRF Facebook page. This, in turn, convinced the child of another IDRF volunteer to donate money from her savings to IDRF.

8.8: Reflections on Europe's Role in India's History

European contact with India goes back over 2,500 years. Alexander the Great, king of the ancient Greek Kingdom, sent Scylax to explore India through land and sea routes in 515 BCE. The exploration stopped at the Indus River *(Sindhu)*, and since then the people in the area were called Hindu.[96] That is why our ancient scriptures – *Puranas, Vedas,* the *Ramayana* and the *Mahabharata,* for example – do not have the word 'Hindu' in their vocabulary. Yet all these scriptures are embraced by modern Hindus.

India's history of the past 500 years is full of adventures of the Portuguese, Dutch, French and the British in trade, and then in conquest. They succeeded in exploring India through many voyages. The first such attempt was by Christopher Columbus, an Italian explorer who landed on the east coast of the U.S. in 1492. That's why the indigenous (native) peoples in the U.S. have in the past been called Indians and we are called Asian Indians as per our ethnicity. Another explorer, Vasco De Gama of Portugal, arrived in India in 1498 at Malabar Coast (present Kerala state) followed by Admiral Afonso de Albuquerque in 1510 at Goa. Subsequent explorations were made by the Dutch in 1605 at Pulicat, Madras (now Chennai); by the Danish in 1618 at Tharangambadi, Tamil Nadu; and the French in 1664 at Pondicherry (all three are on the east coast of India). Most importantly, the British arrived in 1612 and established the East India Company, initially for the purpose of exporting Indian goods but eventually the company intervened in Indian governance. They succeeded in capturing the city of Calcutta (now Kolkata) from the Mughal rulers in 1756, and eventually it became the capital of India during the British Rule in 1772 under Warren Hastings as the first Governor General. The British started grabbing power from local kings – the Mughals, Nawabs, Maharajas, and Rajas. Later, the national capital was shifted to Delhi in 1911. Eventually, the British Empire constituted present-day India, Pakistan, Bangladesh, Burma (Myanmar), and Ceylon (Sri Lanka).

The British introduced the first goods (cargo) train in 1837 in Madras (now Chennai), and the passenger train in 1853 in Bombay (now Mumbai). By the end of British rule in 1947, India had a vast network of railways throughout the country. India expanded its railways enormously

---

[96]   This river was known to the ancient Indians in Sanskrit as *Sindhu* and the Persians as *Hindu. India* is a Greek and Latin term for "the country of River Indus." Ancient Greeks referred to the Indians as "Indói", literally meaning "people of the Indus."

after it gained independence, making Indian railways the largest rail network in the world. Similarly, English became the *lingua franca* because of British policy and sanction. Ultimately, Indians' mastery of the English language accelerated the pace of India's success in world affairs.

During the colonial period, the British exploited the Indian masses and our natural resources for their own benefit. Eventually, Indians succeeded in gaining independence in 1947, though with a huge penalty – the partition of the country into a "secular" India and the Islamic Republic of Pakistan, on August 15, 1947. Pandit Jawaharlal Nehru became the first prime minister of India. The political leaders needed about two and a half years to formalize and adopt the Indian Constitution which was written under the chairmanship of Dr. B.R. Ambedkar. Thus, India celebrated its first Republic Day on January 26, 1950, when Dr. Rajendra Prasad became the first president of the country. India chose the path of democracy where people live freely and can choose and practice their own faith, be it Buddhism, Zoroastrianism (followers are typically called *Parsis*), Sikhism, Jainism, Judaism, Islam, Christianity, Hinduism, or its variants such as Sarla's *Arya Samaj* tradition.

8.9: Reflections on Self-Identity

I hope that Hindu-Americans will not shy away from acknowledging their Hindu identity and will simultaneously equip themselves with Hindu ethos and values – pluralism, universalism, service before self, and working without desiring the fruits thereof. As to the split between my Indian-American and Hindu-American identities, it depends upon context: as an IDRF volunteer, I am an Indian, but in my family life, I am a Hindu. This issue can lead to some misunderstanding, and I do not wish to lecture – I only speak about how I have embraced these values in my own life.[97]

> **As an IDRF volunteer, I am an Indian, but in my family life, I am a Hindu.**

---

[97] I have endeavored to embrace the basic ethos of Hinduism such as *Vasudhaiva*

If you were to ask me what it means to be an Indian, and why I still so love my Indian passport, I would need to mention my feelings about the pledge that a new citizen of the United States has to take, owing allegiance to the U.S., and to none else. Because I could not make such a pledge, I decided to retain my Indian citizenship. Perhaps this was too sentimental or emotional, and if I had been a bit pragmatic, I could have become an American citizen and still carried out *seva* effectively in India.

I also worry at times about reconciling my love of India with the events and values that are reshaping India today. While we should take pride in the *Mahakumbha Mela* which occurs every twelve years and draws upwards of 100 million pilgrims, I wonder what has happened to the hundreds of millions of dollars earmarked to clean up the Ganga and the Yamuna rivers. Where is the purity of the human being, and of the air he breathes, and the water he drinks? I am impelled to urge the Indian community at large to take much greater interest than heretofore in ensuring accountability, compliance and transparency in governance.

8.10: Reflections on Contemporary American Politics

I fear that American democracy has become a "dollar-o-cracy" with crony capitalism, divisive politics, and lobbyists holding public offices.[98] The national debates of two presidential candidates, one representing each major political party, seem to be managed by vested interests in recent election cycles. In my view, President Trump's election in 2016 reflects a non-violent, democratic revolution against the political establishment in Washington controlled by the Democratic and Republican political parties. Still, I wonder how a candidate who had never held public office was able to get elected as the country's

---

Kutumbakam (the world is one family) and *Sarve Jana Sukhino Bhavantu* (let all the people of the world be happy).

[98] Notwithstanding the critical role of the dollar in politics, as a U.S. resident for over 60 years, I am happy to assert that I have not come across a situation wherein I was induced to bribe any official.

Chief Executive. I am appalled by much of what has happened during Trump's administration. President Trump has debased America's image in the world, jeopardizing the normal lives of millions of Americans, as well as demoralizing government employees and putting them through undue financial hardships. The lengthy debate through the fall and winter of 2019-2020 in the U.S. Congress regarding the impeachment of President Trump deflected the attention of elected officials from their obligation to focus on society's basic needs such as climate change, depleted infrastructure, gun control, health insurance, and huge income disparities.

In my view, Trump holds the responsibility for losing the 2020 election. He completely mismanaged the COVID-19 pandemic, at times even calling the virus a hoax and going so far as to encourage his supporters to vote in person at risk to their own health and safety. The fact that President Trump refused to gracefully concede the election greatly tarnished the reputation of the United States as a democratic superpower. The resulting attack on the US Capitol on January 6, 2021 was as inconceivable to me as to much of the American population and democratic nations worldwide. The fact that so many Americans traveled from all over the country to the Capitol building that day made it clear that the United States had not ousted white supremacy simply by having elected an African-American president in 2008. Unfortunately, racism has far deeper and widespread roots in the culture of American society. I think that the subsequent second attempt to impeach Trump missed the mark; instead perhaps a Commission on Domestic Terrorism (similar to the one which convened after 9/11) might have made better headway to take corrective steps to prevent these kinds of attacks and liberate American society from racial prejudices and conspiracy theories.

8.11: Reflections on Contemporary Indian Politics

One of the highlights of our last visit to India in 2009 was to personally meet Arvind Kejriwal, renowned crusader of the anti-corruption movement (Chief Minister of Delhi since February 2015).

The corruption in government was so flagrant at the time that Anna Hazare (1992 Padma Bhushan) led an All-Indian Anti-Corruption Movement in 2011. This movement succeeded in the enactment of The Lokpal Act in 2013, which is an anti-corruption act which helped lead to the May 2014 victory of the Bharatiya Janata Party (BJP), led by Prime Minister Narendra Modi, and opened a new vista for India's future. While Modi had a strong record of governance as Chief Minister of Gujarat, I hope that comprehensive improvements in governance remains a priority for the government. The emphasis on transparency through digitization and required use of the unique identification card (*Aadhaar*) for financial transactions as well as for procuring goods and services at a subsidized rate should help in combating pervasive corruption, so it gives me hope for a much better India in the long run.[99]

Similarly, India's democratic traditions remain strong, with the peaceful transfer of power, both at central as well as state level, happening smoothly without disruption to normal public life. I admire the independence and integrity of the Chief Election Commissioner in conducting the elections. Indian parliamentary elections are held every five years, allowing several weeks for completion of the voting process. Vote counting is done only upon completion of all phases, and the Indian electronic voting machines have become renowned for their reliability.

However, corruption remains in elections as it is generally believed that money is still involved and continues to play a vital role in procuring votes. And I must admit that rampant corruption is still faced by the Indian masses at virtually all levels of society. Modi, in the interests of remaining in power, does fall short of the goal to have a "clean" government down to the grassroots levels if political parties and their candidates are not held accountable for electoral expenses.[100] In IDRF's

---

[99]   Serving healthy lunches to children at government schools through The Akshaya Patra Foundation is a step in the right direction (60% of funding is provided by the Central Government and 40% by the community at large). Millions of meals are served every day.

[100]   It pains me to admit that India's bureaucracy rarely functions well in the absence of greasing the palms of the administrators.

own dealings with numerous NGOs in India, we have faced serious challenges concerning the quality of governance. For example, the administration of the Foreign Contributions Regulation Act (FCRA) can be so nonsensical that in one instance we were left with no option but to approach the Prime Minister's Public Grievance Office – we never heard back. In another instance our emails addressed to the concerned Home Minister and copied to the Head of FCRA department were not even acknowledged despite multiple reminders.

But the community at large also bears responsibility, and can make a difference themselves, as illustrated by our successful experience with an NGO in Wardha, MH. The NGO was required to have a license to sell its produce at their shop. They discarded the easy choice of receiving a license through the common practice of paying a bribe. Instead, they followed the Gandhian Way by blocking the entrance and exit doors of the issuing office until they got their license. A year later, the same NGO needed a license for running a cafeteria. By that time, word had spread widely about this NGO and, as a result, they received their next license right away with no hassles. This example illustrates the power of community engagement in combatting corruption and improving the quality of governance.

In order to provide a corruption-free government at all levels, the government should undertake massive reforms, including administrative, educational, electoral, and judicial. Notwithstanding his shortcomings, I am pleased that Modi was re-elected as Prime Minister in May 2019. This victory emboldened him to undertake long overdue reforms.[101] Three recent examples, of which I am particularly proud: (1) amending the Constitution of India to remove the special status for the states of Jammu and Kashmir, which places them now under the supervision of the central government; (2) adopting the Citizens' Amendment Act (CAA), which provides a faster route to citizenship for

---

[101] Based on my three decades of experience with IDRF, I have strong reservations about the validity of governments' claim of "*Swatch Bharat Abhiyan.*" The government ought to be more accountable and transparent than heretofore. In brief it should spell out its budget, invite open bidding with civil society (community) organizations and work closely with them.

persecuted religious minorities relocating to India from Pakistan and Bangladesh; and (3) honoring the recent Supreme Court ruling about *Ram Janmabhoomi*, which creates a clear path for the reconstruction of a temple destroyed by the Mughal emperor Aurangzeb five centuries ago.

In a nutshell, while much work remains, the Modi government has significantly enhanced the prestige of India, *yoga* has become a household word, Indian IT professionals are respected all around the world, and India's rapid economic growth into one of the top countries in the world is widely acknowledged.

8.12: Reflections on India's Economy and Development

Early Indian economic and industrial policy immediately after independence (first under Prime Minister Nehru and later under the leadership of Indira Gandhi) worked because it was, essentially, a policy of import substitution. However, by 1991, this strategy totally collapsed. Since then, unfortunately, despite liberalization, little comprehensive development has occurred. The Indian economy began to stall due to factors including coalition politics and the need for politicians to pander to their vote-banks. The Indian Institutes of Technology (IITs) are still graduating top-notch engineers, but there is very little innovation happening in India. These same engineers, when they make their way to the U.S., can flourish because of the culture of innovation in this country, the ease of setting up business and industry, and the reward system in place here. Steps are being taken in India towards a more open economy, but it has been slow going.

The Indian Planning Commission was headed by people whose mindset was largely Western, and the strategy and development policy they were following was based on the Western model: they virtually ignored the environment, the well-being of poor farmers and tribal people, and the health and well-being of women. The replacement of the Planning Commission with NITI Aayog (National Institution for Transforming India) in February 2015 reflects the overall vision of the Modi government. Translating this vision into practice is likely to take many years due to a variety of political pulls and pressures. For instance, if the government means business, it should make the utilization of schemes such as MPLADS (Member of Parliament Local Area Development Scheme) or MLALADS (Member of Legislative Assembly Local Area Development Scheme) transparent and available digitally to the public to prevent fraudulent use of dedicated funds.

I worry that policymakers in India do not have the requisite knowledge or a good understanding of the realities on the ground. Bad policy has led to an increase in the rate of farmer suicides, due to the increased need for farmers to borrow from unregulated moneylenders in order to buy costlier seeds and costlier farm equipment. I think micro-credit should be given primarily through civil society organizations, such as self-help groups, and not by banks – and I see the work of IDRF as important and relevant in this context.

The many development challenges faced by India today are further aggravated by the increase in population and by climate change. For instance, around the time of India's independence, the population was estimated to be 330 million. According to the most recent census, the population is now 1.35 billion, more than quadrupling in the past 75 years, despite the government's vigorous efforts to encourage family planning. The *'chhota parivar sukhi parivar'* (small family, happy family) movement has been embraced by educated families more so than by Muslim fundamentalists and rural populations.[102]

8.13: Reflections on the Pandemic

The COVID-19 pandemic shattered the whole world in 2020. I admit my ignorance about the history of the Spanish flu pandemic of 1918-1920, where at least 50 million people (roughly 5% of the world

---

[102] My family set a good example. My own family, within three generations, had seen a significant decline in family size from nine (my siblings) to four or five (nephews/nieces) and eventually to two (grandchildren) – see our family tree in Appendix 1 for more information. IDRF's experience in Haryana state regarding family planning clearly reflects its success as detailed in Chapter 5.

population at the time) died.[103] I must give credit to the dedication of the medical scientists and public health officials for the tremendous advancements of the past century, which severely limited the loss of life compared to that of previous pandemics. This includes the global cooperation and funding that led to the rapid development and testing of vaccines, an incredible accomplishment, on an accelerated timeline never before seen. Thanks to the Emergency Use Authorization (EUA) of the US Food and Drug Administration (FDA), vaccines were available to health care workers beginning in December 2020. By June 2021, vaccines became available to virtually all Americans over the age of twelve

I find that the constraints I already endure as a visually impaired person mean that I find my house a paradise and not a prison. Confinement due to COVID did not pose a serious challenge for Sarla and me, as retired people who were already at home most of the time. Our home has artifacts and art in every room, which friends have jokingly called a "mini museum." We are delighted to live among the many rugs, paintings and other pieces of art collected during my work trips at the World Bank, our many travels as a family, as well as gifts from our wide circle of family and friends. Over the years we spent collecting these treasures, we could never have foreseen that I would lose my eyesight. Nonetheless, I am fortunate that I can pass my time on the treadmill recalling in detail the items in our home and remembering the good times – and good friends – from the past.

8.14: Reflections on Total Visual Impairment

Looking back, I wish I had paid more attention to learning and to maintaining skills in the use of new technology. In the late 1970s, I was one of the few at the World Bank who knew something about computers and was on a committee to incorporate and increase the use

---

[103] I listened to the audiobook version of *Pale Rider: The Spanish Flu Pandemic of 1918 and How it Changed the World* by Laura Spinney in 2020, as the COVID-19 pandemic intensified in the US.

of computers at the Bank. However, in the 1980s my attention shifted, and my personal skills using new technology began to fall behind. Now, with the loss of my eyesight, I am becoming adept at using some of the cutting-edge technology that has been developed to help those with disabilities. I also enjoy listening to audio books and savor some old Hindi film music.

My memory lane, however, is still vibrant. I have travelled so far from my humble beginnings – it was over six decades ago when I undertook my first overseas trip. Since then, I have travelled across all six continents. I have enjoyed seeing Alaska and Hawaii, numerous state and National Parks, monuments, and historical landmarks on the U.S. mainland.[104] Not many could afford such extraordinary travel, and it is indeed inspiring to note that I understood the importance and relevance of seeing the world, and made sure that Sarla, Sanjay, and Gautam were exposed to diverse international cultures.

I have travelled by air and road with family and friends and feel blessed to have wonderful memories about the life I once had. I can still enjoy the fresh air sitting on the porch, but I intensely miss being able to see the natural beauty (flowers, trees, chirping birds) all around me. For the past decade, I have been confined to the four walls of my home. I could feel bitter or depressed and experience nightmares. But I do not. My home is my paradise. What, you may wonder, is sustaining me? It is the selfless spirit to serve the downtrodden. In other words, life is worth living if one makes a difference in the lives of others.

Life is worth living if one makes a difference in the lives of others.

---

[104] After 39 years of marriage, Sarla and I took a wonderful nineteen-day cruise to Alaska, a vacation without any financial worries. I wished to return to Alaska with the kids and grandkids but, because of the tragic loss of my eyesight in 2010, such a trip has not been possible. I regret that I could not take Sarla to Australia, nor could we visit Kenya and see the wildlife there – these are a couple of the trips I wish we had taken.

In the long run, we shape our lives, and we shape ourselves.
The process never ends until we die. And the choices
we make are ultimately our own responsibility.
Eleanor Roosevelt

CHAPTER 9

Sarla's Reflections

9.1: Sarla's Upbringing and Family Tragedies

MY ELDEST SISTER, Sharda *jiji*,[105] often read this poem by Rabindranath Tagore to me and to her daughter, Poonam, when we were both children:

Where the mind is without fear and the head is held high
Where knowledge is free
Where the world has not been broken up into fragments
By narrow domestic walls
Where words come out from the depth of truth
Where tireless striving stretches its arms towards perfection
Where the clear stream of reason has not lost its way
Into the dreary desert sand of dead habit
Where the mind is led forward by thee
Into ever-widening thought and action
Into that heaven of freedom, my Father, let my country awake!

We were too young to understand this poem, but just to please her, I memorized it and used to recite it to her. She encouraged us to read stories of freedom fighters, including Gandhiji, Nehru, Sardar Patel, Lokmanya Tilak, Veer Savarkar, and many others. Their stories and deeds inspired us and gradually I understood Tagore's poem as if it echoed my father's dream for his children.[106]

---

[105] Also known in scholary circles by her full name, Dr. Sharda Vedalankar.
[106] Viswakavi Rabindranath Tagore's compositions were chosen by two nations

My great-grandfather, Munna Lal Arya, was born in Bihar Sharif, a small town in the eastern Indian state of Bihar. He started our successful family jewelry shop in 1884 which is still thriving today.[107]

The original jewelry shop which has been in Sarla's family since 1884. Photo taken in 2015 when Anjali and Gautam took their family to visit Sarla's ancestral home in Bihar Sharif.

His success enabled him to build a large home which included a library that became a gathering spot for people to talk about current affairs and Europe's role, including British colonial rule, in the modernization of India.[108] As the patriarch of the family, a large oil-painting of my great-grandfather adorned our home's courtyard.[109]

---

as their national anthems: India's *Jana Gana Mana* and Bangladesh's *Amar Shonar Bangla*. In 1913, he became the first non-European to win the Nobel Prize in Literature for *"Gitanjali,"* a profoundly sensitive, fresh and beautiful collection of poems.

[107] It later took the name "Munna Lal – Mahesh Lal Jewellers," named after my great-grandfather and my father. The shop is now overseen by my nephew, Prem Arya.

[108] The ancient Nalanda University (Buddhist Monastery) was the world's earliest residential university (500 AD to 1200 AD). Relics of this university are only few miles away from my home in Bihar Sharif. It was destroyed by Muslim Turkic general Muhammad Bakhtiyar Khilji who massacred and burnt Buddhist monks and Brahmin scholars to ashes during his raids across the North Indian plains.

[109] Later, my whole family moved out of Bihar Sharif and resettled in Ranchi, presently the capital of Jharkhand state. Thus, Satya *bhaiya* got an opportunity

My grandfather died accidentally at the very young age of 19, while my grandmother was just 17 years old and pregnant with my father. My grandmother was forced to become a recluse because of her widowhood and she became quite bitter. My father, Mahesh Lal Arya, inherited great wealth because of the jewelry shop's success, and our lives were comfortable: we lived in a big house with a large garden, and with many servants to attend to our needs. However, a horrible tragedy struck my family in 1946, when my eldest sister Sharda *jiji*'s husband, Chandra Gupt Vedalankar *jijaji*, died at age 33. My father, who was full of life, was never the same person after this tragedy. As a result, he insisted that his eldest daughter (my eldest sister) should not be subjected to the social taboos, since he had seen his mother confined to the compound as a widow from the young age of 17 until age 73.[110] My father died in 1948, and my mother soon followed in 1950. I was just 9 and 11 years old, respectively, when my parents died.

I was just 9 and 11 years old, respectively, when my parents died.

The sense of belonging to one's family is quite strong in India. With the nuclear family now becoming common, inter-generational living may be a thing of the past in India. But my education and my training at home prepared me to travel to far-off places without fear, echoing Tagore's poem.

My parents had great influence in deciding what type of education we needed. My grandmother and mother were not literate. My father had completed high school but, being the only child, he was somewhat pampered and got a lot of attention. A tutor came to supervise us daily as we did our homework. My parents were patriots and dreamt to see

---

to fulfill his aspiration towards education. Then my ancestral family home was demolished and replaced by a school building that was donated to the D.A.V. School System.

[110] My father saw how his mother was kept away from social life, so he never wanted his daughter to face that situation. He encouraged her to go for higher studies. Later, she even established Sunderwati Mahila (girls) College in Bhagalpur, Bihar where she was the founding principal of that college and continued to lead the school for over three decades. It is the most prestigious college in the region. My father's progressive vision for his daughter was fully realized.

India free from colonial rule. They followed the *Arya Samaj* tradition and wanted all of us children to learn Sanskrit and read our sacred texts, such as the Gita, and do *havan* (worship around the fire). We were all good students, and we worked hard to please our elders.

Later, we were sent to far-off places to study in *Gurukuls* where we continued studying Sanskrit until we completed college. All eight of us were students in *Gurukuls*, where students and teachers lived together on the campus. My five brothers studied in Gurukul Kangri Viswavidyalaya, near Haridwar, in the school started by Swami Dayanand's disciple, Swami Shraddhanand. My two sisters studied at the Arya Samaj Kanya Mahavidyalaya, up to the B.A. degree, in Jalandhar, Punjab. I was sent to Kanya Gurukul Mahavidyalaya, in Dehradun, Uttar Pradesh (now located in the state Uttarakhand) in 1948. Four of my siblings went to the United Kingdom to pursue higher studies. My eldest sister, Sharda *jiji*, received a scholarship from Bihar to complete her PhD in the UK, the first woman in the state to do so.

I started traveling alone from Bihar Sharif to Dehradun, without an escort, at age twelve. It was rare to send a twelve-year-old alone to a faraway place without any adult supervision. I continued to study there until I completed my undergraduate degree in 1958. Later, I completed an M.A. in Political Science from D.A.V. College (Dayanand Anglo Vedic College) in Kanpur, UP. The D.A.V. colleges imparted knowledge of Indian history, languages, and culture. I received a gold medal in 1958 for being the best student, as well as many other medals throughout my studies.

As I was very young when my parents died, my siblings and I were raised by my eldest sister, Sharda *jiji*, and second brother, Satya *bhaiya*. She was 20 years my senior and became like a second mother to me. My brother accepted the responsibility of our family's finance and business after my father died and supported the education of all my siblings. He was guided as well by Sharda *jiji*.

Sarla's siblings and their spouses. Front row (l-r): Sharda, Satya, Om,
Dharam and Saras. Back row: Vishu, Meera (Vishu's wife), Shantiprakash
(Saras' husband), Rammani (Satya's wife), Sarla, Ratna (Dharam's
wife), Vinod, Mridula (Santosh's wife) and Santosh. Picture taken in
1982 at Padma's wedding (daughter of Sarla's brother, Om).

9.2: Marriage and Voyage

I was introduced to Vinod by Satya *bhaiya* in November 1959. At
that time, Vinod was working as a researcher in Delhi. He came to my
hostel in Kanpur with his sister and we met at the railway station
cafeteria. We talked, and we watched a movie together, and later we
exchanged a few letters (in Hindi). I told him I must complete my M.A.
I asked him only one question, and that was
whether he smoked. He said "no." He was
approved by my family, and we got married
on May 16, 1960. We did not know each
other at all, except for the fact that his simple
nature attracted me. What impressed him
about me was that I wanted to complete my education. He discussed
the options of going to Australia, UK, or the U.S. on scholarship. I had
never heard of MIT until then, and so it all seemed novel and exciting
when he decided to attend MIT.

> **We did not know**
> **each other at all,**
> **except for the fact**
> **that his simple**
> **nature attracted me.**

Vinod accepted a Ford Foundation fellowship, and we flew to the U.S. via Zurich in August 1960. My ticket was purchased by my brother. We landed in Boston, and an MIT representative received us at the airport and took us to our new home. Soon we met Dr. Sukhamoy and his wife Lolita Chakravarty. Later we met Mrs. Helen Padelford, who had started the Host Family Program at MIT to welcome foreign students. She remained in touch with us regularly and invited us for Thanksgiving and Christmas. I later attended their daughter Caroline's wedding at Harvard Chapel, and we are still in touch with her. There were a handful of Indian students at MIT then. I babysat Diana and Avi, daughters of Professor and Mrs. Noam Chomsky, a reputed American linguist.[111] I also had the misfortune of meeting Lillian Bono in the International Students Office on Brattle Street in Cambridge. She cheated me by making me believe that she needed to borrow $700 for some emergency. I lent her the money, as a result, I had lost that scholarship amount.[112]

I taught Hindi at the Berlitz School of Language in Boston. Bill Johnson, a PhD student at Harvard, was my first student. He too had a Ford Foundation scholarship and he intended to do research on the Tata Steel Industry in Jamshedpur, India. We became good friends and we are still close with his wife, Margie. Bill passed away in 2014.

I enrolled myself in the M.S. program in Communication Arts at Boston University in the winter session of 1961. I was a recipient of generous grants from the Kaltenborn Foundation. This new field was exciting, and I dreamt of working in radio or perhaps television. These plans were ultimately derailed by the needs of our son, Sanjay, born in 1961, with cerebral palsy. Sanjay required extensive physiotherapy and speech therapy as well as medical treatment to control seizures. We

---

[111] Being a newly-married woman and having no experience in handling kids, it was quite a challenge to play with a two-year-old child and a one-month-old baby. Professor and Mrs. Chomsky were very nice to me.

[112] She invited me to visit the state governor's office, where the state official photographer took my photo with the governor. When I insisted that she return my money she denied that she had borrowed it and said it was a fee she was charging us for the Public Relations work rendered to me, which was a complete hoax.

needed time to understand and cope with these issues. After Vinod's two-year leave expired in August 1962, he took Sanjay alone back to India. His *bhabhi* and mother took care of Sanjay until I returned in March 1963, after completing my studies.

I needed to leave Boston temporarily to finish my research on "U.N. Radio" at the United Nations headquarters in New York City. I found an ad on the bulletin board from a Mrs. Weiss, a human rights advocate, who wanted to hire a student for three hours a day that would help her with household tasks in exchange for boarding and lodging. I took the job. My weekends were free. I became fond of the Weiss family and learned a lot from them, especially about Jewish traditions. In February 1963, a police officer knocked on their door early one morning and told them they were housing an illegal immigrant. Mrs. Weiss called me into the room and said that I need to show my passport, which I had accidentally left behind in Boston. I was told that my visa had expired and that I was to be deported. All of this was very frightening, but Mr. Weiss, who was a lawyer, suggested I should go to Boston and appear at the Immigration Office with my passport and a letter from my advisor, Professor Gillis.

> **I was told that my visa had expired and that I was to be deported.**

I took the next bus to Boston and was met at the bus station by my friend, Tilak Raj Bawa. He accompanied me to the immigration office where I was fingerprinted and asked to swear that I was not a communist. All of this was confusing and humiliating. Professor Gillis suggested that I be offered a three-month extension of the visa, but this event made me afraid to stay any longer than necessary in the U.S. I defended my thesis successfully, got a photo taken, and said goodbye to friends and professors. Within 48 hours of my thesis defense, I left for India.

> **I was fingerprinted and asked to swear that I was not a communist.**

*Sarla's graduation from Boston University with her
MS in Communications, May 1963.*

9.3: Life in Transition: Delhi

We established our home at 25/14 East Patel Nagar, New Delhi, close
to a park and only about three miles from the Planning Commission
office where Vinod was working. Initially, we neither had a telephone
nor personal transport, such as scooter or motorcycle, while owning a
car was a distant dream. We fortunately got our Vespa scooter because
we preordered prior to leaving India in 1960 (yes, back in those days,
the waiting list for a scooter was over four years!). These five years in
Delhi were difficult. We struggled to find the right doctors and care for
Sanjay and we had no help from the family. However, we had three or
four friends who helped us. Shravan Kumar and Sunitha Pahuja's home
became our sanctuary after our return from the U.S. We bonded so
well and their son Mukul and daughter-in-law Abha are still in contact
with us. My sole focus was on finding suitable doctors and medical
treatment for Sanjay.

Once back in India we decided to fall in line with the national
motto *"chhota parivar sukhi parivar"* (small family, happy family). So,

we wanted to have a second child and our dear daughter Leena was born on April 28, 1964. Yet "man proposes, and god disposes." Unfortunately, our beautiful little baby girl passed away on February 6, 1965 from leukemia. As a mother, I cannot get through with the pain of losing my baby – she is always in my thoughts.

> As a mother, I cannot get through with the pain of losing my baby – she is always in my thoughts.

Living in the nation's capital, New Delhi, led to constant and frequent visits by nieces and nephews, mostly unannounced – one of them even stayed for six months! We were often asked to find suitable matches for our visiting relatives, including for my sister's daughter, Poonam.

I recall taking an arduous train journey alone with Sanjay to Christian Medical College in Vellore, Tamil Nadu, for a medical consultation. Dr. Mary Verghese was the doctor. She was wheelchair bound and I wondered what had happened to her. She gave me her autobiography, *Take My Hands*. I read it, felt inspired, and trusted her. We were advised that it would be better to have Sanjay's hand and foot surgery performed in the U.S. This was a turning point in our lives because of the meager medical facilities available in India in those days. Thus, we were obliged to leave our motherland and venture into the unknown to seek a better future for Sanjay. In retrospect, was it a right decision? Yes, notwithstanding medical mishaps and challenges from his disabilities, Sanjay is leading a good family life in Boston.

9.4: Managing Our Child with Disabilities

We landed in Boston without Sanjay in 1967. He stayed in Pondicherry (now Puducherry) at the Sri Aurobindo Ashram with Vinod's sister, Sarla *jiji*, who was an ashramite, until we could bring him back to Boston in 1968. Mrs. Padelford again welcomed us back in Boston. Our goal was to give Sanjay a better life. This meant that I had to take care of him, and I remained a homemaker for the following 25 years. My day-to-day life was completely structured around Sanjay's needs. Any disability suffered by a family member alters the whole family dynamics. Life is no longer "normal." To understand this intellectually is easy, but to assimilate it emotionally is a lifetime's work. Raising one child with special needs while providing normal opportunities for the other child felt like touching the sky and the earth at the same time. But, of course, we had to cultivate relationships with others as if our life was "normal." Initially, we did not understand that cerebral palsy is not just a visible disability. Yes, the person walks and talks differently; but it is also a progressive condition, presenting new challenges which emerge in adolescence. Sanjay's epileptic seizures and speech impediment both appeared in his middle school years. I kept learning how to help him, while having to maintain normalcy at home.

> **Raising one child with special needs while providing normal opportunities for the other child felt like touching the sky and the earth at the same time.**

Due to his cerebral palsy, epilepsy, and speech impediment, Sanjay could not cultivate a social life. He had few friends until his high school days. He needed special, assistive equipment to allow him to drive safely and, as a result, he got his drivers' license only when he was 21 – much later than his peers. He compensated for the lack of a social life by being extremely studious through high school, college, and graduate school, ultimately receiving his BA and MBA, and passing his CPA exam. He joined the Environmental Protection Agency (EPA) as an internal auditor. Eventually, however, he was compelled to take early retirement from the federal government after 15 years of service due to the long-term side effects of a seizure medication, Dilantin, which he had been taking for decades. Sanjay faced his challenges valiantly and patiently. Now he has a family, and I know that the wisdom he has gained through his trials and tribulations is an asset to his wife Renu, daughter Anisha, and all of us.

9.5: Settling in the Washington, DC Area

Our families, Vinod's and mine, were both freedom fighters. When I look back on raising our sons, I believe we were able to instill in them a sense of their Indian heritage, and the importance of duty and sacrifice by teaching them Hindi and by visiting India every two years to show the children industrial progress alongside widespread poverty. I even bought *Amar Chitra Katha* comic books to expose them to Indian mythology through moral teachings.

One attraction of coming to live in Washington, DC was that it is the capital city. Things happen here. Embassies of many countries reside here, and our children had an opportunity to know classmates from other countries. They heard their native languages and felt some kinship with them, because we also spoke Hindi at home. We also enrolled them in India School, where I taught language and history. It facilitated their visits to India and helped them to know their cousins.

Naturally, we exposed our sons to the philanthropy that Vinod started in 1975 following Indira Gandhi's Emergency proclamation. Our sons started helping us in 1977, initially by licking envelopes and mailing our annual fund-raising letters, and later with their advice and insight over the years. Our desire to contribute to India's progress was not just acceptable to them, but it seems to have made them proud of our commitment to such an ideal.

Activities of our family included picnics with friends, apple picking, hosting friends for dinner, hosting outside guests and, of course, checking the children's homework. Sanjay and Gautam both learned to swim. Gautam learned to play the piano, he ice-skated, and helped us plan trips to India. All four of us loved to watch National Geographic films in the city on Friday evenings (though Gautam would admit later that he would often fall asleep watching the films!). Museum visits were a favorite and frequent outing. Both brothers played board games and *carrom* board, a traditional Indian game. Our family also attended cultural programs at Gandhi Center on special occasions such as October 2nd (Mahatma Gandhi's birthday). It is an active center that promotes goodwill and talks about Gandhiji's contribution towards non-violence.

Once the boys were grown, I learned more about opportunities for physically challenged young adults and completed a two-year certificate course on "Aging and Disability" at Montgomery College in 1986. Vinod took early retirement from the World Bank in 1988. As a mother of a child born with cerebral palsy, I dedicated my career and life towards the well-being of the disabled. That's why I started part-time work with the JFGH (Jewish Foundation for Group Homes) as a direct care worker, despite my two masters' degrees. I worked there until 1996 in their Bender group home with four disabled men – Howard, Michael, Ted, and Steve.

During these years, I also spent much of my time keeping in close touch with Vinod's large family of eight brothers and sisters and their forty children. Vinod and I felt honored to have my Sharda *jiji* visit us at our Carderock home, soon after her retirement in 1982. Also, we were fortunate to have my Satya *bhaiya* and *bhabhi* visit our family to spend some time with us here in our home in 1987.

Gautam, Sanjay, Vinod, nephew Raju and his wife Uma, Sarla, Satya bhaiya and his wife Rammani bhabhi, Rajat (Sarla and Vinod's grand-nephew). Photo taken in our backyard in 1987 when Satya bhaiya and bhabhi visited us.

We frequently hosted all kinds of visitors. For example, Vinod sponsored the immigration of a friend's daughter, Achala Mittal, (without consulting me!) and she lived with us for five months until she joined her medical program. Another guest, Narayana Paduval, was employed as a research assistant at the World Bank under Vinod's sponsorship, and stayed with us for a month while he got settled. Many IDRF and RSS volunteers stayed for weeks and even months at our home. This arrangement of food and lodging we offered our visitors surprised our American friends. And, at times, I felt that my personal ambition was sacrificed in helping others – I deeply regret this, even now. But as the chores and challenges seemed to fill my days and years, so did the joy of friendship and a busy social life.

> **At times, I felt that my personal ambition was sacrificed in helping others – I deeply regret this, even now.**

We feel privileged to have met Nek Chand Saini (Padma Shri 1984), an artist who was once a road inspector from Chandigarh, Punjab. The artist in him discovered novel resources for his creativity in scrap waste material. The Nek Chand Rock Garden, located in his hometown of Chandrigarh, has received numerous public recognitions. In the 1980s, he was specially invited by the Smithsonian Institution, Washington DC, to design and build their children's museum. Being a vegetarian, he had formidable task of arranging for his meals, so I organized a group of five or six Indian friends who provided him vegetarian meals once every week during his three to four month stay in DC.

We founded a gourmet dinner group in 1974 which met six to eight times a year for shared meals with local friends. We created the 'Food for Thought' cookbook with all our U.S. friends, featuring recipes from our members, complete with stories about the family history and their ethnicity. This book was released on the auspicious occasion of Gautam's wedding. With my friend Sheila Love, I joined the AAUW (American Association for University Women) to support scholarship programs. I thoroughly enjoyed the various programs offered by the Asian American Forum in Bethesda, an ideal blend of Asian cultural norms and American professional management. I also joined a book club at a local independent bookstore, Politics and Prose, which provided a platform for people to gather and discuss a book or topic of interest. These activities were enough to keep me busy and engaged. I am proud to say we had no cleaning lady or gardener for our first 25 years in Washington. Each one of us did our work and kept our house tidy and neat and the boys kept up with their chores. Sanjay became really good at mowing the lawn, carrying groceries upstairs, vacuuming the home, and keeping us company with great affection. As Gautam got older, he took over those same chores.

In America, we made lifelong friends. Among others, I have the deepest gratitude towards Pervin and Adi Davar; Alka and Dilip Paul; Andrea and Marvin Haber; Carol and Peter Lowe; Neelam and Prakash Chitre; Dorothy Grayson; Femma and Gerald Lo; Kusum and Rana Batra; Darshan Krishna; Malini and Hemant Joglekar; Jugnu Jain; Lona and Joram Piatigorsky; Betty and Jim Parker; Laskhmi, Krishna and Nilima Jayaraman; Barbara and Kamaal; Leena and Bob Housmann; Connie and Al Michel; Margie and Bill Johnson; Madhu and Shardanandji; Mohini and Ram Gehani; Roy, Shanta and Prabha Agarwal; Rama and Rameshwar Paul; Ruth Tabrah; Ashi and Ram Rastogi; Savita Srivastav; Sudha and Prem Garg; Vimla and Ram Agarwal; Sookie and Jay Lee; Surjeet and Hardyal Singh; Sudha and Adesh Jain; Indira and Girish Parekh; and GR Verma and family. In addition, members of our gourmet dinner club and members of the Asian American Forum have remained good friends. All in all, these friendships enriched our life, reflecting the cultures and diversity of our community.

Vinod and Sarla with the Jayaraman family, our friends since 1961.

Roy and Shanta Agarwal (friends since 1963) with their daughter, Rashi, and Dr. GR Verma (colleague of Vinod's at University of Rhode Island from 1969 and one of the most generous and consistent donors to IDRF with a true selfless spirit of 'seva').

I have been keenly aware of my identity as an Indian. This is reflected in my dress, the food I cook, my culture and language, but most of all in my attitude. I feel so good to be Indian. Duty has been profound in my head – a simple example of this is my feeling that no one who comes to our home should ever leave with an empty stomach. Mrs. Padelford was a church woman who influenced me by the way she cared for students at MIT and I learned a lot from her after coming to the U.S. Most of my American friends were very kind to us and we are ever grateful to them for sharing their affection.

> **I have been keenly aware of my identity as an Indian.**

We joined VHP (Vishwa Hindu Parishad) and attended their conferences around 1984 in New York City, and 1993 in Washington, DC. The Vivekananda centenary conference in Singapore in 1988 was most memorable. There we met an American Hindu, Sadguru Sivaya Subramuniyaswami, who spoke on Hinduism and impressed both of us. In 1979 he founded the magazine "Hinduism Today" and we became a life member. In September 2001, we visited the Hindu Monastery – Saiva Siddhanta, Kapa'a, in Kauai (Hawaii) and fortunately were blessed by him. I vividly remember this trip because we were scheduled to return to the mainland on September 11, 2001. But due to the horrible attack on New York's Twin Towers that day, the entire air traffic system was paralyzed, and we were compelled to remain in Hawaii for several more days.

The idea of *Vedanta* (the ancient philosophical thoughts of the Hindus) has inspired us to rise above our petty concerns. For example, we made it a habit not to exchange gifts at Christmas, but only to write an annual letter to each other. But we did exchange gifts with friends. We did not visit temples often but traveled to many countries around the world. The remembrance of trips taken together with our sons, and my solo trips to UK and France with my friend Dorothy Grayson, with Sookie Lee to the Netherlands and Mexico, and Arizona trips with Shanta Agarwal, and a trip to Mount Rushmore in South Dakota with Margie Johnson, added great joy.

The new century started with dramatic ups and downs. The birth of our grandchildren Anisha (2002), followed by Rahul (2003) and Tara (2006), followed by Gautam and Anjali moving from Boston in 2006 to be near to us in Washington, DC – all major events which brought us great joy and for which we feel immense gratitude.

Sarla and Vinod with their three grandchildren at
Vinod's 75th birthday party in August 2008.

Now, our family unit is complete. Our daughters-in-law – Renu and Anjali – are professional women (Renu in medicine and Anjali in the law), hard-working, and caring.

We had to face another extraordinary challenge when we were forced to confront the frail human ego of a well-known, wealthy person in 2007. We were told time and again that the wealth of this opponent was greater than justice. Perhaps the opponent did not know Vinod's adherence to truth, dignity, and honor. Vinod was even willing to accept any punishment imposed by state and federal authorities, if found guilty of any wrongdoing. Finally, justice prevailed in accordance with U.S. law, and its guarantee of fair trial. It was a very traumatic process for three trying years, and it took a toll on our health. However, we continued to focus on IDRF's mission, helping the marginalized people of India to move forward with hope.

We were told time and again that the wealth of this opponent was greater than justice.

9.6: Our World Travels

We travelled often to India, especially during the years when Vinod was working at the World Bank, as they offered biennial home leave (trips to the employee's homeland) as part of their generous benefits package. Vinod meticulously planned these trips which coincided with both Sanjay and Gautam being at formative stages in their lives, and we wanted to expose them not just to our extended family and Indian culture, but also to other cultures across the globe. We often went through Europe, stopping at one or two cities to visit and return via the Pacific Ocean and the west coast of the United States, again to visit one or two cities. In this way, we were able to visit the UK, France, the Netherlands, Germany, Spain, Portugal, Italy, Russia, Egypt and Greece on the way to India and visited Japan, Singapore, Hong Kong, Thailand, Taiwan, China and Hawaii returning via the Pacific.

We have so many wonderful memories from these trips – for example, we were amused and can never forget the amazing spectacle of the world famous "Lipizzaner" dancing stallions in Vienna, Austria. Once a weapon of war but has transformed into an art form, it was the perfect choreography between man and stallion. The show was so popular that we booked our tickets several months in advance. Another spectacular view we had was through the highest and longest stretch of railway, the Bergen Railway in Norway. It was a seven-hour trip crossing one of Europe's most beautiful mountain ranges, the Langfjellene. The train climbed almost 4000 feet and went through 182 tunnels crossing the wild frontier.

I remember visiting Lisbon and learning about the history of the Portuguese as traders in India from the early 1500's – a museum in Lisbon had an extensive collection of items from India. We even managed to find a Hare Krishna Indian restaurant in downtown Lisbon! We really enjoyed tasting ethnic foods in these different countries as, back then, we did not have all of these foods available to us in suburban Maryland. Our travels also allowed us to make keen observations of people, who often stared at me because I wore a *sari* almost every day on these trips.

I heard the word "Gandhi" every now and then while waiting in line and talking to the local people. They identified my nationality as Indian by mentioning Gandhi's name.

In the summers when we were not traveling to India, we would often visit National Parks around the U.S. and friends on the East Coast. Our travels kept our sons engaged in reading about places and planning the sightseeing. Our travels broadened our knowledge of geography, agriculture, and ethnic communities. Alaska was a highlight of all our trips.[113] Even after two decades we have vivid memories of our exciting trip to the northernmost point of Alaska accessible to tourists. We traveled in a small airplane carrying 6-7 passengers and returned by bus during the night with 30-40 tourists. We reached our hotel at 3 am with bright sunshine, the view spectacular throughout that journey.

Sarla and Vinod in Alaska around the summer solstice
(longest day of the year) in June 1999.

We bought useful items from Selfridges UK for our home when we could afford it, including our 16-person dinner set which we still use today, over 40 years later! The sales lady told us we can bake, cook, and put the items in the dishwasher – oven to table to dishwasher. We bought most of our furniture from Scan, a modern Scandinavian furniture store

---

[113] For travel details, see Appendix 7.

which no longer exists; the pieces were simple and modestly priced. One such item was our round dining table which extends to seat anywhere from 4 to 10 people. Many of our happy moments took place around this table, from countless dinner parties to family gatherings to sharing our happy and sad feelings with our friends. I do wonder, sometimes, what more memories our dining table will bear witness to?

9.7: Enduring the Cruel Realities of Life

Vinod's total loss of eyesight has inevitably impacted my life, confining me to our home. I am no longer free to organize my daily routine because I must attend to his needs: from early morning till late evening, and I must make sure that he is served breakfast, lunch, dinner, and coffee/tea. Thanks to his willpower, he remains as independent as possible. His iPhone with voice command and his walking stick are his dearest companions now. Initially, I used to be concerned about him using the treadmill in our basement, but he gained my confidence after some minimal supervision by caregivers. I need to be around while he takes care of his daily chores, but there is a limit beyond which he cannot manage on his own. He needs me now to be a caregiver: for instance, when meals are served on his plate, I need to orient him, treating his plate like a clock with its numbers so he knows where each food item is.

Our longtime friend François Gautier, founder of Foundation for Advancement of Cultural Ties (FACT), and the Shivaji Maharaj Museum of Indian History, Pune, visited us in June 2014. His visit aimed at raising funds and we arranged a dinner for that purpose at a restaurant in Virginia. While this program went very well, in an irony of fate, I met with an accident at the restaurant that impacted my driving capacity forever. As if this wasn't enough, a few months later I had to go through a hysterectomy surgery necessitating me to take complete bed rest. We are now

We thank the Almighty for embedding the passion to serve humanity that keeps us going strong!

confined to our home but, thanks to our mission and God's blessing, we have learned to enjoy our current life within the four walls of our home. We thank the Almighty for embedding the passion to serve humanity that keeps us going strong!

9.8: Closing Thoughts

We would like our family to honor the following principles:[114]

1. Believe in God – develop faith in HIM – *Satyam Shivam Sundaram* (God is Truth, Love, and Beauty).
2. Follow your higher impulses through love of your children and family.
3. Practice compassion, public service and act in accordance with your values. You may feel in your heart as you age – the World is My Family (*Vasudhaiva Kutumbakam*).
4. Be thankful for all you have with deep gratitude; God's grace has been throughout our lives.
5. Practice the discipline of hard-work and moderate consumption and good grooming with daily routine of prayer, fitness, and volunteer work.
6. See the patterns of '*Yin and Yang*' – day and night, good and bad, joy and sorrow, etc. That is life.
7. Blend the American and Indian cultures and take the best from both worlds. We are blessed to have an opportunity to live in United States. Duty and sacrifice are two pillars of Indian culture while personal growth and individualism are necessary conditions in the American culture.
8. Cultivate the desire to keep learning: it breeds humility – we will never know enough at any point of life.

---

[114] For our daily prayer, see Appendix 11.

9. As we age, we lose physical strength and memory. Making and keeping a habit of writing the highlights of your family each week will guide you through many memorable moments.

10. Understand yourself – nature and nurture – one comes from our genes and the other is accrued in the context of the environment we grow up in and is given to us by our place of birth, our family, and our own efforts.

AFTERWORD: REFLECTIONS
FROM A FEW FRIENDS

Narender and Aruna Jain

YOUR BIRTHDAY CELEBRATION is an occasion to record a few words on half-a-century of our association. We met after my marriage to Aruna – Sarla's friend. Your four score years of commitment and hard work exemplify life of a KARMA YOGI. Deeply rooted in Indian culture, you sacrificed your career, family-time and resources to serve Bharat Mata during her myriad crises. You have been my *AADARSH* – "Idol" is not adequate to express my feelings. You mentored me in my times of indecision.

Your life demonstrates that retirement is not the END of a productive career in a premier organization like The World Bank. You could have chosen a life of luxury with a World Bank pension. Instead, as they say in Urdu, "*tere samne aasman aur bhi hain*", you chose a life of hard work and sacrifice in which you achieved the pinnacle of success. Under your stewardship, IDRF has given millions for disaster relief to the destitute. It provided for development and education of thousands who are less fortunate. The good work has continued despite your misfortune which would have been a personal disaster for lesser mortals but it did not break your will to serve.

In handling the recent IDRF crisis you proved that adversity either grinds down a person or polishes him up – depending on the stuff he is made of. Philosophically, God did not will you to see the glee on the face of a treacherous friend-turned-tormenter, when he dragged you to a court of law. Sarla stood shoulder-to-shoulder with you. When you were engaged in academic pursuits, she was fighting Sanjay's battles. Now she is your window to the world: she holds your hand and lives your dreams. She maintains friends, bringing individual value to the relationships. She keeps an enviable communication network. Gautam and Anjali have followed in your footsteps of sharing without seeking, and sharpening focus on taking your work further as none would. Your loving grandchildren add the much-needed *joie de vivre*. Aruna joins me in wishing you a happy birthday, good health, a life fulfilling Century of good work, wonderful companionship and much more during the years to come.

Carol and Peter Lowe

Dear Vinod, here is a love letter to you and Sarla for your 85th birthday, truly a milestone in the life of a wonderful man. Peter and I have known the two of you since 1968, 50 years of wonderful friendship. Through those years we have come to understand, admire and respect you very much. We have been there for the good times and the troubling times. As we have aged together, we can look back on a shared history of raising children, and now enjoying grandchildren.

As you remember, our friendship began at the University of Rhode Island. Peter was older than most of the graduate students, so we found friendship with many of the young professors who had come to URI. Gautam was born at that time and Sarla was "surprised" that I would give a gift to the mother for presenting the world with a new child! Sarla was so devoted to the care of Sanjay who required many extras, her determination to provide the best for him was an inspiration to me as I too struggled with one of my children.

Vinod, you were working on finishing up your thesis and you asked me to read it for clarity. I didn't understand a word of it, but the work impressed others and you moved onto the World Bank. We too had moved to the DC area by then, so our friendship was able to grow. I particularly remembered one of your moves, the one to Carderock where we taught you and Sarla to paint a room. Sarla spent a lot of time with the children because Vinod's position required lots of travel. Our children were older, we were older and our responsibilities increased.

Still, we have found times to do fun things; our trip to the American West where we stayed at a Navajo Indian Reservation around Canyon de Chee, our trip to Canada, our trips to Rhode Island are wonderful memories of our activities as a couple. So too are the memories of the many dinner parties and of course your 50th wedding anniversary when our grandchildren played together in trees.

The American philosopher Thoreau says that 'friendships are like gardens, they have to be tended and weeded.' Our friendship has been more like a garden, there have been very few weeds to pull.

Malini and Hemant Joglekar

I met Vinod and Sarla for the first time in 1972 and, almost immediately, we became very close family friends. One of the main reasons was that our children were similar in age. Our first impression of Vinod was of a very devoted, loving husband and father and a somewhat serious, studious person. We had heard of him as a brilliant economist – PhD from MIT – who had just started working for The World Bank. Although we did not know much about his discipline, his way of explaining it made it easy to understand the problem and its solution. He aptly demonstrated the depth of his knowledge. It also showed the sincerity and compassion for his fellow human beings. He had to travel a lot around the world for his work. However, when he was in town, we used to enjoy picnics, Smithsonian visits, daily YMCA swimming trips, as well as other family outings together.

In 1987 Vinod took early retirement. Wanting to dedicate his time and energy to serving the underprivileged, unfortunate people of India, his mother country, he started IDRF. Knowing Vinod came from a family of freedom fighters and social reformers, we were not surprised by his decision to retire early. Since starting IDRF, he has completely devoted himself to various developmental projects in India. This devotion has included moral and financial support along with personal visits to the projects. Donors felt confident and comfortable knowing that every donation was used vigilantly for furthering the cause of a worthy organization. That is why IDRF is going on 25 years and has been able to provide millions of dollars in all forms of support in India.

The great saint Samarth Ramdas Swami had said "Death is inevitable but one must leave behind a unique identity that will be remembered forever." Vinod is a living example of that wisdom. He is IDRF and IDRF has become his identity. Of course, there is always a strong woman behind a man's success. That strong woman is Sarla. She has been with him by his side, through thick and thin, always supporting and, at times, even directing.

We wish them both a long successful life together and it is our privilege to know them so closely.

Jaipal and Sheila Rathi

I consider myself an enthusiastic admirer of Vinod whom I have known for more than a quarter of a century. I started my *seva* work in the form of a school/hospital project in India in early 1980s and was exploring ways of sending the money to our project through a charitable non-profit organization in US. In that context I contacted Vinod and learned about India Relief Fund (IRF) which he had just founded at the time. This was the beginning of our ever-lasting relationship. I remember to have very quickly grasped the strength of his character and his ability and willingness to guide novice social workers like myself. I gradually came to know his lifelong *sadhana* of serving his motherland and how committed he was to continue doing that for the rest of his life. I was a young man with a lot of enthusiasm to serve the society but with very little knowledge and no experience. But I always found Vinod available to me like a guru ready to teach his disciple all that I could absorb to become an accomplished social worker like himself. Little did I know at that time that this path of serving the unprivileged masses in India, although generally full of inner joy, does present tough challenges from time to time. It is at such times that one needs a role model and a guide to hold your hand to stay focused in the path.

As the time progressed our relationship became more and more intimate. Being in contact with Vinod, I never failed to see that he always preached by his own examples an uncompromising adherence to truth no matter what happens. Sometimes I saw in him my guru showing me the path to *Daridranarayana* (God in the form of poor and destitute) that I secretly aspired to seek as a part of my spiritual practice. Vinod is not known to people as a religious or spiritual man but his actions and conduct closely resemble those of highly evolved *sadhus*. I see him as a *sadhu* in plain clothes.

His vision impairment bothered me a lot but no one can fail to notice that the soul residing in his body never felt defeated, which is a compelling evidence of a life well lived. Vinod preaches the same truth but without uttering a word about it and, I suspect, without even being aware that he is doing it. I feel that our association during this sojourn on earth has been simply re-establishing our soul connection from where we left off the last time around. I thank Vinod from the core of my heart for coming into my life and greatly enriching it. I wish him many happy returns of the day full of inner joy, peace, and all the blessings of God. Amen!

Ashok Bhagat

Vikas Bharti is an India-based NGO that IDRF has supported financially for several decades. Dr. Vinod Prakashji is one of the individuals who in his heart wants to empower the deprived section of the people and contributed a lot towards streamlining Vikas Bharti since its inception. He has been one of the strong pillars since our nascent phase. Vinod and his admirable wife Sarla not only extended financial support but also visited Bishunpur to uplift the courage and enthusiasm of the workers of the organization. His motivational encouragement triggered and injected intense energy to our workforce which enabled the organization to achieve one milestone after another. His obsession and strong determination for the social and economic development of the tribal people of Jharkhand is incredible.

When I came to Bishunpur, leaving my family members behind in Uttar Pradesh to work with the tribal people of Jharkhand, Sri Vinod took partial responsibility to educate my daughters, for which I shall remain indebted to him in the years to come. He also helped me a lot during the marriage ceremony of my daughters.

Sri Vinod always advocated for innovations, he generated new ideas and thoughts for the upliftment of the poor section of the population. He always inspired us to adopt new technologies to match with the present-day situations. It was his strong desire and inspiration that Vikas Bharti Research and Study Centre was established 13 years ago in Ranchi. Now this center is contributing to the smooth and efficient functioning of the organization. Right from the beginning he guided us to be a leader in transparency.

Vinod has supported us to create a sustainable development model for small marginalized communities through horticulture and women's participation. He helped establish a 10-acre Training and Demonstration Center where indigenous technology and bio-fertilizers are used to cultivate fruit plants, vegetables, medicinal plants, and flowers. Research helps farmers understand the best ways in which drought-resistant crops can be cultivated by experimentation with inter-cropping to grow plants suited to the climate.

Many such innovative models in education, health and livelihood sectors were developed in kind association with Sri Vinod and replicated in different areas of Jharkhand. He is still working for the betterment of poor Indian families despite suffering from his own health problems. This depicts the strong self-belief and devotion of a great man.

Achala and Anil Singhal

It has been my honor to know Dr. Vinod Prakash for the past 5 decades. He has influenced my life from my very early years, as a family friend who became more than a real Uncle could ever be. His humility and willingness to help others, working silently and going out of his way to help whosoever needs help, is a thing which flashes to me as soon as I think of him. My first memories are when he taught my mom algebra in Delhi, India in 1960. Then he went to U.S.A. and whenever he and his wife came to visit us in India, I was inspired to go to U.S. and do higher studies just like him.

Lo and behold, as soon as I became a doctor, he sponsored me to come to the U.S. in 1977. I came with similar determination that after studying and earning some money, I will go back to India and serve my motherland. He and his wife not only sponsored me, but also taught me the American ways of life and gave me immense love so that I did not feel that I was away from my own parents. Their love for me continued even after I got married and had my daughter. In fact, it was very nice to see my serious uncle becoming so light-hearted and joking with my five-year-old!

With his inspiration and good training, we returned to India in December 1989 to settle at the foothills of the Himalayas where there were no good medical facilities. We helped Swami Rama in setting up Himalayan Institute Hospital from its very inception. This hospital is now a medical college and tertiary care hospital. We were able to do all this because of our role model, Dr. Vinod Prakash, and his constant love, care and concern for us.

We are always so proud to tell everyone that he is my uncle and he is the founding president of IDRF. He has collected millions of dollars for development projects across India. Rather than charging money for services, he even adds the bank interest to people's donations! He has continued to be my idol and inspiration for my entire life and for my family. I pray to Almighty to give Uncle a healthy, happy and satisfying life of at least 100 years, so that he can continue to do his own good work as well as inspire others by his exemplary actions.

Appendix 1 – Family Tree

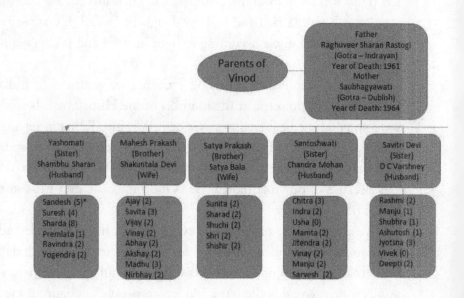

Parents of Vinod

Father
Raghuveer Sharan Rastogi
(Gotra – Indrayan)
Year of Death: 1961
Mother
Saubhagyawati
(Gotra – Dublish)
Year of Death: 1964

Yashomati (Sister) Shambhu Sharan (Husband)	Mahesh Prakash (Brother) Shakuntala Devi (Wife)	Satya Prakash (Brother) Satya Bala (Wife)	Santoshwati (Sister) Chandra Mohan (Husband)	Savitri Devi (Sister) D C Varshney (Husband)
Sandesh (5)* Suresh (4) Sharda (8) Premlata (1) Ravindra (2) Yogendra (2)	Ajay (2) Savita (3) Vijay (2) Vinay (2) Abhay (2) Akshay (2) Madhu (3) Nirbhay (2)	Sunita (2) Sharad (2) Shuchi (2) Shri (2) Shishir (2)	Chitra (3) Indra (2) Usha (0) Mamta (2) Jitendra (2) Vinay (2) Manju (2) Sarvesh (2)	Rashmi (2) Manju (1) Shubhra (1) Ashutosh (1) Jyotsna (3) Vivek (0) Deepti (2)

* () shows number of children in next generation

232

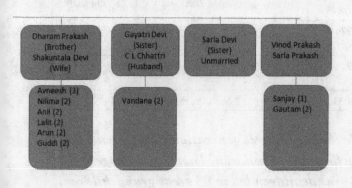

Annex:

Sibling Name	Life Span (Age)	Marriage Year	Spouse Name	Spouse Life Span (Age)
Yashomati (Sister)	1905-1980 (75)	1922	Shambhu Sharan	1900-1966 (66)
Mahesh Prakash (Brother)	1909-2005 (96)	1935	Shakuntala Devi	1918-1998 (80)
Satya Prakash (Brother)	1911-1978 (67)	1938	Satya Bala	1916-2008 (92)
Santoshwati (Sister)	1918-1985 (67)	1939	Chandra Mohan	1915-1973 (58)
Savitri Devi (Sister)	1921-2010 (89)	1943	D C Varshney	1913-2003 (90)
Dharam Prakash (Brother)	1922-2007 (85)	1946	Shakuntala Devi	1932-1994 (62)
Gayatri Devi (Sister)	1924-1997 (73)	1956	C L Chhattri	1915-1994 (79)
Sarla Devi (Sister)	1928-2005 (77)	Unmarried		
Vinod Prakash	1933	1960	Sarla Prakash	1939

What a dramatic change in three generations! My parents had nine children. In turn they had 43 children. That is an average of 4.8 per couple. These 43 grandchildren led to 93 great-grandchildren, an average of 2.1 per couple.

Appendix 2 – Glossary

Atma santushti: inner contentment or deeper joy of the inner consciousness

Bhaiya/Bhaisaheb: respectful term for elder brother

Bhabhi: Sister-in-law, brother's wife

Bhagya: Fortune, fate, destiny

Bharat: India, also known as *Hindustan*

Chachaji: Father's younger brother respectfully called *chachaji*, and his wife is called *chachiji*

Grihasth Jeevan: Hindu way of life has four stages: *Brahmcharya* (student life), *Grihasthashram* (married/domestic life), *Vanaprasthashram* (retirement), and *Sanyashram* (full renunciation)

Janeu: A 'sacred thread' worn by boys starting at the adolescent age when they go through the "sacred thread" ceremony/rite of passage

Jiji: respectful term for elder sister

Jijaji: Brother-in-law; sister's husband is respectfully called *jijaji*

Karma: Action or deed or duty, leading to the cause-effect cycle

Mamaji: Mother's brother; respectfully called *mamaji* and his wife is called *mamiji*

Neem: *Azhadiracta Indica* – a tree whose leaves are used for a variety of medicinal purposes, and its twigs used as a dental brush; a drought-resistant tree that grows all over India, especially in semi-arid areas

Sarvangasana: A shoulder stand in yoga, considered the second best to *sirsasana* – headstand – for whole body blood circulation

Saree:	Traditional Indian dress for women – rectangular, long piece of cloth in varying length from six yards to nine yards (usually), tied round the waist, and draped over the shoulder, in a variety of styles based on region or dance traditions, etc.
Satyagraha:	A policy of passive political resistance, especially as advocated by Mahatma Gandhi against British rule in India
Suryanamaskar:	Sun salutation in yoga; the body is stretched in a series of twelve postures

Appendix 3 – Arya Samaj

Personal Note: My family as well as Sarla's family are *Arya Samajis*. Although my family adheres to the principles of *Arya Samaj*, Sarla's family not only practices it but also ritualistically does *havan* (worship around the fire) every day in the early morning. Her father served as the president of the *Arya Samaj* of Bihar state and sent all his children to the *Gurukuls* to be educated in this tradition.

Arya Samaj

Indian society in the 19th century witnessed many social evils, such as child marriage, *sati* (burning a widow on the funeral pyre of her deceased husband), infanticide, *purdah* (veil) system and polygamy. A number of social reform movements were directed towards the eradication of such evils, *Arya Samaj* prominent among them. Founded in 1875 by a social reformist, Swami Dayananda Saraswati (1824-1883), *Arya Samaj* was based on the idea of infallibility of the Vedas. This movement advocated education and established two distinct but interrelated institutions: (1) Modern – Dayananda Anglo Vedic (DAV) Schools and Colleges; and (2) Traditional – *Gurukul* (schools where teachers and students live on the same campus, following an ancient Indian tradition). Saraswati's book *Satyarth Prakash* (The Light and Meaning of Truth) made a great impact on people and became the guiding philosophy of this reform movement. *Arya Samaj* has many adherents even now and they all swear by the following ten principles:

1. *Paramesvara* (God) is the fountain of all things knowable.
2. Worship is due to *Isvaraa* (God), who is all truth, all knowledge, all beatitude, incorporeal, the support and imperishable, immortal, exempt from fear, eternal, holy, the cause of the universe and sun.

3. *Vedas* are the books of true knowledge and it is the paramount duty of every *Arya Samaj* follower (*Arya*) to read or hear them read, and to teach and preach them.
4. An *Arya* should always be ready to accept the truth and renounce untruth when discovered.
5. *Dharma*, after consummate deliberation, should be his/her guiding principle in all actions.
6. The primary object of the *Samaj* is to go to the world for improving the physical, intellectual, spiritual, moral and social condition of humankind.
7. An *Arya* should manifest love for all and appreciation of justice in his/her behavior towards others.
8. An *Arya* should endeavor to diffuse knowledge and dispel ignorance.
9. An *Arya* should not be content with his/her own improvement but look for it in that of the others as well.
10. In matters which affect the general social well-being of humanity, an *Arya* ought to discard all differences and not allow his/her individuality to obtrude; but in strictly personal matters, everyone may have his/her own way.

Arya Samaj followers eschew caste distinctions. They do not believe in the hereditary *varna* (so-called caste) system, instead desiring to uplift the masses through education. As members of the *Arya Samaj*, our families gave up the caste name "Rastogi" and so none of the family members use it.

Sources:
1. *Encyclopedia of Hinduism* Volume A.
2. Neeta and Satyapal Khera, *Sandhya and Havan* (with English translation and transliteration)

Appendix 4 – The Rashtriya Swayamsevak Sangh (RSS)

Personal Note: As a teenager, I became an RSS *swayamsevak* (volunteer) and offered *satyagrah* (non-violent protest). In 1949, I participated in the mass movement against the Indian government's ban on the RSS. I remained out of touch with RSS while away from home, from 1955 until the imposition of Emergency in June 1975. This Emergency brought Indian-Americans together and I took charge of the India Relief Fund (IRF) upon the lifting of Emergency in March 1977. A decade later, I started a new organization called India Development and Relief Fund (IDRF) that aimed to improve the development of the marginalized people in India. I remained an integral part of the *Sangh Parivar* until 2003. We had the privilege to welcome *Sangh* leaders to our home and arrange meetings with community members.

The Rashtriya Swayamsevak Sangh (RSS):

The *Rashtriya Swayamsevak Sangh* (RSS or *Sangh*) was founded on September 27, 1925, by Keshav Baliram Hedgewar, a medical doctor, in Nagpur, India with the goal of organizing and strengthening the Hindu society, which he felt had been weakened by a variety of forces over the centuries. RSS has a combination of social, cultural, and nationalist agendas. RSS was established as a "kind of educational body whose objective was to train Hindus who, on the basis of their character-building experience in RSS, would work to unite the Hindu community so that India could again become an independent country and a creative society."[115]

RSS is not registered as an organization. However, the various trusts, which in turn actually manage the activities carried out under the banner of RSS, are registered. Its affiliates – Vishwa Hindu Parishad (VHP), Bharatiya Janata Party (BJP), Akhila Bharatiya Vidyarthi Parishad (ABVP), Bharatiya Kisan Sangh, Swadeshi Jagaran Manch and Bharatiya Mazdoor Sangh, among others – are registered, and

---

[115] See source 1 Malkani

information about them is readily available. In addition, RSS affiliates have a vast network of dedicated social service organizations to serve the needy throughout India – from Jammu and Kashmir to Tamil Nadu and from Arunachal to Kerala.

The RSS thus summarizes its mission: for the welfare of entire mankind, Bharat must stand before the world as a self-confident, resurgent and mighty nation.[116] Even at the inception, the *Sangh* was viewed by its founder not as a sectoral activity, but as a dynamic powerhouse energizing every field of national activity. Expressed in the simplest terms, the ideal of the *Sangh* is to carry the nation to the pinnacle of glory through organizing the entire society. Verily, this is the one real national as well as global mission of RSS.

Sources:
1. *RSS Story* (1980) by K.R. Malkani
2. *Dr. Hedgewar the Epoch-Maker* (1981) by B V Deshpande, S R Ramaswamy, H V Seshadri
3. *How others look at the R.S.S* (1989) by Keshav Hedgewar
4. *RSS: A View to the Inside* (2018) by Walter Andersen and Shridhar Damle
5. *The Brotherhood in Saffron* (2019) by Walter Andersen and Shridhar Damle

---

[116] See http://rss.org/

Appendix 5 – My Research Works

1. **An Estimate of Stock of Precious Metals in India** (*Indian Statistical Institute- Calcutta, 1959*)

2. **A Demonstration Planning Model of India, J. Sandee- United Nations Expert** (*Studies Relating to Planning for National Development- Indian Statistical Institute, Calcutta 1960*)

3. **Incentives and Labor Productivity in Soviet Industries** (*Center for International Studies- Massachusetts Institute of Technology- Boston, May 1961*)

4. **An Estimate of Tangible Wealth in India** (*Reserve Bank of India- Papers on National Incomes and Allied Topics- January 1963*)

5. **Fixed Capital Coefficients and Replacement Requirements** (*Indian Statistical Institute- New Delhi, May 1964*)

6. **A Consistency Model of India's Fourth Plan- In Collaboration with Alan S. Manne** (*Sankhya: The Indian Journal of Statistics, Vol.27, 1965*)

7. **Role of Incentives in Soviet Industrial Productivity** (*The Indian Journal of Labour Economics- July-October 1965, University of Lucknow, India*)

8. **Production Concentration and the Consumer - Comments on a point touched by the Monopolies Inquiry Commission** (*Artha Vijnana- Journal of the Gokhale Institute of Politics and Economics- June 1966, Poona, India*)

9. **On Measures of Productwise Concentration** (*Artha Vijnana- Journal of the Gokhale Institute of Politics and Economics- September 1966, Poona, India*)

10. **Statement in U.S. Senate Hearing as Former Joint Director, Monopolies Commission, Government of India** (*Economic Concentration- Hearings Before the Subcommittee on Antitrust and Monopoly of the Committee on the Judiciary, United States Senate, 19th Congress- April 1968*)

11. **Concentration of Economic Power in India** (*Center for International Studies- Massachusetts Institute of Technology- Boston, August 1968*)

12. Ph.D. Thesis (unpublished) **Manufacturer's Inventories in a Developing Economy:** An Intertemporal Macroeconomic Study of Indian Large-Scale Manufacturing (*Thesis accepted by Department of Economics, M.I.T. on March 11, 1970 with Appreciation*)

Appendix 6 – My Favorite Books

The following books influenced my personality and values.

A. Print Books:

- *Asian Drama: An Inquiry into the Poverty of Nations* – Gunnar Myrdal
- *Creating a World without Poverty: Social Business and the Future of Capitalism* – Muhammed Yunus
- *Dr. Hedgewar the Epoch-Maker* – by B V Deshpande, S R Ramaswamy, H V Seshadri
- *Education for Values, Character and Integrity* – edited by Shambhu Dutta and Dr. Kalpna Prasad
- *Friday Morning Reflections at the World Bank: Essays on Values and Development* – David Beckman, Ramgopal Agarwala, et al.
- *India's Contribution to World Thought and Culture* – edited by Lokesh Chandra et al.
- *Small is Beautiful: Economics as if People Mattered* – E.F. Schumacher
- *Waging War on Corruption: Inside the Movement Fighting the Abuse of Power* – Frank Vogl
- *Wings of Fire: An Autobiography* – A.P.J. Abdul Kalam with Arun Tiwari

After I lost my eyesight in June 2010, I have relied on listening to audiobooks. The books listed here helped me find light in the total darkness.

B. Audiobooks:

- *The Adversity Advantage: Turning Everyday Struggles into Everyday Greatness* – Paul Stoltz and Erik Weihenmayer
- *Beyond Religion: Ethics for a Whole World* – Dalai Lama

- *Beyond the White House: Waging Peace, Fighting Disease, Building Hope* – Jimmy Carter
- *Confucius from the Heart: Ancient Wisdom for Today's World* – Yu Dan
- *The Price of Inequality: How Today's Divided Society Endangers Our Future* – Joseph Stiglitz
- *Self-Healing: My Vision and Life* – Meir Schneider
- *Steve Jobs* – Walter Issacson
- *Train Your Mind and Change Your Brain: How a New Science Reveals Our Extraordinary Power to Transform Ourselves* – Sharon Begley
- *Bounds of their Habitation: Race and Religion in American History* – Paul Harvey
- *Pale Rider: The Spanish Flu of 1918 and How it Changed the World* – Laura Spinney

Appendix 7 – Important Events (1959-2010)

1959	Vinod earned Master's in Statistics from Indian Statistical Institute (ISI) Calcutta; Vinod and Sarla got married in India, and moved to MIT, Boston, USA
1961	Sanjay's birth
1962	Vinod and baby Sanjay returned to India and rejoined ISI, Delhi
1963	Sarla completed her Master's in Mass Communication from Boston University and returned to Delhi
1965-66	Baby Leena was born and passed away from dreadful leukemia
1967	Vinod and Sarla returned to Boston, USA and he continued work on Ph.D at MIT
1968	Vinod and Sarla moved to University of Rhode Island, USA and Sanjay rejoined his parents
1969	Gautam's birth
1970	Vinod earned his Ph.D from MIT
1971	Vinod joined The World Bank and the family moved to Washington, DC
1972	Sailed to UK on QEII; India holiday (Sarla's niece Jyoti's marriage, Sarla and children stayed for three months)
1975	Family visited California, Hong Kong, Thailand, India (including Assam tea gardens), UK, Germany
1976	Sarla became U.S. citizen
1977	Visited Greece, Italy, Denmark, India, Taiwan, Hawaii, Houston
1979	Visited Egypt, India (including Kerala and Kanyakumari), Japan
1981	Visited India, Norway, Sweden, Philippines, Japan
1982	Visited India (Sarla's niece Padma's wedding), Canada (Calgara and Banff)

1983	Visited Soviet Union, India, Netherlands, France; Sanjay graduated from American University
1985	Visited India, China; Gautam spent summer as volunteer for "Aditi (Indian exhibition at the Smithsonian)
1987	Visited Mexico, Spain, Portugal, India
1988	Vinod took early retirement from World Bank at age 55 and started IDRF; Vinod and Sarla visited Philippines, Indonesia (attended local wedding), Austria
1989	Visited Singapore, India (Bengaluru, Goa, Chennai, M.P.); Vinod stayed with Walter Andersen in Delhi
1990	Visited Bengaluru for *Vishwa Sangh Shivir* (VSS, global gathering of RSS volunteers) and visited Ayodhya, Varanasi, Khajuraho
1991-2	Visited India (Nagpur, Orissa, witnessed avalanche near Uttar Kashi); Gautam graduated from Yale and joined McKinsey in New York
1993	Global Vision 2000 (DC) at centenary of Vivekananda's visit to U.S.; Vinod visited site of Earthquake in Latur (Maharashtra); Sanjay earned MBA at Pace University and started working at EPA in New York; Gautam joined Bessemer Venture Partners and moved to Boston
1994	Family traveled to many cities in India; Sanjay got engaged to Renu in Delhi
1995	Sanjay and Renu's January wedding in DC; Vinod and Sarla traveled to Vadodara for VSS gathering; traveled to New York and Boston
1996	Visited site of devastating cyclone in A.P., India
1997	Gautam and Anjali's May wedding in DC; Sarla's trip to Mexico with Shanta Agarwal
1998	Vinod and Sarla accompany Gautam and Anjali to India (wedding reception in Delhi and Aurangabad); visited Vancouver and Victoria, Canada

1999	Visited India (visited site of Odisha super cyclone); Sarla's trip to Ireland, France, Wales and London with Dorothy Grayson; Vinod and Sarla's trip to Alaska, Sanjay and his family settled in Boston
2000	Sarla's trip to South Dakota with Dorothy Cunliff and Margie Johnson to see Mount Rushmore; Vinod and Sarla traveled to Taos (New Mexico), Arizona, Nebraska
2001	Visited India (Sarla's grandniece Shweta's wedding); visited site of Gujarat earthquake; Vinod and Sarla traveled to Mumbai for VSS gathering
2004	Visited Somnath temple, Porbandar (Gandhiji's birthplace), Dwarka, Golden Temple (Amritsar); Gautam started Monsoon Capital
2006	Visited Portland (Oregon), India (Rajasthan, Bengaluru, Ranchi for 86th birthday of Sharda *jiji*); Gautam and his family moved to DC
2007	Visited Sea World and Disney World (Florida) with Sanjay, Renu, Anisha; Visited India (Sarla's grandnephew Rajat's wedding)
2008	Visited India (including Chitrakoot, MP)
2009	Visited India (Kerala inauguration of Vivekananda International Foundation, Delhi to be blessed by Mātā Amṛtānandamayī (hugging mother); and Gandhidham following Gujarat earthquake)
2010	Vinod's blindness in June and no more travel

Additionally, Vinod has traveled to six continents for his work. Countries he visited include: Austria, Bangladesh, France, Iran, Italy, Malawi, Nepal, Saudi Arabia, South Africa, South Korea, Switzerland and Yemen.

Appendix 8 – IDRF's Grants for Disaster Relief and Rehabilitation, 1993-2022

	IDRF's Disaster Relief and Rehab		
	Disaster Name	Year	IDRF's Grant
1	Latur Earthquake	1993	$303,000
2	Andhra Pradesh Cyclone	1997	$28,500
3	Odisha Supercyclone	1999	$620,075
4	Kargil War	1999	$312,941
5	Bengal Bihar Floods	2000	$26,160
6	Rajasthan Drought	2000	$23,000
7	Gujarat Earthquake	2001	$3,040,459
8	Tsunami	2004	$1,141,500
9	Surat Floods	2006	$20,000
10	Bihar Floods	2009	$30,000
11	Karnataka Floods	2010	$13,500
12	Uttrakhand Floods	2013	$98,000
13	Jammu and Kashmir Floods	2014	$48,000
14	Chennai Floods	2015	$85,500
15	Nepal Earthquack	2015	$107,000
16	Siachen Glacier avalanche	2016	$7,500
17	India floods	2017	$100,900
18	Kerala floods	2018	$15,000
19	India Floods-Gujarat	2018	$39,000
20	Bul Bul cyclon-W. Bengal	2019	$3,550
21	Kerala Rehab	2019	$71,780
22	Bihar Floods	2019	$27,000
23	Fani floods-Odisha	2019	$29,940
24	Kerala -Rehab	2020	$25,000
25	Fani-Rehab	2020	$20,000
26	COVID-USA	2020	$67,000
27	COVID-India/Nepal	2020	$137,000
28	COVID-India/Nepal	2021	$1,430,432

29	W. Bengal Cyclon	2021	$9,060
30	Telangana-floods	2022	$10,000
31	COVID Rehab-India	2022	$214,250
32	Sri Lanka Crisis-Relief	2022	$35,000
Grant Total			**$8,140,047**

Appendix 9 – IDRF's Finances, 1988-2022

Year	Revenue			Expences		
	Contributions	Others	**Total**	Grants	Admin expense	**Total**
2022 (unaudited)	$3,809,664	-$60,988	**$3,748,676**	$3,619,319	$112,760	**$3,732,079**
2021	$6,143,101	-$14,602	**$6,128,499**	$4,550,873	$114,803	**$4,665,676**
2020	$2,655,770	$33,796	**$2,689,566**	$1,760,686	$97,426	**$1,858,112**
2019	$2,000,848	$30,783	**$2,031,631**	$1,493,132	$97,896	**$1,591,038**
2017	$2,066,556	$4,324	**$2,070,880**	$1,884,860	$89,121	**$1,973,981**
2016	$2,438,373	$12,444	**$2,450,817**	$2,067,266	$58,649	**$2,125,915**
2015	$1,548,944	$22,277	**$1,571,221**	$1,413,809	$55,017	**$1,468,826**
2014	$1,200,766	$17,488	**$1,218,254**	$1,289,125	$67,591	**$1,356,716**
2013	$1,578,837	$8,911	**$1,587,748**	$1,288,127	$46,496	**$1,334,623**
2012	$1,120,144	$23,950	**$1,144,094**	$1,086,600	$42,012	**$1,128,612**
2011	$816,769	$5,431	**$822,200**	$1,039,780	$46,059	**$1,085,839**
2010	$704,974	$58,432	**$763,406**	$1,864,075	$38,534	**$1,902,609**
2009	$492,061	$96,233	**$588,294**	$2,473,525	$171,197	**$2,644,722**
2008	$584,394	$324,354	**$908,748**	$1,255,960	$106,830	**$1,362,790**
2007	$970,536	$342,768	**$1,313,304**	$1,483,445	$54,904	**$1,538,349**
2006	$953,700	$324,936	**$1,278,636**	$1,759,319	$39,601	**$1,798,920**
2005	$2,123,197	$292,398	**$2,415,595**	$2,495,626	$57,457	**$2,553,083**
2004	$1,385,334	$439,512	**$1,824,846**	$1,325,773	$56,834	**$1,382,607**
2003	$756,540	$298,280	**$1,054,820**	$1,267,951	$71,186	**$1,339,137**
2002	$701,555	$391,600	**$1,093,155**	$1,269,443	$41,321	**$1,310,764**
2001	$3,793,086	$412,673	**$4,205,759**	$2,068,593	$15,324	**$2,083,917**
2000	$3,876,873	$72,196	**$3,949,069**	$1,700,398	$15,260	**$1,715,658**
1999	$1,373,142	$57,285	**$1,430,427**	$808,726	$7,460	**$816,186**
1998	$976,526	$26,476	**$1,003,002**	$374,400	$13,157	**$387,557**
1997	$431,048	$21,086	**$452,134**	$305,006	$10,775	**$315,781**
1996	$289,037	$5,180	**$294,217**	$237,730	$2,490	**$240,220**
1995	$344,662	$2,864	**$347,526**	$329,653	$2,438	**$332,091**
1994	$245,932	$3,094	**$249,026**	$358,068	$1,803	**$359,871**
1993	$405,566	$804	**$406,370**	$263,190	$2,010	**$265,200**

1992	$87,079	$697	**$87,776**	$103,074	$946	**$104,020**
1991	$86,679	$765	**$87,444**	$77,201	$729	**$77,930**
1990	$51,994	$864	**$52,858**	$65,706	$345	**$66,051**
1989	$45,830	$336	**$46,166**	$22,552	$939	**$23,491**
1988	$16,010	$42	**$16,052**	$8,882	$318	**$9,200**
Grand Total	**$46,075,527**	**$3,256,689**	**$49,332,216**	**$43,411,873**	**$1,539,688**	**$44,951,571**

Appendix 10 – Awards and Recognition

Name of Award / Recognition	Year	Name of Organization giving the Award	Reasons and Accomplishments for which Award was given
Community Service Award	1994	Associations of Indians in America (AIA), USA	Outstanding fund-raising to support relief/rehab for Latur earthquake victims
Outstanding Contribution Award	1995	Rashtriya Swayamsevak Sangh's Vishwa Sangh Shibir-Vadodara, India	Support for Latur Earthquake Victims
Sardar Ballabh B. Patel Award for Outstanding Community Service and Volunteerism.	1997	Council of Asian Indian Associations of Greater Washington, USA	Dedicating his sons' wedding gifts (1995 & 1997) towards the empowerment of underprivileged in India
Award for Relief and Upliftment of Poor in India	2000	National Council of Asian Indian Associations, USA	Grand success in fund-raising for providing support to the Kargil war heroes
Utkal Mitra Samman	2002	Orissa Society of the America, USA	Special contributions toward the welfare of super cyclone victims in Odisha
Recognition of outstanding contribution	2003	Gujarat State Disaster Management Authority, India	Appreciation of rehabilitation work for Gujarat earthquake victims
Social Service Award	2003	Uttar Pradesh Samaj of Washington DC, USA	Sustained leadership and service toward self-empowerment of the downtrodden in India
Bharat Seva Award	2003	Federation of Indian Associations of Tampa Bay, USA	Outstanding social solidarity and relief work whenever India was struck by disaster

Manav Seva Sarvodaya Award	2004	National Council of Asian Indian Associations & Indian Cultural Coordination Committee, USA	Deep commitment towards changing lives of impoverished in India
Award for Social Service	2004	Indian Cultural Coordination Committee, USA	Demonstration of sustained leadership in social service
Distinguished Social Service Award	2007	Federation of Indian-American Association, USA	Sustained Contribution to Community
Award from Jeevan Prabhat	2009	Arya Samaj-Gandhidham, Gujarat, India	Outstanding contribution towards resettlement of earthquake affected children
Dharma Seva Award	2012	Hindu American Foundation (HAF), USA	Commitment and service to the Indian community at large
Social Service Award	2013	National Federation of Indian-American Associations (NFIA), USA	Exemplary social services through IDRF
MIT's 1861 CIRCLE (personal award)	2013	Massachusetts Institute of Technology (MIT), USA	Recognition of philanthropy to M.I.T. since my graduation in 1970, (PH.D. in Economics)
Mahatma Gandhi Seva Medal	2014	Gandhi Global Family, India	Exemplary contributions in meeting community and national needs
Certificate of Appreciation	2014	Indian Cultural Coordination Committee (ICCC), USA	For extraordinary support and commitment of the mission for the people in India

Manav Seva Sarvodaya Award	2018	National Council of Asian Indian Associations (ICCC) & Governor of Maryland, USA	For 30 years of IDRF's service
Distinguished Community and Humanitarian Service Award	2018	Ekal Vidyalaya USA's India Gala, USA	Outstanding dedication to the community and exemplary humanitarian service to the marginalized
County Citation Award	2020	Montgomery County Council, Maryland, USA	For IDRF's commendable relief work done to serve the multi-cultural and diverse communities in the Washington DC Metro Area during these challenging times
Outstanding Humanitarian Award for COVID Relief Efforts	2022	Greater Washington Association of Physicians of Indian Heritage (GWAPI)	For IDRF's COVID relief efforts in Washington DC Metro area
Outstanding Social Services	2023	Swami Vivekananda Rural Development Society	For providing extraordinary services to the underprivileged

Appendix 11 – Our Daily Prayer

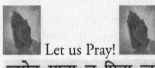

Let us Pray!

त्वमेव माता च पिता त्वमेव,   त्वमेव बन्धुश्च सखा त्वमेव।
त्वमेव विद्या द्रविणं त्वमेव,   त्वमेव सर्वं मम देव देव।।

Tvameva mātā cha pitā tvameva; Tvameva bandhush cha sakhā tvameva

Tvameva vidyā dravinam tvameva; Tvameva sarvam mama deva deva.

Oh God, Thou art my mother and Thou art my father also; Thou art my brother and my friend Thou art.

Thou art knowledge and wealth unto me; Thou art my all-in-all, Oh Lord of Lords.

ॐ असतो मा सद्‌ गमय।
तमसो मा ज्योतिर्गमय।
मृत्योर्मा ऽमृतम्‌ गमय।।

Om asato mā sad gamaya ◆ Tamaso mā jyotirgamaya ◆ Mrityormā amritam gamaya.

OM! Lead me from the unreal to the real;

from the darkness (ignorance) to the light (knowledge); and from the death to immortality.

ॐ सर्वे भवन्तु सुखिनः सर्वे सन्तु निरामयाः।
सर्वे भद्राणि पश्यन्तु मा कश्चित् दुःखभाग्भवेत्।।
ॐ शान्तिः शान्तिः शान्तिः

Om sarve bhavantu sukhinah; sarve santu nirāmayah
Sarve bhadrāni pashyantu; mā kashchit duhkh-bhāg-bhavet.

Om Shantih Shantih Shantih!

OM! May all be happy; may all be free from afflictions;

may all see the goodness of others and in everything; may no one suffer sorrow,

OM! Peace, Peace, Peace.